Women at WORK

An incisive and challenging examination of the situation of women workers in Australia

KAYE HARGREAVES

Paperback: 978-1-958381-90-8
eBook: 978-1-958381-91-5
Library of Congress Control Number: 2024910981

This is a work of nonfiction.

Don't Be Too Polite, Girls!

We're really on the way, girls, really on the way,
Hooray for equal pay, girls, hooray for equal pay!
They're going to give it to most of us in spite of all their fears,
But do they really need to make us wait three years?

Chorus
Don't be too polite, girls, don't be too polite!
Show a little fight, girls, show a little fight!
Don't be fearful of offending, in case you get the sack,
Just recognise your value and we won't look back.

I sew up shirts and trousers in the clothing trade,
Men don't do the job so I can't ask to be better paid.
The people at the top rarely offer something more,
Unless the people underneath are walking out the door.

They say a man needs more to feed his children and his
What are the needs of a woman who leads a double working
When the whistle blows for knock-off, it's not her time for
She goes home to start the job that's not yet paid and never

(an extract from the song 'Don't Be Too Polite, Girls!' by Glen © 1969)

Table of Contents

Preface

While working towards my sociology degree, completed in 1972, I had a variety of jobs which gave me first-hand experience of the exploitation of casual labour, almost no knowledge of trade unions (whose absence from the workplace was puzzling), and a lasting desire to get behind the scenes to see how mechanisms I had taken for granted in society really worked. I realised that I was one of the majority who understood little about, and therefore had minimal control over, the social institutions by which we lived from day to day either as workers, consumers or residents.

Like many women in the early 1970s I was also deeply affected by the women's movement. It taught me to look closer to home than most sociologists are comfortable doing, and I listened more to other women and with them began to make more sense of my own experiences. International Women's Year came and went, but I knew from my own and other women's experience of work that changes were continuing. However, I was concerned that the working lives of thousands of women, habitually ignored by sociologists and journalists, were a significant part of Australia's history that could easily be lost. Writing a book about them would be one way of giving their struggles some of the recognition they warrant. In personal terms, deciding to commit myself to such a project was the result of resolving an emotional crisis in favour of being independent.

I set out to see how women in Australia experienced work and in order to gain a thorough knowledge of the crucial issues sought information from a variety of sources. My starting point was a 1976 report by Des Storer, a former research officer at the Centre for Urban Research and Action. Called 'But I Wouldn't Want My Wife to Work Here', it was the result of a study of migrant women in several industries in Melbourne. I planned to gather information with a broader scope, about Australian-born women as well as migrant women, and about those working in clerical and service industries as well as in factories.

During 1977 and 1978 I interviewed a hundred women working in a range of jobs. These interviews were tape-recorded and then transcribed. Extracts from them have been used to bring to life points made in discussion of statistical information and research findings. Only brief mention is made of the situation of the interviewees to preserve anonymity, and all quotes without identified sources are from these interviews.

I spoke to many other women informally, both individually and in groups, in their homes, in their workplaces at lunch times, at union meetings and at meetings of women's organisations. Their comments, while not quoted specifically, contributed much to my understanding of the issues covered here.

I was also given access to information held by various specialist organisations, including the Women's Trade Union Commission (Sydney), the Women's Electoral Lobby (Sydney), the Lidcombe Workers' Health Centre, the Trade Union Research Centre (Newcastle) and the Working Women's Centre (Melbourne).

Interviews and other research were done in Brisbane, Lismore, Newcastle, Broken Hill, Sydney, Canberra, and Melbourne. While I must, therefore, admit to an eastern States basis, I can also say that although women's jobs are affected by regional characteristics, the issues that emerge are remarkably similar nationwide. This has been confirmed at several national conferences where women from all over Australia have shared their experiences of work. At each conference or meeting further details and variety of experience are brought forward, but the fundamental issues of women's right to work, child care, health, union involvement and increasing awareness and organisation all recur.

Chapter 5, 'Migrant Women', draws heavily on the work of the Centre for Urban Research and Action (CURA) and I have quoted many extracts from an article that I wrote when research officer there.

In 1979 when I began working as one of the coordinators of the Western Region Centre for Working Women, situated in Melbourne's western suburbs, I had further contact with many women working in factories there, along with women active in unions in Melbourne. I would particularly like to thank all those people whose co-operation, practical support, encouragement and criticism were immeasurably helpful to me throughout the four years of research, writing and rewriting.

Kaye Hargreaves
Melbourne, 1980

Introduction

Having a job, or looking for one, has become part of the experience of a growing number of women in Australia.

Despite the entry of women into the paid labour force, the experience of women both in the workplace and in society generally is very different from that of men. Women experience the institution of work differently from men and, generally speaking, it is a worse experience. The response of women in the workplace and in the community generally during the 1970s has presented challenges both to the labour movement and to the nature of contemporary social relationships. These factors combine to make it important to focus on women in the workforce.

The sexual division of labour

The tradition in Australian society, no less than many others, has been for certain types of work to be done by women and other types to be done by men the 'sexual division of labour'. Although work is now often considered to be one of the most important ways of establishing a person's social identity and position, women have more often been defined in relation to their role as child-bearers and nurturers and as supporters and sexual partners of men. 'Women's work' has been the work contained in that role, and mostly such work has been unpaid, women having to remain economically dependent. However, some women have also always worked in the paid workforce, mostly women from working-class backgrounds or married to working-class men. This fact has been frequently ignored by social scientists and historians because, at least until recent oral histories, working-class people have rarely had the opportunity to describe their own situation when history is being recorded. While many of these women especially the deserted - have had to struggle against poverty, all women in the paid workforce have been socially and economically at a disadvantage: because the jobs available to them, the preparation in the form of social expectations, education and training, and the wages offered for women's work, have been based on the assumption that it is normal for women to have male breadwinners.

Industrial growth and development over the past, say, fifty years changed the type of work available and increased the number of paid jobs for which labour was demanded. Many of these 'new' jobs were filled by women. In fact, many of them were created as areas of traditionally unpaid 'women's work' were industrialised and taken out of the home. For example, some manufacturing industries such as the production, processing and packaging of food, and the clothing and textile trades, grew until the mid-'60s. The service industries those concerned with dealing with people such as caring for the young, the aged,the sick or the disadvantaged, providing food, cleaning up after people along with the white-collar occupations providing back-up services to business and public administration, became major employers of women with supportive functions not too far removed from women's traditional role.

So despite the opening up of jobs to women, the sexual division of labour has been maintained with few challenges to it in the twentieth century, apart from during the second world war when women were recruited into jobs normally done by men.[1] Some women, remembering the period immediately after the war, speak of societal pressure on them to go back to their domestic roles and relinquish the gains they had made towards the right to work and equal pay. Attempts to resist this pressure were generally unsuccessful and those two issues remained key demands for women both within unions and in the community at large.

Despite equal pay decisions, inequalities persist. Most women are poorly paid because a low value is placed on the sort of work they do. For reasons which will be explained in this book, a narrow range of industries and occupations has been open to women, usually involving less-skilled jobs with fewer prospects and little status. Women have usually worked with other women, or, if working alongside men, have had quite distinctly supportive jobs. These are all features of the segmented labour market within which women are employed.

Demands for the right to work are more important and controversial than ever in the early 1980s as the economic recession deepens. In its contemporary usage, 'the right to work' has meant, especially to women, a variety of concepts, including equal access for men and women to all occupations and all promotions, opposition to discriminatory hiring and firing, and opposition to unemployment and the social and economic system which creates and perpetuates it. It strongly opposes the idea that in times of unemployment women should leave the paid workforce and go back to an unpaid domestic role, based on the notion that a woman's place is in the home', or to use Hitler's famous phrase, women's domain is 'kinder kirche, küche'.

Industrial and community organisation around issues such as women's right to paid work, equal pay and child care were muted, to say the least, in the 1950s and 1960s and, largely as a result of economic growth and social changes, there has been developing public acceptance of working women. This book will cover these changes in the two post-war decades, and look in more detail at the legacy of those events for women, especially in relation to the industrial work force.

A major change for the female labour market in recent years has been the rapid increase in the number of women entering paid jobs, especially the number of married women, and the related increase in the number of part-time jobs. This trend has become even more pronounced against the deterioration of the general labour market. This deterioration, however, has not appeared to be as bad as it really is because of the extensive hidden unemployment; the underemployment of women in particular remains invisible in statistics because many unemployed women have a family role to slip into.

Women's role

The traditional female role of child-bearer, childraiser, nurturer, and emotional supporter of the family is still predominantly credited by society. The parenting role assigned by society to women is much greater than that assigned to men. While it is normal for men to enter the labour force as soon as they have finished their education and to stay in it until they reach retirement age, the corresponding pattern for women has been to leave their employment on marriage or for the birth of a child and, in some cases, to return to paid work later. While there have been significant changes in the past thirty years, such as women marrying younger, completing their families in a shorter time, returning to paid work sooner and having a substantial part of their lives remaining in which to work, the pattern of relating paid work to the family role has continued.

While much has been said about the decline of the extended family in assisting with child care so that parents can have jobs, the main involvement of the community in child care remains the compulsory education system which takes children aged from five to sixteen years for somewhat less than the normal working day. Other forms of community responsibility for child care, such as creches, day-care centres, after school and school holiday programs, and pre-school child-care facilities have been slow to develop in Australia, and have all too often been geared towards the needs of two-parent families with one spouse, assumed to be the husband, employed, and the other not in the paid labour force except possibly part time. In other words, they have not been geared to the needs of women who combine parenthood with full-time paid employment.

This, along with men's reluctance still changing only very slowly - to share in domestic responsibilities, has meant that women in Australia have a 'double working life' with two jobs, one paid, the other unpaid. To assume, as economists and writers generally do, that only paid work is work denigrates the value of the unpaid work done by women. To women who have borne the workload of raising a family it is galling to hear of women 'stopping work to have a family' or 'going back to work after raising a family'. Of course, this is far from being a uniquely Australian problem. It has been documented or discussed in many Western industrial countries as well as South America, Japan, South-East Asia and the Soviet Union.

The focus in this book is on women in the paid workforce. However, it is impossible to separate the 'two jobs'. While there are many women - about three out of every five - who are full-time unpaid workers in the home, all but a few of those at some stage take paid work. This may be before their children are born, after the children go to school, when the family has a financial set-back, when the children leave home, or when suitable child-care arrangements can be found. An increasing number of women are living as single people or are separating from their husbands, becoming the sole supporters of their children and finding that employment is the only way out of the inevitable poverty of life as a supporting parent receiving social security benefits. So, while at any one time a large proportion of women are not in the paid workforce, few women stay out of it permanently. The trend has been for the time out' to be reducing, although the worsening unemployment situation may well be discouraging women from returning to paid work.

This intermittent aspect of women's experience in paid work has many implications. For instance, programs designed to raise the confidence of women re-entering the labour market later in life are essential. Provisions for part-time study or refresher courses for women engaged in the care of their children should be more widespread. Systems of seniority should take into account the accumulated years of a woman's experience, rather than treating her as a raw recruit each time she resumes her job. Lack of such supportive services has helped to keep women confined to the lower levels of a narrow range of occupations.

As few women stay out of the labour market altogether, and conversely even fewer are able to leave their unpaid work behind while they take paid jobs, they suffer excessive demands on their time and their emotional and physical energy. The difficulties facing women at work are reinforced because the two jobs leave no time for union involvement, community action, education or job training.

Some women have paid the price for this with their health. Fatigue and emotional stress are only just beginning to be recognised as major occupational health hazards for women. Some women have tried to accommodate their employment to their domestic responsibilities as best they can by taking part-time jobs or doing shiftwork. They have paid a price in terms of reduced incomes, fewer fringe benefits, reduced job security and more limited employment opportunities and prospects for advancement. These options are unsatisfactory 'solutions' to the competing demands that women face.

So the relationship between unpaid and paid women's work is unavoidable, a key to the understanding of the present situation of women workers.

Why do women work?

The changes concerning paid working women that have taken place since the second world war especially the increasing proportion of women in the paid workforce and the earlier child bearing - have been only very slowly accompanied by changes in attitudes and social expectations. Until recently a discussion on women in the paid workforce would have started by asking the question 'Why do women work?' That question would have referred only to paid work while taking for granted the unpaid work associated with the domestic role of women. Furthermore, it would have seen paid workforce participation as a deviation from the unstated norm - something puzzling or problematical. The answer would probably have been that there were three reasons for women working: economic, social and career reasons. Since these motives are surrounded by many myths, an examination of some of them is worthwhile.

The first and most obvious reason is economic necessity. It has been a double-edged sword in the battle for women's rights. As an argument for the right of women to paid work, it has been used to counter the claim that women work only for 'extras', 'pin money' or 'personal spending money'; in other words, things that they do not really need'. Helen Prendergast, of the Women's Trade Union Commission, asserted in a talk for International Women's Year in 1975 that the attitude that 'women don't need to work' was discriminatory and false. It ignored the needs of female breadwinners and those for whom one income was not enough. On an ideological level, the claim that women work to support themselves and their families has lent support to the concept of women having economic power rather than being necessarily dependent. It has also reinforced the idea that women are working in earnest and their industrial claims should be taken seriously.

On the other hand, it has also been argued that women are forced to work' through economic circumstances, a fate just a little better than death. The corollary of this view is that as soon as economic circumstances can be improved women will no longer have any reason (or right) to work in paid jobs. Consistent with this is the demand for significant differences in the rates of pay for men ('breadwinners') and women ('dependants'), a situation which existed for about the first three-quarters of the twentieth century, much to the detriment of women. Not until 1977 did the Australian Council of Trade Unions drop its policy of trying to ensure that women were not forced to work and affirmed instead the right to work of any-one who wished to do so. It was as if women had been required to pass a means test before being eligible for paid work. That means test included not only financial status but also marital status and prospects.

The most prominent situation of need was having a husband who was on a regular but very low wage which was inadequate to support a family, or who was sick, unemployed or in irregular employment. Having a husband who drank, gambled or for some other reason failed to support his family would also have been included, although little prominence would have been given to this outside all-female circles.

Another reason that would have been given for women working was economic choice: for example, when a young married woman works to save up for a deposit on a house or for various other consumer goods related to establishing a home and family. Other examples would be the older married woman with children working for a few months to buy something special, or working part time to provide extras for the family. This concept that women choose to work to pay for things that they are thought not really to need has been used to undermine the job. Security and working conditions of women. It has duly come under much attack.

Conventional explanations of why women work would also have mentioned social reasons, such as the need to break down the isolation of being at home, the desire for the social contacts and relationships that are formed in the workplace, and the search for personal confidence, self-esteem and independence that, to some extent anyway, come with having a job. These reasons have been regarded by many people opposed to the entry of women into the paid workforce as trivial or even frivolous and self-indulgent. More recently, the problems of women lacking self-esteem and confidence have met with greater understanding.

The last major reason given for women working would have been the pursuit of a career or vocational calling. This has always been accepted as the right of a minority of exceptionally devoted, talented or privileged women. As such, it has been irrelevant to the majority of women who have been restricted to the more mundane or routine jobs offering little in the way of inherent satisfaction or career prospects.

In all cases, paid work has been seen as secondary to the role of women in society, avoidable and best avoided unless economic necessity is really pressing. Most importantly of all, in the way the question has been framed, workforce status has been defined as secondary to marital status. In some respects these reasons economic, social and career are still valid today, for both men and women usually work for a combination of them. However, what is not valid is the underlying assumption that the entry of women into the paid workforce is undesirable and preferably subordinated to the domestic role.

The women's movement

In the early twentieth century the suffragette movement in Australia included some demands for workplace equality and throughout the century feminists in the labour movement, such as Muriel Heagney, have also struggled for equal rights. The re-emergence of the women's movement in the 1970s was a reflection of changes in birth control, other demographic changes and the increased number of women combining paid work with their traditional child-rearing role. The movement made women active in trade unions aware that the situation of women in the workforce is inseparable from that of women in the home and in the community in general, with the result that they began to insist on rights and policies that link these areas of women's lives. A working women's charter emerged which set down key issues such as child care; sharing of domestic work between men and women; elimination of sexual stereotypes and bias against women in education, training and employment; introduction of maternity leave; retraining programs for women re-entering the paid workforce after having children; and full participation of women in trade unions. The underlying principle of the various formulations of the charter was the right of every woman to paid work and to realise her full potential on the job and in society generally. And for this to be possible, the work traditionally done without pay by women - the physical and emotional nurturing of children and adults alike

- must no longer be the sole responsibility of women. In other words, there was a challenge to the sexual division of labour.

These issues are included in the Charter for Working Women, which was adopted by the ACTU in 1977. The ACTU charter affirms support for ... the right to paid work for all who want to work, irrespective of age, marital status, sex, sexuality, race, country of origin, religion, political belief or appearance'. The issues it takes up, as part of the 'affirmative action' needed to ensure women's equality in the work place are:

1. Entry to the workforce
   - Education and training
   - Child-care provisions.
   - Protective legislation to be reviewed

2. Workforce participation
   - Elimination of employment discrimination
   - Equal pay for work of equal value
   - Equality of promotion opportunities
   - No discrimination in retrenchment and redundancy procedures
   - Work patterns flexible working hours
   - On-the-job health and safety information
   - Regular medical services for workers
   - Maternity and paternity leave

3. Trade unions
   - Increased recruitment of female members
   - Trade union education - encouragement of female attendance and availability to both men and women of courses on problems of working women
   - Encouragement for women to stand for office in trade unions

This book looks at these issues and examines some of the actions taken and still need in order to put into practice the aims of the women's movement as articulated in the charter.

During the 1970s trade unions gradually became more willing to adopt the principle of the right to work and to demand action on all the issues needed to make women's right to work a reality. Also in the 1970s there was greater public acceptance of this right, until the impact of the current recession.

Given the high unemployment inherent in this recession, and the technological changes and new international division of labour that are presenting challenges not only to the reforms achieved by women in the 1970s but to the quality of the living and working lives of all Australians, the last chapter looks at the progress of the charter to date, and the likelihood of further achievements in the future.

CHAPTER 1

'Really on the way'

Working Women - a Historical Perspective

From the early days of colonisation in Australia, women were in demand as domestic servants. Beverley Kingston, in My Wife, My Daughter and Poor Mary Ann[1], has shown that domestic service in private homes, hotels and boarding houses was the major area of women's paid work in the second half of the nineteenth century.

Terms of employment were semi-feudal: hours were long, supervision was strict and the work itself was heavy, dirty and laborious. Remuneration ranged from keep to small wages, and was entirely unregulated.

It is not surprising, therefore, that domestic service declined as more women turned to factory employment and the influence of the labour movement resulted in slowly improving working conditions. By 1880, according to Kingston, no industry other than domestic service employed workers for sixteen to twenty hours a day, six or seven days a week.[2] There were several attempts to form domestic servants' unions. The Female Employees' Union of NSW, established in 1891, aimed to include all women workers.[3] At about the same time, in Victoria, the Domestic Workers' Union met in the Female Operatives' Hall (which no longer exists) next door to the Trades Hall.[4] Most of these unions were short-lived, and attempts to form them ceased after about 1911. The only successful female unionisation took place in institutions like hospitals, where employment resembled industrial conditions that unions were accustomed to, such as fixed hours and wages.

Kingston estimates that in 1901 almost half of the paid female working population were still engaged in domestic service of some sort. However, the proportion continued to decline, especially in private homes, so that by 1947 only 18 per cent of the female paid workforce was engaged in domestic work and over half of its members worked in hotels, restaurants and boarding houses.[5] Although these areas are notoriously difficult for unions to organise because, for instance, of their family-type situations, terms and conditions of employment gradually came to resemble those of the more industrial occupations.

However, not all domestic service work was converted into paid occupations in the marketplace. By 1920 the pattern of domestic work being done by housewives without pay was well established and remains today a part of women's working lives.

Statistics on the number of women in the paid workforce go back as early as 1918 when the Government Statistician estimated that about half the women in Australia worked in paid occupations at some stage of their lives and about 20 per cent continued to do so all their lives. Between 1861 and 1901 approximately one in three women aged between fifteen and sixty-four had been breadwinners.

The growth of manufacturing industry saw the rise of trade unionism amongst women. A union of 'tailoresses', garment workers from a number of factories around Melbourne, was formed in 1874 following the first known strike of women workers in Australia. Although short-lived, the union achieved higher pay and improved conditions and was partly responsible for an inquiry being set up to investigate sweated labour in the clothing industry, and the introduction of Victoria's first Factory Act.[8]

Edna Ryan and Anne Conlon, in their book Gentle equal pay for women workers and the importance of the 'male breadwinner' concept. They show that the campaign made slow progress throughout the twentieth century. In the Harvester Judgment of 1907, a basic wage was introduced, supposedly providing for the needs of a man and his family.[10] The high proportion of female breadwinners was ignored. In 1912. Mr Justice Higgins explicitly stated that the rate of pay for any given job should take into account whether it was primarily a 'men's job' or a 'women's job', so that men could be protected against unfair competition from lower-paid women. In 1919 the female rate was set at 54 per cent of the male rate.

Before the second world war there was little pressure on unions to fight for equal pay. Some unions with predominantly female membership had consistently made claims for equal pay: for example, the Clothing Trades' Union made a claim in 1926, and the Clerks' Union sponsored a conference of the Council of Action for Equal Pay in 1937. However, the Depression of the 1930s, with its high unemployment and abundance of cheap female labour, saw many male Historical Perspective unionists responding by fighting for the exclusion of married women from the workforce. One of the consistent champions of equal pay and the right of women to paid work was Muriel Heagney who published Are Women Taking Men's Jobs? in 1935.[14] In it she argued for the right of all women to work for the rate for the job, irrespective of sex. She led the Campaign of Action for Equal Pay, attempting to counteract propaganda blaming women for the Depression, and trying to change the half-hearted approach of most trade unions to the rights of women workers. She won support from unions who mounted an equal pay case in 1940.

Between 1939 and 1941, with the advent of the war, over 94 000 women entered the paid workforce, mainly in defence production. 16 The call for pay gained more support as unions sought to ensure that women entering traditional men's jobs did so only for the duration and at male rates of pay. In 1941, Muriel Heagney put to the ACTU a six-point policy for women workers, which included the right of women to earn a living in industry at a rate of pay based on the job itself rather than on the sex of the worker, equal access to occupational training, removal of regulations restricting the entry of women into certain jobs, removal of restrictions on married women, and the right of women to economic independence. In 1942, the Women's Employment Board was set up to ensure that the entry of women into 'men's jobs' did not undercut the eventual position of men in the post-war labour market. There were many stoppages and disputes by both women and men over pay and conditions during this period.

Daphne Gollan, a labour historian and former research officer with the Federated Ironworkers' Association, has noted the 'invisibility' of many of these women's struggles, which were discounted as unimportant by government and unions alike. Speaking at the Second Women and Labour Conference in Melbourne in May 1980, she commented that although women workers were organising in the 1930s and 1940s they remained 'invisible' because they lacked the support of an autonomous women's movement.

The post-war period

In the years immediately following the war there was pressure by employers on women to leave their jobs or revert to their former rates of pay. There was some resistance to this, but generally I was not successful. Economic interests and government propaganda emphasised women's role in recreating home life, increasing the population and enjoying the promise of a new era of consumer goods in the home. General prejudice against married women in the paid workforce was widespread. Unions were preoccupied with the campaign for the forty-hour week and the basic wage case. Furthermore, the government was embarking upon a massive program of immigration which was to provide not only a labourforce but an expanding domestic market for locally manufactured goods. So at the outset of the post-war period, women made up 22 percent of the workforce, and were generally receiving 75 per cent of the male basic wage. However, as post-war expansion began, women's participation in the paid workforce altered considerably.

The recruitment of large numbers of migrants from English- and later non-English-speaking countries in the 1950s and 1960s had a huge impact on the labour market, probably more so for women's employment than men's. By 1971 migrant women made up 25 percent of the female labour force and they were concentrated in the manufacturing and service industries that have traditionally been associated with early industrial development and have therefore employed women in low-paid, labour intensive work, with poor conditions and a low level of labour organization.

The single most striking feature of the thirty years of post-war industrial expansion was the increased entry of both migrant and Australian-born women into the paid workforce, a trend which has been prominent in most industrialised countries. In Australia, the proportion of women who worked in paid jobs remained fairly constant at just over 25 per cent throughout the first half of the twentieth century, apart from the wartime increase and the fall during the Depression. Women made up about one-fifth of the total labourforce and most of them were unmarried. However, after the war the proportion of women in the paid workforce rose steadily, reaching 26 per cent by 1954, 35 per cent by 1966 and exceeding 40 per cent for the first time in 1973. Most noticeable has been the increase in the number of married women in the labourforce. In 1933 only 5 per cent of married women worked in paid jobs. By 1961 this had risen to 17 per cent and it continued to rise throughout the 1960s to reach 32 per cent in 1971.

Although this pattern was made possible by changing attitudes to women's role in society and changing child-bearing trends, a more fundamental cause was the demand for labour by the economic system in a time of industrial expansion and economic growth. Indeed, attitudes, although changing, have lagged behind reality. Some of the married women in the labourforce were young women staying in their jobs for a few years before having children. Others were women returning to jobs after their children had reached school age. Increasingly, in recent years, married women with children are also joining the paid workforce. La Trobe University sociologist, Katy Richmond, in her analysis of the participation of women in the paid workforce, said that the number of children a woman had was becoming slightly less of a bar to having a job, although women still entered the labourforce sooner and in greater numbers if they had smaller numbers of children. These married women with children began to occupy the majority of the increasing number of part-time positions.

By contrast, the participation of men in the labourforce has declined over the years, dropping from 83 per cent in 1965 to 78 per cent in 1978. This is probably due to two factors: more men continuing their education after the age of fifteen, and increasing incidence of early retirement.

In the past thirty years, because work patterns of women strongly reflect child-rearing roles, labour force participation rates of women have varied significantly according to age.

In 1961, almost two-thirds of the women in the 15-19 age-group and half of the women in the 20-24 age-group were in the labourforce. However, only a quarter of women in the 25-34 age-group, the peak child-rearing years, were in the labourforce. The participation of women aged 35 and over in the labourforce was only slightly higher. However, by 1971, while participation in the labourforce was highest for women in the 20-24 age-group (59 per cent), more women aged 25-35 were remaining in the labourforce (39 per cent), and the trend of women returning to the labourforce after completing their families was firmly established, with 44 per cent of women aged 35 to 44 being in the labourforce.

However, the high proportion of women returning to the paid workforce was not sustained in the 45-and over age-group, partly due to retirement and partly due to the different expectations of this generation of women. 28 The pattern for this age-group could be expected to change in the 1980s, unless it is counteracted by high unemployment and withdrawal of married women from the labour market.

Overall, the age of women in the paid workforce is lower than that of men with, by 1978, one-third of women workers being under the age of 25. This has several important consequences. It means that the female workforce is vulnerable to a higher unemployment rate, that female earnings will on average be lower than those of men, reflecting the type of work available to young people, and that older women in the workforce will have to contend with the image of women workers as being inexperienced, unable to take responsibility, not interested in promotion and unlikely to stay in a job.

Many myths about women in the workforce have prevailed but with the changes of the post-war years together with the renewed activism of women in the labour movement in the 1970s, they have been under sustained challenge. One such myth was that unionism is a male concern. In 1969, only 36 per cent of women in the paid workforce was unionised - a low figure in comparison with 58 per cent of men. However, the 1970s saw a dramatic rise in women's membership and activity in unions.

The issue that did most to bring the realities of women in the paid workforce to public attention after the war was the campaign for equal pay. When most women resumed work at 75 per cent of the male rate, some unions aimed at achieving gradual increases but generally did not give the issue a high priority. In the 1969 Equal Pay Case, women doing the same work as men were granted equal pay. However, as most women were doing different work from men, only about 15 per cent were covered by the judgment.

In 1973, equal pay was extended to cover work of 'equal value'. However, subjective judgments and social attitudes influence the way the 'value' of sex- stereotyped jobs is assessed. For instance, the ability to lift heavy objects (a male worker's stereotype) is valued more highly than the manual dexterity needed. To do fine detail work (a female worker's stereotype). For many years, nursing, which is only recently becoming desegregated, has been grossly underpaid, while men in comparably skilled trades have commanded quite high pay.

The reasons for this, however, do not lie simply in social attitudes to work. Wages are not set by a rational, judicial process of calculating work value. They are determined by the relative bargaining power of employers and employees, sometimes within the Arbitration framework, sometimes outside it. Women have not been in a strong industrial bargaining position. The reasons for this are complex, but they all relate to the barriers facing the labour organisation of women: family demands, the interrupted career pattern of women, concentration in labour-intensive industry, prevalence of part-time work and the traditional resistence of the male-dominated union movement.

Women in the labour movement took up the approach of Muriel Heagney, insisting that all workers irrespective of sex or marital status be paid 'the rate for the job', with women having equal access to training and employment in the full range of jobs. Their most significant victory came in 1974 with the decision of the Arbitration Commission to extend the adult minimum wage to women, thus dispensing with the 'male breadwinner' concept.

However, inequalities of income still exist, due to the segregation of women in the labour market into 'male' and 'female' jobs which has made equal pay a difficult concept to apply. The next step should not be further arbitration but greater attempts to break down this sex-stereotyped labour market.

The 1970s: a changing labour market.

The major increases in female employment in the 1970s occurred in the traditionally heavily 'female' areas such as clerical, sales and service industries, with a small minority of women moving into traditionally 'male' industries, while there was a loss of female employment in the intermediate areas of manufacturing and communications.

Demographic changes for example women having on average two children, completing their child bearing by their mid to late twenties, and re-entering the paid workforce at twenty-five to thirty-four combined with the demand for female labour in the expanding white-collar industries, led to widespread, although by no means unanimous, community acceptance of women's right to paid work and to the changing role which that entails.

Despite the numbers of women entering the paid workforce and the growing attention given to equal opportunity legislation, women are still concentrated in a few industries and occupations, generally in lower paid, less skilled, routine jobs with few prospects for promotion and training. Changing employment patterns for women during the 1960s and 1970s reflected structural change in the economy – the relative decline of manufacturing and the growth of the service industry and tertiary sector rather than the opening of a widening range of occupations to women, although this is occurring on a small scale.

The most notable change in distribution of women in the paid workforce in the 1970s was in the manufacturing industry, which employed 23 per cent of women in 1971 and only 16 per cent in 1979.31 Although women were still the mainstay of the workforce in the relatively low-paid labour intensive jobs in manufacturing industry, such as the clothing industry, textiles, food processing and light manufacturing industries, over sixty thousand lost their jobs between 1971 and 1979.32 Unemployment overall rose sharply in this period, with women having a higher unemployment rate than men despite the numbers of women in the labour market. As many of these women, especially the married women, entered parttime jobs and as unemployment increased, a debate developed about whether the increase in part-time work represented increased job opportunities for married women or deteriorating employment for full-time job-seekers. By 1976, two-thirds of the female paid workforce consisted of married women. Since then there has been a slight decline, possibly due to the impact of unemployment. However, in 1980 married women were still over three-fifths of the total female labour force.

Sandra Prerost, a union research officer, has stated that the 1970s were characterised by a transition From 'blue-collar' to 'white-collar' employment for, while the expanding service sector allowed women to enter the paid workforce, especially in part-time. Occupations, it did not compensate for the displacement of other women from manufacturing industry In the first half of the 1970s, employment in wholesale, retail and finance grew, while in the second half growth was most notable in the community services sector. The entire tertiary or service sector (which covers wholesale and retail, finance, banking, insurance, community services, other services, utilities, communications, transport and storage) employed 76 per cent of the women in the paid workforce in 1971, rising to 83 per cent by 1979.35 Finance and community services became increasingly female intensive industries, while other industries employed fewer than 5 per cent of the female workforce, so that although women increased their share of employment in some 'male' industries, the increase did not have a significant impact on the segregation of the labourforce.

A study of occupations shows this concentration of women in a few jobs to be even more pronounced, since women are clustered not only in industry grouping but also in certain occupations within those industries. Social researcher Joy Selby Smith has shown that in 1977 there were eighteen occupational classifications in which women formed over 50 per cent of the workforce. These few occupations accounted for 85 per cent of the female labourforce. Looking at it in more detail: bookkeepers, cashiers, stenographers, typists and other clerical classifications accounted for 34 per cent of the female workforce; sales assistants were 13 per cent; house keepers, cooks, cleaners, maids, hairdressers and laundresses were a further 17 per cent; teachers were 7 per cent; nurses and other medical workers were

7 per cent; clothing, textile and footwear process workers were 2 per cent; and telephone operators were 2 per cent.

The result of all the post-war changes increasing participation of women, especially married ones, in the paid workforce, the mass immigration program, changing social attitudes and a changing structure of industries and occupations was labourforce significantly different from that of any previous era.

The growing awareness amongst immigrant ethnic minorities of their disadvantaged position in the labour market and the emerging strength of the women's movement presented unprecedented challenges to the Australian labour movement. Unions were confronted not only with new members but with qualitatively different problems such as the need for child care, the linguistic diversity of the workforce and the persistence of discriminatory attitudes. Furthermore, recently activated migrant and women workers were developing a new style of organising-less formal and hierarchical than the usual union style - based on their own autonomous organisations outside the union movement. They were concerned with issues that specifically affected them as workers, and with developing processes by which they might act on these issues. For working women an important lesson of the 1970s has been that although it is important to air issues in public and to change social attitudes - as the women's movement has succeeded in doing - to have a lasting impact this must be followed up by effective organisation in workplace and in the community.

'Show a little fight'

Towards a Working Women's Charter

If you had raised the subject of the rights of women in the workforce in the 1960s, the issues mentioned after the laughter had died down - would have been equal pay, producing many heated debates, and discrimination, grudgingly acknowledged.

There would probably have been no questioning of the ability of the white, male, Anglo-Saxon or Irish officials to represent female and immigrant members. There would have been no challenge to the idea that child care and domestic matters were the responsibility of women taking priority over their other activities, such as holding down a full-time job.

The 1970s saw discussion at much greater depth about the role of women in the labour market, challenges to traditional female stereotypes, and an upsurge of activism amongst women in the community, including the workplace. The more this went on, the more women realised that equal pay, although an important gain, was only a small step, and that more fundamental changes were needed to bring about equality.

As issues were identified, activists usually called on unions to support women. Although some form of port came from the top of the union hierarchy, it was often token support accompanied by resistance to real change. The most productive change has come from the impact of the women's movement on female unionists which has resulted in the organised labour movement being confronted with new issues, and a more participatory style of organising. Both results have been controversial, and both are still emerging and changing.

The new wave of feminism which developed in the 1960s in Australia was, more than in the United States, set on an economic base. It sprang initially from the campaign for equal pay, leading to the 1969 equal pay decision which effectively excluded the majority of women from equal pay. Since then the women's movement has taken a radical stance about women's position in the paid workforce.

Activists such as Zelda D'Aprano, together with the Victorian Employed Women's Organisation Committee (VEWOC), an organisation of representatives of unions with female members, attempted to achieve union action over the unsatisfactory equal pay decision. The inaction of the male union leadership over this issue led D'Aprano and others to believe that pressure would have to come from women themselves.

Thus the Women's Action Committee, a precursor of the Women's Liberation Movement, was formed in March 1970. Its demands were centred on economic equality. For instance, the committee sought 'one rate for the job performed, equal opportunity in employment, maternity leave of one year with no loss of seniority or superannuation and paid maternity allowance to equal full salary for six weeks, child care, kindergarten and child-minding facilities to be increased, part-time work to be made available for women who require it, and retraining courses to be set up for women returning to the workforce'. The group also called for girls to be made aware of the length of their working lives, and to be encouraged to undertake apprenticeships in all trades.[1]

These demands are clearly forerunners of the Working Women's C Charter which developed throughout the 1970s and led to the establishment of a Working Women's Charter Campaign in 1976. From 1971 onwards a pattern was established of women workers organising independently of the male-dominated union leadership to formulate issues and to lobby the union movement to take action in needs of women.

The ACTU and the alternative trade union women's lobby

In 1971 a women's committee was established in the public service union's peak council, the Council of Australian Government Employee Organisations (CAGEO), the first women's caucus and the Media Women's Action Group were formed, and another biennial ACTU congress was held.

In May 1971, before the ACTU congress, a group of a hundred women got together for the first time for an Alternative Trade Union Women's Conference. It was concerned with unions' past inactivity around women's employment issues. In particular, the conference acted as a pressure group on the ACTU to revitalise the fight for equal pay for work of equal value.

One participant reported that the group was rather mild, requesting rather than demanding that the ACTU take into account the one-third of the workforce who were women. Lobbying was 'not in opposition to the ACTU'. It aimed rather to 'highlight the need for action' to improve the position of women in the workforce. Apparently the feeling was that although the ACTU had been paying lip service to women, it could be persuaded to treat them more seriously. The women's lobby wanted the ACTU to take up substantial issues such as women's right to work, equal pay (interpreted as 'the rate for the job'), provision of high-quality and twenty-four-hour child-care facilities, job training without discrimination, a shorter working week, shopping time and maternity leave. They also questioned the lack of women union members, officials and ACTU delegates.

The principal conflict between the women's lobby and the ACTU was over the equal pay issue and it persisted until the 1977 congress. The ACTU's policy was to extend the 1969 'equal pay for equal work decision to 'equal remuneration for men and women workers for work of equal value', which opened the door to the very murky problem of establishing work value, and gave employers the obvious loophole of claiming that women's work was less valuable than men's. But further than this, the ACTU's wage policy emphasised the single-breadwinner family, and sought to discourage the necessity for dual incomes to make ends meet. This assumed a family consisting of a male breadwinner and a married woman who had 'freedom of choice in relation to employment without being forced through economic circumstances to work'. No such choice was offered to men. The women's lobby, on the other hand, wanted Working Women's between men and women in the workplace and in domestic roles, with special provisions such as maternity leave and training to re-enter the workforce. The wage policy consistent with this is one that pays the rate for the job' irrespective of the sex or marital status of the worker. Child-care provisions are a desirable part of this scheme. By contrast, the ACTU policy on child care at that time was to call for child care services to cater for 'the needs of working women who under present economic circumstances have to work' (my italics). The women's lobby's resolution was defeated at congress by six votes, 339 to 333, with the executive voting to retain the original policy.

Some 'left-wing' unions responded to the new feminist wave. In 1971 the Building Workers' Industrial Union, the Australasian

Meat Industry Employees' Union and the Australian Building and Construction Employees' Federation put forward items on child care facilities to congress. The ABCEF proposed an item on women's right to learn skilled trades and to enter these occupations. The Sheet Metal Workers Union (SMWU) proposed an item on The Needs of Women Workers', which covered one rate for the job, maternity leave, child-care and abortion reform, and called on the ACTU to convene conferences on the problems and needs of working women. Policies on maternity leave and child care were passed by the ACTU but the family-wage concept was retained.

Another outcome of the 1971 congress was that the existing equal pay committees were extended to cover all problems of women in industry, and a national conference was to be convened the following year. It was held in November 1972. Although most of the participants were women, most of the debate and motions came from men.

Participants in a workshop spelt out what women expected from the union movement:

Women expect the union movement to treat them human beings, having equal rights with men to share in the benefits gained by the unions for all their members. Where injustices to women exist, they expect the union movement to work for their removal as assiduously as they would for their male members. They expect no preferential treatment only equal consideration as responsible members of the workforce, disregarding the biological accident of sex. They also expect their brother unionists to take an enlightened attitude towards the problems of women members, to treat these problems seriously and in particular to try to eradicate male prejudice towards working women wherever it exists, whether in the unions themselves or on the part of employers.

No one would disagree with women asking to be treated as human beings and taken seriously. However, there would have been no need to put this down on paper had women not felt that they were being treated as less than human. The grievances that women express are often more concerned with intangibles such as being put down, denigrated, brushed off, laughed at or ignored. All but the most thick skinned would steer clear of involvement in any organisation in the face of such treatment.

The group suggested that women should be recruited to unions by means of publicity and education. Although all the usual reasons for the low participation rates of women in unions were discussed, there was little criticism of the failure of unions to produce concrete benefits for women and make involvement worthwhile or accessible to them. It is sad to note that by the time the discussion reached the stage of making recommendations, the feeling of assertiveness on the part of the women demanding to be treated as Towards a Working Women's Charter 33 human beings had evaporated, to be replaced by a suggestion to appoint an industrial psychologist to propose ways of involving women and recruiting members. In other words, women were to be manipulated, while the unions basically would not change.

An entirely different approach was being taken at the same time within the women's movement. It entailed women getting together, discussing their problems, realising that their problems were shared, and giving each other mutual support. It achieved a spectacular growth in personal strength and self-confidence which was a springboard to commanding respect and being able to take up specific issues. Women's caucuses, or groups of women, within industry, were seen by some as the way they could get together to promote the rights of women.

A women's caucus can provide the opportunity for women to involve themselves in union politics, through learning to frame demands for themselves, and through separate and non-intimidating meetings, learning to speak out with confidence about matters which concern them.

In 1972, a women's caucus was formed in the Canberra branch of the Australian Clerical Officers' Association and it outlined cases of discrimination in the public service. This was one of the influences which led to the ratification, by the newly elected Labor government the following year, of the International Labor Organisation (ILO) Convention No. 111 on Discrimination in Employment and Occupation.

Another landmark of the period was the introduction of the Federal Maternity Leave Bill, whose benefits unfortunately reached only a small section of the workforce - Commonwealth public servants.

In 1973 another biennial ACTU congress and a CAGEO conference were held. At the CAGEO conference the women's committee, established two years earlier, reported for the first time. According to CAGEO secretary, Paul Monroe, proposals for improved conditions for women were passed because the men did not know what had struck them'. At the next conference, in 1975, 'the women just got the numbers because it was considered progressive for men to support female issues". The ACTU was rather different: the politicking was intense, and was represented in the press as a conflict between social progressives of the broader labour and women's movements and the conservatives of the union hierarchy. This is how the *Australian Financial Review* saw it:

The ACTU has in fact watered down several of its key 'social' programmes. The decision to reject as policy the concept of an equal minimum wage for men and women has left the Federal Labour

Minister, Mr. Cameron, out on a limb, and has further estranged the blue-collar union movement from the growing movement of militant women workers.

Reporter Bob Mills judged that, by refusing to abolish the family-wage concept, the ACTU had shirked the equal pay issue, exposing its affirmations on the subject as mere rhetoric: Faced with the bald issue of whether or not it should push for equal pay and conditions for women, the ACTU Congress yesterday took the expedient step of voting for a continuation of the existing system'.

According to Mills, the reason for this was defensive, 'more arrived at ensuring there would be no erosion of the wage levels of the male workforce'.

The second Alternative Trade Union Women's Conference was held in September 1973, and was at tended by three hundred women who firmly established the function of lobbying the ACTU congress. Their argument was that while wages were still based on the 'family wage' concept, with men automatically getting a family wage and women, no matter who was supported by their wage, always being paid a fraction of this, equal pay could never become a reality. Other inequalities between the sexes, for instance in job opportunities, would also persist. Tessa Mallos, the Actors and Announcers Equity delegate to congress, was chosen to put the women's case. Her amendment was that: "The ACTU take immediate and urgent action to see that women are granted a minimum wage equal to that of men, and that the concept of a family wage be abolished immediately' and that: 'women should receive equal margins, bonuses, and flow-ons and all mention of sex classifications should be abolished from awards and advertisements for jobs'.

The conservatives at congress argued that male wages would be eroded by any attempts to introduce equal pay, and that the male was still predominantly responsible for providing for dependants. Mallos argued that no one knew how many women supported dependants, and that the present structure was based on a prejudicial attitude'.

Harold Souter, who was then secretary of the ACTU, said that they should not pursue equal pay until there was adequate child endowment to make up for the loss of the "family component" in the National Wage Case'.

Congress' decisions showed the same ambivalence about women that unions had shown for several years. While pointing out that workforce participation had increased and that for the first time the majority of women in the workforce were married, congress repeated that women should not be forced to work'. It advocated a mothers' allowance. This policy has been consistently opposed by feminists on the grounds that it would limit rather than broaden the role of women in society, and that the amount would never be a true recognition of the economic value of the work performed by women in the home. Interestingly, the congress decision indicated no amount for the allowance. Apparently, a suggestion that it be equal to the minimum wage was dropped.

In other comments, the ACTU policy on women attacked the devious plan' of employers to entice women into the workforce and lower the standard of wages and conditions. Congress objected to this on three grounds, namely, the continued exploitation of cheap female labour, the lack of job satisfaction and job opportunities, and the long-term slash in standards for male labour'. The last point, it seems, was decisive.

Although 36 per cent of the workforce at that stage was female, only 3 per cent of delegates to congress were women. Bob Mills, reporting in the Australian Financial Review, commented that it was therefore not surprising that issues affecting women had been shelved or sidetracked. It was no longer universally accepted that women could be adequately represented by men, even though many male union officials claimed to be doing just that.

There has been continuous tension around the question of whether women should channel their efforts for change through the union movement. The 1973 congress showed that normal representation was not enough. This led the Women's Electoral Lobby (WEL), the Union of Australian Women and the National Towards a Working Women's Charter 37 Council of Women to appear in the 1974 National Wage Case in support of the extension of the minimum wage to women, to produce one adult minimum wage. The ACTU and the Australian government, represented by Mary Gaudron, supported the application. Edna Ryan, who appeared for WEL in the case, said that union officials had resented her involvement and that the issue at stake, apart from that of participatory versus representative unionism, was that because of the persistence of the 'male breadwinner' idea within the union movement, the unions had, on this crucial matter of the minimum wage, not been representing women adequately.

As Edna Ryan explained:

... as long as we have certain unions which keep defending the primary breadwinner against the secondary breadwinner role, as long as we have government departments doing the same thing where training and retraining are concerned, as they are at present with a recession on, women are never going to get equality.

Intervention by women's organisations did 'tip the scales' in the 1974 National Wage Case, and made way for the general application of the principle of 'the rate for the job'. The Conciliation and Arbitration Commission felt that it did not have the information necessary to enable it to discriminate between the various needs of workers and considered that the care of family needs was primarily a government responsibility, to be taken up through child endowment, taxation, pensions, and so on. State Industrial Tribunals in New South Wales, Victoria, Queensland, South Australia and Tasmania followed suit the next year.[1]

Rhonda Galbally has pointed out in her thesis on the charter that another pattern to emerge from the trade union women's lobby was that 'left-wing' unions, such as the Amalgamated Metal Workers' Union, the ABCEF and the BWIU, would propose profeminist policies to congress aimed at achieving a more equitable role for women in the workforce. However, in most cases, this action was directed at the ACTU rather than at their own membership. The ACTU in turn emphasised the need for government action. So responsibility was being forced upwards, resulting in very little practical action amongst the membership.

One of the unions to support the Mallos amendment at congress had been the AMWU which followed this up by holding its first National Women's Conference in 1974. Shop stewards were asked to campaign to secure the same award and over-award payment for men and women, and many other resolutions were made covering general social policy as well as issues specifically related to the workplace.

The most detailed discussion was given to the question of child care. The NSW Labour Women's Conference had circulated a questionnaire on child-care needs, and the union undertook to distribute it to other States. This was one minor victory in a very long struggle for union support in the campaign for child-care facilities. The conference also aimed to establish a charter for women working in the metals industry, to lead to the development of a national trade union policy for women in industry by the time of the 1975 ACTU congress.

However, according to Rhonda Galbally, the conference was marred by members of the union's male executive taking control and rejecting proposals for the election of a chairwoman and the appointment of a female organiser. 12 By 1980, women's committees Towards a Working Women's Charter 39 existed in New South Wales and Victoria, and the union decided to appoint a women's organiser in each State. The history of this decision shows that progress is possible but very slow.

There was growing interest in the problem of how to encourage women in the union movement to be more active. The interim committee of the National Council for Trade Union Training arranged a five-day seminar on 'Women in the Union Movement', attended by twenty-four women and one man. Catherine Martin of the West Australian, reported:

If the feelings of the women at the seminar can be taken as a guide, unions can expect them to be seeking maternity (and paternity) leave, flexible working hours, part-time work, and child-care facilities.

They want a society in which women are not penalised for their dual role as worker and child bearer and which expects that provision should be made for women to fit employment in with child-rearing years without total loss of rights to leave and other privileges.

In canvassing increasingly familiar issues such as lack of child care, domestic responsibilities precluding union involvement, and discouraging attitudes of husbands and union officials towards the participation of women in union activities, the women of the conference were critical of both unions and employers, finding that the second-rate position of women was reflected at all levels of society.

The year 1975 was, of course, International Women's Year. By then the proportion of women in Australia's paid workforce had increased to 40 percent and the influence of the women's lobby in the union movement was increasing.

Harold Souter convened a meeting of unions with a high female membership to discuss activities for International Women's Year. He stressed that any program undertaken would have to give the greatest benefit on a continuing basis to the Trade Union Movement generally and the female workforce in particular'. 14 His motivation seems to have been to contain the growing restiveness of women within the safe confines of normal union business, for the meeting called for union representation in International Women's Year activities rather than women's participation in union activities. One outcome was a letter to Prime Minister Whitlam asking for a survey to be done to calculate the economic contribution of women in the home, information which could be used in support of the ACTU's policy of a mothers' allowance. Th long-term effect of this would be to maintain a very strict division of labour between men and women, to discourage women from entering the paid workforce, and therefore to keep them out of the union movement's hair. Such a policy was vigorously opposed by the IWY secretariat and by Elizabeth Reid, the adviser to the prime minister on women's affairs.

Despite the 1974 National Wage Case, and the increased discussion about women in the workforce and in society in general throughout 1975, the ACTU persisted with its 'family wage' policy. Lobbying by feminists and labour women's groups intensified and, building on the experience of two previous congresses, a group of women trade unionists met to 'continue to challenge the powerlessness of women in the traditional trade union structure in order to bring about the changes necessary for women'. The group followed ideas expressed at the Women and Politics Conference in 1975 that in addition to the development of women's caucuses in trade unions, alternative Towards a Working Women's Charter 41 women's actions are a vital component of working women's striving to overcome the obstructions of traditional trade union practices which militate against the democratic rights of women'.

Policies were proposed to the 1975 congress by individual unions as well as by independent organisations. The Union of Australian Women proposed a working women's charter that was presented to congress by BWIU. The AMWU also proposed resolutions about equal pay, discrimination, encouragement of female participation in unions and the need for child care. The conservative view was defended by the Shop Distributive and Allied Employees' Association which reaffirmed the call for a mothers' allowance.

The decisions of the 1975 congress were a patch work of all of these different recommendations conditions for working women were to be improved but the fundamental opposition to dual-income families remained. The press reaction was generally favourable and did not take up the economic and social contradictions within the package' on women. ACTU President, Bob Hawke, was portrayed as repentant, expressing disappointment that there were no women on the ACTU executive and only twenty-four women amongst the seven hundred congress delegates. His new attitude was contrasted with his debate a few years earlier with Germaine Greer, and his 'male Chauvinist Pig of the Year' award.

One response to the trade union women's lobby was the establishment of the Working Women's Centre in Melbourne in May 1975. It was funded by a grant from the Federal government to the Australian Council of Salaried and Professional Associations (ACSPA), the peak council of white-collar unions. Federal funding also enabled the Women's Trade Union Commission to be set up in Sydney in September 1975. Both organisations acted as focal points for research, publicity and consciousness-raising around the issues of women in the workforce and unions.

A group which emerged from the Working Women's Centre called the Working Women's Action Group drew together all the demands which had arisen over the five years since the Women's Action Committee had been formed in response to the 1969 equal pay decision. The demands of the WAC and the 1971 and 1973 Alternative Women's Trade Union Conferences together with the 1974 AMWU Conference issues were all formulated into a cohesive, concise charter.

Two unions, the AMWU and the BWIU, had proposed to the 1975 ACTU congress that a women's charter be adopted. This was accepted, and following congress all affiliates were asked for suggestions for the charter. However, the executive declined to endorse a proposal that women's organisations be directly represented on the body to develop the charter. This meant that the charter developed by women's organisations would not necessarily provide a basis for the ACTU charter. The process suggested by Pat Clancy of the BWIU as far back as 1969 was not adopted: The best way to develop such a charter would be by consultation with the women workers themselves'.

Working women's conferences

The aspect of consultation with women workers themselves came about not through the union movement but through a process of meetings, discussions, action groups and conferences run by and for women. Although most of the participants were women workers, some sponsored by their unions, the conferences were organised autonomously, outside the structure of the union movement. This process was to coalesce into the Working Women's Charter Campaign which acted parallel with the development of the ACTU Charter for Working Women, influencing it at some points.

While unions continued to discuss the problem of women, women's conferences were discussing the problem of unions. In 1975 the problems of women at work, including trade unions, were discussed at both the Women and Health Conference in Brisbane and the Women and Politics Conference in Canberra. A major national conference of working women has been held each year since then. The Working Women's Charter was presented to a conference organised by the Women's Trade Union Commission in 1976 in Sydney around the theme 'Unions Are For Women Too!' It was attended by over 600 women. In 1977 the Working Women's Charter Campaign convened a conference in Sydney attended by about 2000 women from all States. In 1978 the Women and Labour Conference in Sydney drew over 2000 people, and throughout 1979 a group of women met once a month to plan the second Women and Labour Conference of May 1980, which also drew over 2000 people.

The Women and Politics Conference of 1975 had covered some of the recurrent themes around women and unions. Speakers made it clear that the question of women in unions was inseparable from the broader question of the role of women in the labour market and in society generally. The segregation of women into a narrow range of industries and occupations was said to allow the persistence of ghettos of low-status, lowly paid women workers. This in turn would allow employers to discriminate against women on the grounds that they were not interested in promotion, were good at routine work and did not need higher pay.

Robert Goot, an industrial advocate conducting a workshop on unions, said that because of the very limited number of women in trade union decision-making structures 'women's issues don't get pushed'. However, this view was not shared by all female unionists, some of whom expressed enthusiastic support for their unions: 'Our union fights for us all and in our award it's she means he and he means she; there's no differentiation whatsoever in our union in any way.'

Other common responses to criticisms of unions were: 'It's all we've got and we should try to improve it from within'; 'I think that [a] union is the only body that a worker can rely on. Try to work hard within the union itself and make it work better and be more practical. One of the important issues discussed was the inaction of unions which led women workers to form their own action groups, within the union structure if possible, or outside it if too much resistance was encountered. One woman spoke of deplorably squalid working conditions which had led to the formation of a working women's group within the AMWU in South Australia. In this case the union had supported the women. Delegates from twenty factories were elected to a women's committee which met every three months during working hours. The women attending were paid by the union for their time off work.

This type of development has the potential to either strengthen or challenge the prevailing union leadership, so is usually judged by its impact on internal politics. Although many women argue that to activate two-fifths of the workforce can only strengthen unions in general, it is quite clear that there will be no automatic loyalty to the status quo, and some union executives will be challenged or reformed by the involvement of women rather than simply buttressed or supplied with more 'numbers'. Edie Van Horn, a feminist labour organiser, speaking of the Coalition of Labour Union Women (CLUW) in the United States, which has attracted its share of hostility from established unions, mentioned this point: And now, they are beginning to realise that we really mean to strengthen their union, and that this is our intention to strengthen the union - not to tear it down, and not to build a kind of anti-union auxiliary, but a movement that will encourage women to become more involved and more skilled in terms of activity in their own union.

The statement was no doubt a tactical one, aiming to get support for women in unions.

One of the questions yet to be explored is how extensive the conflict will be when migrant and women workers build up enough strength to start challenging instead of asking for support. This point aroused much conflict and debate in 1976 at the Women's Trade Union Commission Conference, 'Unions Are For Women, Too!' The conference tackled the question: Why have women played such a small part in their unions? Part of the purpose of the conference was to demonstrate to the union movement that women unionists were active, aware and willing to organize around issues that affect them. The 'problem', the lack of involvement by women in their unions, was generally not seen as a failure on the part of women. On the contrary, unions were criticised for their lack of protest against the exploitation of, and high unemployment amongst, women, and their failure to recognise women as breadwinners. However, despite the criticisms, the main aim of the conference was to increase the status of women in the eyes of male unionists without being too 'threatening'. Information was distributed about new directions being taken by women workers' groups, about sexism, problems still remaining with 'equal pay', experiences of migrant women, discrimination, parental leave, black women and unions, part-time work, trade union training, fatigue as an industrial disease and other related issues.

The working women's charter

The charter presented at the 1976 conference began with a statement of the right to work for everyone who wishes to do so.

This fundamental right was in reaction to the ACTU's continued support of the mothers' allowance, and growing exploitation of the potential rivalry between married and unmarried women, between men and women, and between youth and married women. Equal pay and equal opportunity were spelt out in the charter, along with the introduction of a thirty-five-hour week, flexible working hours, part-time work and reasonable shiftwork opportunities. These points created difficulties for women from some unions who saw part-time work as eroding workers' right to full-time work and associated benefits. The charter also included child care, paid parental leave, family leave to allow for time off in case of family emergencies, sex education, birth control, abortion on demand and comprehensive research into health problems.

A second version of the charter was drawn up by Towards a Working Women's Charter 47 Sydney participants after the conference. Demands covering the discriminatory use of protective legislation and provision of unemployment benefit to unemployed women with male partners were added, and the demand for equal pay was clarified to one for 'the rate for the job', leaving less room for evasion.

The charter was expected to fulfil two roles. The first was as a document to be used as a log of claims. Documentation of demands was seen as a first step towards pressing unions, government and employers. for explicit action. The charter would be a focal point for organisation, consciousness-raising and communication between women workers. The second role, that of action, was stressed and the title Working Women's Charter Campaign was adopted.

Organisation around the campaign had a number of levels. Four States (Victoria, New South Wales, Queensland and South Australia) had State campaign committees which met monthly to plan specific actions, allow communication and support from diverse workplaces and to encourage co-ordination between women's committees that had been set up in various unions. Some workplaces had particularly active women's charter groups. Another level of organization existed between States, although practical difficulties meant that this level was effective only for communication rather than for joint action.

At the 1977 Charter Campaign Conference many issues were discussed but the conference decided to work on five key areas of the charter: the right to work, the right to organise, the problems of migrant women, child care, and industrial health and safety. One workshop dealt with the ACTU's charter which was to be presented to congress that September, and some lobbying about that was generated. However, on the whole the focus of the conference was the work being done by women at the shop-floor level, within unions and rank-and-file women's committees.

The history of the Working Women's Charter Campaign is one of creative tension between the women's movement and the labour movement, both acting autonomously but influencing each other, overlapping and working together at many points.

Since the adoption of the charter by the ACTU there has been less activity outside the union movement, however numerous groups have formed to work around the charter or various parts of it.

The ACTU Charter for Working Women

Jan Marsh, an ACTU research officer, was given the task of circulating affiliates for suggestions for the ACTU charter. Only seven unions responded. The Working Women's Charter Campaign and the Melbourne Working Women's Centre also sent suggestions but the charter, as presented to the ACTU in September 1977, was primarily the work of Jan Marsh. It began with a preamble stating that:

It is recognised that some policies supported by the ACTU to achieve equality apply also to male workers. However, until such time that male and female workers have equal responsibility for domestic duties and child rearing, many of these policies must be directed principally towards female workers. The pursuit and achievement of recommendations in this charter should contribute to the change in attitudes required before equality regardless of sex can prevail in practice.

It went on to declare:

The ACTU supports, consistent with its policy, the right to paid work for all who want to work, irrespective of age, marital status, sex, sexuality, race, country of origin, religion, political belief, or appearance.[2]

As outlined in the Introduction, the charter covered three areas. The first section included factors which inhibit or restrict women's entry into the paid workforce, and recommended equal opportunities in education and training, a review of 'protective' legislation, and provision of child-care facilities. The second section dealt with inequalities in actual conditions of work. It recommended equal pay for work of equal value, flexibility in the pattern of work, provision of comprehensive, multilingual health and safety information, medical services, and maternity and paternity leave. The third section dealt with women's involvement in unions. It recommended more recruitment of female members, trade union education about the problems of women, and active encouragement of women to stand for office in unions.

Overall, the document was cautiously worded and dealt inadequately with the substantial problems of migrant women by including a point about English lessons in the section on education and training. The important area of occupational health was also limited in that it called for information rather than action to eliminate hazards from the workplace. However, the charter did encapsulate most of the major issues that had been identified over the preceding few years.

One successful amendment to the charter called for a charter conference to ensure that it was a document for action. However several other amendments, both pro- and anti- feminist, were rejected by the ACTU executive. The feminists - primarily white-collar unions such as the NSW Teachers' Federation, and left-wing blue-collar unions - aimed to widen the charter to encompass demands of the Working Women's Charter Campaign and the Working Women's Centre: unemployment benefit for all unemployed people, sex education and abortion. Anti-feminist right-wing ions, such as the Federated Clerks' Union, aimed to reinforce the role of women as homemakers.

The ACTU Charter Conference, 1978

The ACTU Women's Charter Conference was held in March 1978. Preparation for the conference was undertaken by a liaison committee which included several women in prominent positions in their own unions, who were also activists in the Working Women's Charter Campaign.23 According to Rhonda Galbally, there was a polarisation between most of the women delegates on the one hand and the representatives of the ACTU executive on the other.

The conference agreed that child care, equal pay and maternity leave were priority areas for action.25 Responsibility for action on the charter was delegated to the Trades and Labour Councils of each State but by 1979 only the Victorian Trades Hall Council had an active women's committee to implement it.

The main achievement to date has been the winning of fifty-two weeks' unpaid maternity leave in a test case at the Arbitration Commission in April 1979. Although the leave is unpaid, and therefore lags behind both the public service and the labour laws of many other countries, it does offer pregnant women protection against being sacked, and gives them the Towards a Working Women's Charter 51 right to return to their jobs after the birth of a baby. The provisions do not apply automatically, but must be inserted into each Federal award by individual unions.

In the area of child care, the ACTU has become involved in two projects in Melbourne. One was initiated by the Working Women's Centre and ACSPA, and aims to set up a child-care centre. The other has drawn together a number of unions and community workers with the aim of improving child-care services in the western suburbs. Both of these projects are discussed further in Chapter 8.

The Victorian Trades Hall Council Women's Committee In Victoria, a women's committee has been meeting throughout 1979 and 1980, with a major task being to prepare booklets and posters about the charter for distribution in the workplace to the large number of women who are unaware of its existence. The committee is hampered by the fact that distribution of material on a large scale can only be done by the organisers of each union, rather than by a central committee. Therefore, those unions that have their own women's committees, or that have a strong commitment to their women members, are more likely than others to promote the charter.

The Victorian committee achieved a significant amendment to the 1977 charter when, in 1979, they successfully proposed that the charter should include the policy that comprehensive sex education and family planning advice be made available at the workplace', and that 'there should be free, safe legal abortion for those who choose it'.

The Wollongong Working Women's Charter Campaign

In Wollongong, a city south of Sydney which is dominated by the steel industry, a charter committee is women the right to focusing on a campaign to gain work in Australian Iron and Steel company where, in 1980, less than 2 per cent of the production workforce 28 The committee includes women comprised women. unionists but is based in the local women's centre. It In April 1980 some supports the aims of the ACTU charter, but would like to see them extended. for Equal Opportunity, alleging that the company had women lodged complaints with the NSW Counsellor failed to employ women on an equal basis with men. They estimated that 2000 women had been denied jobs with the company over the previous six or seven years. The legal action was being handled as a class action' according to the provisions of the NSW Equal Opportunity legislation.

A 'jobs for women' campaign was set up to win and community organisations, bringing together sev support from a wide range of unions, women's groups eral of the general issues of the charter - the right to work, unemployment, discrimination, and the problems of migrant women.30 It is addressed to the particular nature of Wollongong which is an industrial city where the major employer is a traditionally 'male' heavy industry and the wide range of manufacturing, service and tertiary sector industries which typically employ women are absent.

The Newcastle cleaners' strike

In Newcastle, similarly an industrial city to the north Towards a Working Women's Charter 53 of Sydney, dominated by BHP, the Working Women's Charter Campaign supported industrial action by women employed at BHP by a firm of contract cleaners.

The women, of whom half were English-speaking and half Yugoslavs with little English, were members of the Miscellaneous Workers' Union. Until March 1976 there had been 34 full-time cleaners working a total of 1190 hours a week on the BHP site. Then the company changed this to 39 cleaners working part time for a total of 720 hours. When the cleaning contract came up for renewal in July 1977, a rival contractor offered to do the job in 566 hours a week. When contractors change, the same women are usually kept on the job. However, the new contractor proposed to employ full-time workers only and sack the remaining 23 women.

In June 1977 the women went on strike, taking their cleaning equipment with them so that it could not be used by strike-breaking labour. They formed a strike committee, published bilingual leaflets, and went around to job-sites in Newcastle raising money and support. They were joined by members of the Working Women's Charter Campaign from Sydney.

Under great pressure financial hardship, the threat of unemployment, hostile press reactions and tension between the two ethnic groups - the women continued their strike for eight weeks, during which they gradually gained the confidence to crowd into the union office, taking over available desks and telephones.

The women went back to work after the eight weeks to allow a hearing at the Industrial Commission. The hearing ruled that 18 women should be employed full time at BHP and that the contractor should employ all the remaining women on other sites around New castle. Accordingly, the women worked for another month. In this time their two shop stewards, one Aushands and were obliged to resign their union postralian and one Yugoslav, were both made leading itions. Other women spoke of intimidation by supervisors.

At a union meeting at the end of the first month the women realised that in fact only 16 or 17 women had been employed at BHP, and that the contractor had been sacking older women from other sites in order to employ the women from BHP. They complained that they were expected to work much faster to do the work that had once been done by 34 women, and still maintain the same standard. They felt depressed about their ability to protect their jobs and control the amount of work required of them. They decided to go back to the Industrial Commission and ask for 20 full-time cleaners to be assigned to the job. The company applied to have the number reduced to 16, and the court decided that the number should be kept at 18.

The union organiser involved in the dispute said that the decision was a great victory, especially for the small number of women still active'. He attributed this to the sustained involvement of the women themselves in the dispute and at the court hearing. Three women gave evidence and were 'magnificent although terrified'. One of the women, a Yugoslav, was questioned through an interpreter and 'tipped the can on the company'

Many issues can be seen in this one dispute. One important point is that the right to work must be fought for on the job when loss of employment is threatened. Too often, the right to work is seen only Towards a Working Women's Charter 55 as a problem of unemployed people.

The second major point is that the right to work' rapidly raises the question of 'workers' control'. The women in Newcastle initially went on strike to keep their jobs but as the dispute went on they claimed the right to determine how many hours the job needed and therefore the conditions that each worker should have. It is a reflection of the serious impact of the recession on women that the Newcastle cleaners were not fighting to improve their conditions, but to prevent them deteriorating even further. Industrial cleaning is heavy work, and the pressure on the women to keep up the same amount of work after their numbers had been reduced was leading to health problems such as tiredness, stress, sore arms and legs and frequent recourse to analgesics and tranquillisers.

A further point is that in the course of the dispute the union organiser worked hard to give the women maximum support and encouragement, but never took over or prevented the women from pursuing the dispute for themselves. The strength that the women gained from this experience can be seen by the fact that although union activists were harrassed and moved to different jobs by their supervisors and two shop stewards were forced to resign their positions, another woman came forward to take on the job of delegate. So union organisation was retained despite the immense pressures against the women. As the organiser commented:

Of all the disputes that involve women workers, the crying need is for female union organisers. I don't care how good an organiser is, and I guess I try to do my job as well as I can, women will relate to and respond much better to women Women at Work than they ever will to men. Their experience has proven to them that they shouldn't expect too much from a union organiser, and the trust isn't there. I believe there is a terrible need for more within the unions themselves.

feminists to play more of a role The Western Region Centre for Working Women My own work at the Centre for Working Women, in the Melbourne suburb of Footscray, has been based on a similar principle. The centre is an autonomous cooperative of women whose aim is to work with unions to support women workers at the shop-floor level. The aim of the centre is not to take on the role of a female confidence-union organiser but to encourage the development of consciousness-raising, building, and opening access to information so that the women themselves can create the demand for better representation, more support, more effective organisation and more resources being directed towards their problems as women workers. A process Specifically, the centre's purpose is to discuss, publicise and work towards implementing the ACTU Charter for Working Women. Initially, in 1978, the centre concentrated on the meat industry and established contact with groups of women in five meatworks. With repeated contact and discussion in the lunch break, core groups of interested women were developed. In the meat industry women are outnumbered by men, and have to cope with strong hostility from them. They felt that to be effective, they needed more knowledge of their rights, of union procedures and how to go about asserting themselves on the job and within the union. This led Towards a Working Women's Charter 57 to the centre developing a proposal for a women's course which we would run. It was to be attended by several women from each of the factories, during working hours, with time off from work paid for by the union. It was to have included consciousness- raising, confidence-building discussions of strategies for dealing with problems that arise in being a woman at work as well as information about awards, rights and procedures, and some of the background to the union movement and the women's movement. Unfortunately the courses were not held, mainly because of the erratic nature of the meat industry at that time. Some factories closed, others were functioning on a skeleton staff, and another was relocated all of which caused great uncertainty and hardship to the women. We retained contact with women from one of the factories that was still working and had regular meetings in a local council centre, as well as showing films and videos at our own centre outside working hours.

In early 1979 we started working with women in the clothing industry, and visited about eight factories in the region. Permission to enter the factories and contact the women was gained for us by the union organiser. We would then address them in the lunch room, meet the shop steward and move from table to table, explaining the issues in the charter and listening to the women's reactions. Often we returned with interpreters or with information about some particular aspect of the charter which the women had found relevant - some were concerned about child care, others about discrimination, others about union education courses, others about employment opportunities for their daughters.

At this stage we were basically talking about issue and were hampered by the lack of resources such suitable environment for using those that were avail. as leaflets, posters and short video tapes, and the and unsuitable for holding meetings. However, havable. Most of the factories were small, noisy, crowded ing built up contacts with the women, we were able to community schools and find other locations, such as municipal offices, which were near enough to the factory for women to visit in their lunch break – usually half an hour. This allowed the women to speak freely and overcome some of the physical problems.

The next phase of the centre's work was to emphasize processes rather than issues. We found that initial interest in particular issues rapidly fell away, and women would say they saw no prospect of doing anything; they felt powerless and pessimistic about their ability to change things. The reasons for their pessimism varied from factory to factory. In some, women blamed the men who were so hostile to their involvement in union issues, in others the Australians blamed the migrants or vice versa, the young blamed the old, the old blamed the young and almost everyone blamed the union. While we saw that these divisions were based on very real difficulties, we also saw that they were the product of people's sense of frustration at their own powerlessness.

Our response to this was to keep meeting and to try to bring up relevant examples of situations where this sense of powerlessness and isolation had been overcome, say in another factory or another industry; for example, a dispute in which all ethnic groups had been united, or a situation in which women had stood up for themselves and won support of the men on the job. As we went through these examples it became apparent that we were talking about a process taking Towards a Working Women's Charter 59 place amongst the women in the factory, a process of basic organisation based on their awareness of their common interests. It was leading towards the development of shop committees and women's charter groups on the job. Without this basic organisation and process whereby the women could state and act upon their needs, talk about issues was futile.

We envisaged an expanding network of women's organisations - shop committees in individual factories, charter groups made up of women from different actories in the same industries, women's committees in individual unions, charter groups drawn from different unions and industries always, and most importantly, based on developments at the shop-floor level. Our approach is time-consuming but basically we feel there is no way for women in the labour movement to organise effectively without long hours of multilingual discussion in the workplace. Therefore, implementing the charter means more than simply acting on a policy document. It entails a continuing task of building links between women workers which must of necessity go beyond the traditional centralised 'from-the-top-down' style of action that has excluded women in the past.

CHAPTER 3

'And we'll get our jobs back

The Right to Work

The right to work, as quoted in the Universal Declaration of Human Rights, includes the right to free choice of employment, just and favourable working conditions, and protection against unemployment

For women, who have traditionally worked without pay and without recognition as workers, this entails the right of entry into the paid workforce and the gradual removal of the barriers against participating as equals. It means recognition of women's right to economic independence and recognition of the value and variety of the contribution that women can make in the paid workforce. To ensure that working conditions are just and favourable, women must also have the right to organise as workers and to participate in trade unions.

The barriers that exist at present fall into two groups. Firstly, women's job horizons and options are limited, not expanded, by the early social conditioning, education, training and retraining now available Secondly, the double working life of most women imposes a handicap or penalty on women in the paid workforce. Lacking such provisions as child care, paid parental leave, family leave, refresher courses, flexible working hours and supportive social attitudes, most women are limited in their ability to enter and participate in the workforce.

Furthermore, we live in a time of social and technological change and of economic and environmental crisis. The availability of job security, employment opportunities, income security and social services will all be in question as the twentieth century draws to a close. The right to work, encompassing both the social and the economic role of women, will inevitably feel the profound impact of these forces.

Because it is part of an economic and political system, the right to work cannot be guaranteed by law. For this reason, although many countries guarantee the right to work in their constitutions and Australia does not, the social barriers and difficulties that women face are similar in those countries and in Australia.

Australian women have been fighting for the right to work and for the conditions that must accompany it for most of this century. As Edna Ryan and Anne Conlon put it in their book, *Gentle Invaders:*

When the contribution past and present of women in the Australian workforce is considered, it is dreadful injustice that women have been considered invaders of the workplace. As women have never been less that 20 per cent of the Australian workforce at any time, and have more generally been one third, it is not only unjust but ludicrous that women have been faced with the necessity of demanding either the right to work or the right to be paid the rate for the job.[1]

They conclude that although some legal entitlements equality in the paid workforce will only be achieved through active participation and struggle.

As has been noted, there has recently been an increase of women in the paid workforce, to 37 per cent of the total in March 1980 from the 20 per cent to 30 per cent that was typical of the first half of the century. However, this has not been accompanied by changes that significantly reduce the workloads of women traditional unpaid role. Changing social attitudes and economic pressures have led to women working in paid jobs as well as looking after families, having children, cooking, doing the shopping and housework and so on. But they have not led to a real shift in the burden of domestic responsibilities. This in turn has helped to tie women to sex-segregated, low-paid, dead-end jobs that are an imitation of their unpaid work.

As has been explained in Chapter 2, the numerous versions of the working women's charter developed over the 1970s all led with a statement of the right to work and followed with a list of issues needed to guarantee that right and make it effective, including opposition to discrimination in the hiring and firing of women, positive encouragement in education and job training, and provision of child-care facilities to make participation in the workforce possible.

The right of married women to work

In the past the greatest hostility regarding women's right to work has been towards married women in the paid workforce. As the history of the equal-pay case shows, it has been generally assumed that women do not have a right to economic independence, do not support families either as sole or substantial breadwinners, and are inevitably supported by their husbands after marriage. Any regard for social history would show this assumption to be false. And yet it has been a persistent myth used to justify denying employment to married women, sacking women on marriage, or limiting married women to jobs that men and young people are not seeking.

Stella Nord, a British migrant who has been campaigning for the right to work for many years, was working in the meat industry in Queensland in the 1960s when the right of married women to work was a big issue:

Union policy in the southern district, which was the area all around Brisbane, was against married women. The only time you got a job was when labour was short and there was no one else. But there was no State union policy, and that meant there were quite a number of arguments.

There was a lot of campaigning. At one stage, when it was the union policy, the State one, that we should remain on the job, there was an attitude in certain sections was very bad. There was a seniority system. There were two sections and two separate seniorities. It was a last on, first off principle. At that time the supervisor, the manager, he wanted to pay off someone from the other department. And the delegate, plus, I would say, almost everybody else, said no, they should pay us, the three married women, off, from now on, and allow three from the other section to go in where we were. And the boss dug his toes in and said 'No, you wanted two separate seniorities and here they are.' Anyway, there was a meeting called and I was the only one who put my hand up against it. And there were other married women who would have liked to oppose it, but such was things would be very difficult for them. However, when in the atmosphere that existed that... they really felt that unopposed. You felt like public enemy number one. So the put my hand up it was registered that it didn't go totally straight away.' After that the foreman came round and he delegate came round and told us, You'll have to leave the union.' So we went home, and a big argument went on said, 'You can't go.' And

I said, 'Well, I doubt if I can oppose about the two seniorities, which was a union decision.

So eventually it was decided that they wanted the two seniorities retained. That meant we would go back. And I to go back. They were really terrified, working in that at- was in touch with the others by phone, and they didn't want atmosphere. So I said, "The argument's been fought. We've got the right to go back. If you don't go back now, all that's been wasted. And you want to think about establishing the right to work.' Anyway, they all turned up. We had a terrible time. Matter of fact, we were threatened with being thrown in the Brisbane River if we did turn up. But what did happen was we were pushed out of various queues, for hot water for tea and things like that. But it didn't last long.

What was interesting was, some of the most militant women around there you couldn't move them about married women. It became very noticeable that [the issue of] pregnant women, used mostly by the men, was their favourite [argument]: 'Oh, yes, you've got your old man to keep you. Single girls are walking the streets, forced to go on the game.' It had a real emotive appeal, the single girl 'walking the streets'. Never mind about maybe married women walking the streets too. They do say, however, that if you are widowed or if you are separated, you were counted as single. But if you actually had a husband... you were made to feel that you were taking the bread out of a starving single woman's mouth. And it was a very difficult one to overcome. And it was no good spouting about the rights of married women, well you had to do that, but it didn't get through that type of very emotional thing that was put over... It was so powerful that even if men had their wives working they'd keep it quiet. And I knew for a fact that women were living with blokes. I mean, I'd visited their houses. We all lived in the area, so you'd see the women shopping Saturday. Even a lot of the men knew they were living with blokes.

The issue got so hot it was decided there'd be a mass meeting called. And a meeting was called by the Southern District Council, and quite a lot of lobbying went on. I know I worked my guts out getting in touch with married women in other sheds who were working. Some of them were afraid to come. Some of them did come. But at that meeting, I must say, the influence of the National Civic Council was very strong, and they had NCC support, and the right wing of the Labor Party. And they were mouthing the policy that a woman's place is in the home. I mean that was the gut thing about it. The ones against married women actively went around and asked people to come to this meeting in the Trades Hall. Any road, come the night, I may be wrong, but I reckon overwhelmingly we were outnumbered. They called on the union, the State body, to reverse its policy.

After a while, it must have been about twelve months after this, there was another meeting called. By this twelve months after, a quite a number of married women were working - the number had increased and a number of single women had got married. It's remarkable how in six months things can change. So there was a further meeting and we lobbied again, and this time it was overwhelmingly in favour of the right of married women to work - including a lot of men that were. So that was a bit of a gain.

Actually, when the situation comes up now against married women, I don't think it will ever reach the low level that it was then. So many more married women are going to of work, the percentage is much higher; and not only that, their children, their financial needs are greater; for that there's a higher cost of living, higher cost of education reason I think married women will fight more than what they did then.

But a lot of men have their wives working too, and to a certain extent they've kind of got double standards. Their wife can work somewhere else. If on the job there's rumblings about married women, they keep very quiet about it. They don't... they won't come out and support married They know that they need that money and that they want women, even though their own wife is working somewhere their wife to be working.

Queensland in particular has always been notorious for its attitude to married women in the workforce. The Queensland government for years and years had the policy of not employing them in the public service.

Recently, women's right to work has been recognised by the Conciliation and Arbitration Commission in an historic judgement in the case of a woman who was dismissed by her employer because she got married. In August 1977, Mrs Janine Marshall was sacked from her job with Rockhampton City Council where she had worked for four years. She took her case to the Committee on Discrimination in Employment and Occupation which deferred it while her union, the Municipal Officers' Association, applied to the commission for a variation in their award to provide that an employer should not elicit a promise from an employee to resign on marriage and should not dismiss an employee on marriage.

The case was supported by the Commonwealth, the United Nations Association of Australia and women's organisations such as the Women's Electoral Lobby and the Union of Australian Women. They were particularly concerned because the practice of dismissing women on marriage was common amongst local government authorities in several States. The commission ruled that it had... a role to play in the elimination of discriminatory work practices, and so opened the way for anti-discrimination clauses to be inserted into awards, so that they will have greater legal force than they do now as well as trade union backing.

The Rockhampton Council argued that its policy of sacking married women helped to alleviate youth unemployment. The commission had this to say in response:

No one doubts that youth unemployment is a serious problem, but in our view this problem cannot be solved by the forced retirement of married women workers.

The incidence and spread of youth unemployment is such that the pursuit of a policy to create jobs for young people by the dismissal of married women by certain local government authorities in Queensland could have no significant impact on youth unemployment levels...

Although the local government associations sought to resist the M.O.A. application by reference to the current unemployment situation, it is noteworthy that according to the evidence of Alderman Pilbeam, Mayor of Rockhampton, the policy has been pursued by his Council for 'over the past 100 years', a time span in which there have been periods of full employment.

The award was varied to state that there should be no discrimination on the basis of sex 'other than a distinction, exclusion or preference based on inherent requirements of a particular job'. Sacking of women after marriage was interpreted to be primarily a case of discrimination on the basis of sex rather than marital status. Although Janine Marshall was not reinstated, her case did serve to give women's right to be understood, though, that Australia does not have a work a place in Australian industrial law. It should uniform labour law and it is still up to each union to clauses to protect women's right to work, inserted into take action to have anti-discrimination clauses, or their awards.

The right to work and changing labour market conditions

Many obstacles to women's right to work still remain. and the lack of appropriate education, training and Some, such as the lack of adequate child-care facilities retraining facilities have been regarded primarily as social issues. These will be discussed further below. However, more and more unions are coming to regard them as industrial issues and are adopting policies about them.

The Women Workers' Group of the International Federation of Chemical and General Workers' Unions (ICF) held a conference in 1973 on the right to work and problems that hinder its implementation. In a discussion of some of the developments of recent years one speaker pointed out that these aspects – equal pay, anti-discrimination laws and so on - would continue to advance slowly, as long as 'the pace of technical progress' remained the same and unemployment was avoided. Unions, with the involvement of the large number of their members who are women, could do much to hasten this by influencing public opinion and bringing about the desired political and technological choices.

As the Australian economy has swung from a period of growth to one of recession characterised by rising unemployment, declining manufacturing industry and technological change this process is all the more urgent as the impact on women has been great. The increasing entry of women into the paid workforce has been stemmed. Women have a higher rate of official unemployment than men, along with a far higher hidden unemployment rate, and the old attacks on the rights of married women to work are regaining currency. The ambiguity of women's role as paid workers and unpaid workers in the home is being exploited again as more women drop out of the labour market altogether, discouraged by the lack of job prospects.

To advocates of women's rights this process is a denial of the right of women to economic independence and to the broad range of social experience that the paid workforce represents. To many families who depend on two incomes it is a threat to their economic security.

The crucial questions facing women workers are whether or not employment opportunities will remain and, more importantly, whether the gains made in social attitudes, laws and industrial organisation can be maintained in order to protect job opportunities.

While these questions seem impossible to answer at present, two important points are relevant. Although it is true that the social and industrial advances of women workers depend a lot on the state of the labour market, which is now in decline, they also depend on the level of industrial and community organization that women have achieved. In the Depression of the 1930s fewer women had experienced the paid work- force than now, fewer were unionised and fewer had been active on the job. They were, therefore, less able to withstand the impact of the Depression. The situation may well be different in the 1980s. Secondly, since the women's movement has been primarily a community rather than industrial orgianisation, it is now better place to reach unemployed women and the understand the social impact of unemployment to women.

Despite the demand for their labour, Australian women were slow to make slow to make social and industrial gains in the 1950's and 1960's. The major reason for this was probably the massive immigration program of that period the labour shortage without requiring much government expenditure on social health, welfare and educational services. This was to detriment the migrant workers settling in Australia, particularly the women who joined workforce in large number and were forced to cope without all those services. In a situation of labour scarcity Australian-born women would have been in a better position to bargain and improved social and industrial provisions. The trend in the 1980's will be for employer's to move their capital top areas of plentiful and cheap labour, primarily South-East Asia rather than importing a new and non-unionised workforce, so that again the bargaining position of Australian female workers will become tenuous.

that period reduced the labour shortage without probably that the massive immigration program of health, welfare and educational services. This was to requiring much government expenditure on social, the detriment of the migrant workers settling in Australia, particularly the women who joined the workforce in large numbers and were forced to cope with.

Trends in female unemployment

In May 1979 the Australian Bureau of Statistics estimated that 6.2 per cent of the paid workforce were unemployed and actively seeking work. They numbered some 396 600 people- 186 000 women and 210 600 men. The rate of unemployment was higher amongst women, with 8 per cent of the workforce unemployed, than amongst men, with 5.1 per cent of the workforce unemployed. Throughout the years 1964 to 1974, female unemployment was consistently higher than male unemployment. It ranged between per cent and 3 per cent compared to around 1 per cent for men. Keith Windschuttle, in his book. *Unemployment,* comments on the apparent paradox that despite higher rates of unemployment women have gained more jobs than men, and in those terms are doing 'better' in the labour market. Since the 1960s and early 1970s women's unemployment has increased by three to four times and men's unemployment has increased by five to six times. What has happened is that the increasing entry of women into the paid workforce has continued as unemployment has risen and the higher unemployment rate of women has also persisted, even though it has not risen as steeply as that of men.

Unemployment, as officially measured, is higher amongst single people than amongst married people, whether male or female, but it is higher amongst married women than amongst married men. In May 1979, 5.1 per cent of married women in the labour force were unemployed compared to 2.5 per cent of married men and 12.7 per cent of unmarried women. This points to the especially high unemployment rate amongst young people, notably young women. As many as 20 per cent of women in the 15-19 age-group were unemployed; that is, one in every five, compared to 14.2 per cent of young males. Women in the 20-24 age-group had an unemployment rate of 9.9 per cent, half as much again as the rate for the workforce as a whole.

Clearly the paid workforce is segregated into groups, according to sex and age, whose experiences with work and unemployment are significantly different. Women and young people are experiencing more severe effects of recession than men and older people. However, workers in their late forties and fifties are being edged out of labour market into early retirement. Ethnic origin is the other major characteristic by which the labourforce is segregated. The most drastic discrimination in the labour market is directed towards Aboriginal people. No reliable figures Aboriginal unemployment exist, but several estinates have been made putting the figure at around half of the Aboriginal workforce. This is not simply the effects of recession, but the cumulation of the impact of the white civilization on Aboriginal culture.

More reliable figures are available for Australia's overseas-born workforce. They indicate that recently arrived migrant worker are harder hit by unemployed than white Australian-born workers. The is not much difference between Australian-born men and women. The difference is most marked in respect of married women. Of a number of possible reasons, is that migrant women are concentrated in manufacturing industry, especially those labour-intensive industries that have been hardest hit by technology and structural change, such as clothing, textiles, footwear and light manufacturing, where thousands of jobs have ceased to exist. Another possibility is that because their husbands are likely to be working in unskilled jobs on the minimum wage, themselves facing unemployment, migrant women, if unemployed, will stay in the workforce looking for a job, whereas Australian-born women are more likely to stop job hunting and define themselves and housewives.

This is one example of " hidden unemployment" a phenomenon that is receiving more attention as official statistics lose their credibility either because of technical inadequacies or because of repeated political manipulation.

Hidden Unemployment

It is not uncommon to hear the Minister for Employment stating that unemployment has dropped by several thousand. For instance, in August 1979 the Australian Bureau of Statistics reported a decrease of 6500 in the number of people unemployed. However, this cannot be taken as a sign that the job market is looking up because there was also a drop of 35 000 in the number of employed. So the labour market lost 41 500 people, many whom should be counted as hidden unemployed. The state of the labour market is probably best measured in these circumstances by the rates at which various social groupings are participating in the labour force. Figures released by the Bureau of Statistics in August 1979 showed that only 60.1 per cent of the hospital workforce were employed for looking for employment, the lowest since 1966.

Many articles mentioned in particular hidden unemployment among young people, women and older workers. For example, a paper by the Department of Employment and Youth Affairs stated that:

Empirical studies undertaken elsewhere have shown that women, youth and older workers are particularly likely to react to a reduction in job opportunities by dropping out of the workforce, and so the increasing discouragement resulting from rising unemployment will slowly erode labourforce participation of these demographic groups.

The Australian Financial Review commented on the 21 September 1979 that ironically, falling participation rates make official unemployment figures look better than the actual state of labour market. Discouraged workers, the article continued and do not show up in official figures.

Part-time work may be regarded as another form of hidden unemployment if people really want to work longer hours take part-time jobs because they cannot find full-time jobs. If this is true, then partime work is an aspect of the deterioration of the labour market. Karen Throssell, of the labour resource centre, has argued that this is more relevant to the male labour market, claiming that male workers formely employed full time have taken a step down into part-time work whereas female part-timers are more likely to be entering the paid workforce for the first time or after a long break from their paid work. For them, part-time work may represent the opening up of opportunities for married women For them, part-time work may represent the opening up of opportunities for employment that did not exist previously. This should not obscure the factthat job opportunities for married women who choose to work part time because of their child-care and other domestic responsibilities are still quite limited. If better child-care facilities were available and if more domestic duties were shared, more women would be available for longer hours of paid work. And, given job opportunities, more women would be able to make child-care arrangements and seek jobs with longer hours. Also, greater sharing of child rearing and domestic tasks by men could result in increased support for shorter working hours and for increased pay and benefits for part-time work.

The Australian Bureau of Statistics has found that some part-time workers would prefer to work longer hours but cannot, for a variety of reasons.19 Others were actively seeking full-time jobs. In May 1979 13.2 per cent of part-time workers said they would prefer to be working longer hours, and a further 4.2 per cent were looking for a full-time job. A higher proportion of men wanted longer hours (18.2 per cent) or were looking for full-time jobs (7.7 per cent) compared to women (11.8 per cent and 3.0 per cent). Fewer married women said they would prefer longer hours (9.3 per cent) or were looking for full-time jobs (1.5 percent) compared to single women (21 per cent and 8.6 per cent respectively).

These figures indicate that whilst a small proportion of married women presently employed part time could be regarded as being amongst the 'hidden unemployed' or under-employed, a quarter of the men are in that situation, along with over a quarter of the single women.

Estimates of the extent of hidden unemployment indicate that the official figures should be doubled to get the real level of unemployment. The hidden unemployed are estimated from surveys of the labourforce and of those not in the labourforce. Within the groups already mentioned, they include people wanting longer hours, those discouraged from seeking work because of the lack of job opportunities, those considered too old (or too young) by employers, people with language difficulties, people lacking adequate education and training for the jobs that are available, people who cannot find jobs in suitable locations or within suitable hours, people unable to find childcare, and people who are marking time at school because they have no job to move on to.

With unemployment becoming more long term, the number of people dropping out of the labour market is increasing. Young people in particular girls become demoralised and stay home, perhaps looking after younger brothers and sisters or with the housework. Some drift into pregnancy at an early age because they see no other future for themselves, no other purpose in life. Married women, whose work pattern is characterised by periods in and out of paid employment, are most likely to withdraw from the labour market as they can slip into a family role more easily than men.

One study found that as male unemployment increases, more women join the paid workforce, probably to supplement family income or to have some protection if their husbands become unemployed. However, as male unemployment continues to increase and job prospects for women also deteriorate, greater numbers of women leave the paid labourforce as discouraged workers.

Structural barriers against women's right to work

Even in times of so-called full employment, when official figures for job-seekers and vacancies roughly equal, women have had a high rate of unemployment. The types of jobs available – in a highly sex-segregated labour market - have not been suitable, or they have not been located in areas accessible to women. Surveys done in 1969 of female unemployment in Newcastle, Wollongong, Elizabeth and Geelong, all regional cities outside their State capitals, showed that there was high official and hidden unemployment amongst women. The report proposed solutions such as improving transport to allow women to travel to the available jobs, broadening the range of industries and jobs in the areas concerned in order to increase the number of openings in 'female' occupations, and, lastly, encouraging women move into more non-traditional or predominantly male occupations.… social and work attitudes of employers, unions and the women themselves must change to the extent of recognizing the possibilities of employing females in a wider range of jobs. At the same time, this could require examination of instances of industrial legislation and awards which restrict hours of work and entry of women in respect of certain occupations. The provisions of special training, where necessary, to equip females to carry out the work required should also be considered.

The only study done in that period of full employment to find out how many women would join the paid workforce or register for employment if they thought jobs were available was carried out by the NSW Department of Decentralisation and Development in order to discover whether decentralisation of industry to country towns was viable. 23 A large potential workforce was discovered, consisting of women who were deterred by lack of job opportunities from registering for employment. The study found that an average of 24 per cent of the females surveyed who did not register would have sought work if they thought it was available. But while their services were not called upon, these women did not appear in unemployment figures, did not receive the dole and were not the subject of concern in news editorials.

Since those two reports were published some changes have taken place. For instance, social attitudes about the range of jobs open to women have become more liberal. Committees and boards have been set up with discrimination. Unions have accepted the principles of equal opportunity in education and employment, and the ACTU is undertaking a review protective and restrictive legislation affecting women workers. However, there have been fewer developments in the areas of education and job training.

Statements that the education system does not succeed in preparing people for the workforce, and that it narrows rather than broadens their opportunities, are so common, especially in relation to the education of women, that they need not be listed here. In at least two ways women's right to work is seriously diminished by the education system. Firstly, the system, in concert with broader societal influences, contributes to the narrow range of expectations and skills that girls develop. Special encouragement is needed to compensate for the channelling of girls into subjects that limit their job opportunities. In 1975, Girls, School and Society, a report on the educational opportunities of girls, stated:

Girls achieve at least equally well with boys in school, but the subject choices they make are more limiting than those made by boys in the opportunities they open up for further education and employment.

Girls may also be handicapped by entering the workforce with lower educational level than boys. According to the report:

The greatest disparity between the sexes exists in industrial and technical training which strongly attracts boys leaving school before completing a full secondary course. Girls leaving school at this level are more likely to drop out of schooling altogether.

Secondly, the education system affects those women – in fact most women – who periodically leave and re-enter the paid workforce. As the report stated:

Educational opportunities for women re-entering the workforce are still very limited. There is as yet no serious attempt to give financial support, encouragement or open access to women whose education and occupational opportunities have been restricted by the important social function of child rearing.

If women are to continue this function as well as participating in the paid workforce, then certain provisions are called for. As the report said:

The need for special bridging, preparatory, refresher courses and on-the-job training for women seeking to enter or re-enter the workforce in the past has been accepted in principle both by the TAFE Committee and the Department of Labour although implementation has fluctuated.

The last phrase is a delicate way of saying that not much has been done.

Girls, School and Society also states that the education system has not been designed for recurrent education. This especially affects women, but as technological change increases it will become more important for all workers.

It is not enough simply to make courses available. The second Technical and Further Education (TAFE) report accepted that child-care facilities were a prerequisite for the educational participation of many women. This is a point that has been constantly reiterated when educational and job opportunities for women are being discussed.

Kerry Lovering, Director of the Women's Bureau of the Department of Employment and Youth Affairs, has stated that the major problems most women face in the workplace are associated with the fact that they withdraw from the workforce for child bearing and rearing. She goes on to say that the effect of this break is that many women are absent at an age when experience and skills are being acquired by men to enable them to reach higher positions. Unless remedial action is taken, women are restricted to low- status positions.

She suggests solutions such as maternity leave (to provide women with more job security), retraining for women re-entering the workforce, part-time work to allow mothers with young children to retain their skills, encouragement of women at home to take courses, greater development of women's self-esteem and training in assertiveness.

Another important suggestion she makes is that young women should be able to plan their families and careers with a better understanding than they have now of the social realities. Whereas many girls reject education because they expect to 'marry, stop work and live happily ever after', the facts are that over half the women of child-bearing age are in the paid workforce - 51 per cent of women in the 25-34 age-group and 57 per cent of women in the 35-44 age group. Compared to a hundred years ago when women had on average six or seven children, bearing the last in their early forties, and a life expectancy of less than fifty, women now complete their families earlier and have the prospect of twenty-five to thirty years in the paid workforce. This makes it all the more important that young women be educated and counselled with this future in mind and that resources are devoted to overcoming the problems that women face as a result of their break from paid employment. The major obstacle to such a proposal is that with structural changes in the economy leading to the disappearance of more and more jobs, no amount of education, training, counselling or confidence-building is going to create jobs.

This paradox is evident in the operation of National Employment And Training scheme (NEAT). It was introduced in October 1974 by the Labor government and was intended to provide a comprehensive system of labour-market training to alleviate unemployment, particularly for retrenched workers, disadvantaged job-seekers and persons faced with declining opportunities for their skills'. Those eligible for the scheme included:

- those who require training to update skills or to gain entry to employment, which includes persons not in regular civilian employment because of domestic responsibilities, loss of a breadwinner, sickness, physical incapacity, imprisonment or military service;
- those who are interested in entering special training programmes designed to alleviate specific labour shortages or are lacking in adequate skills;
- those who have been or are likely to be made redundant as a result of technological change within an industry;
- those who are unemployed as a result of structural change in an industry.

Clearly, while very broad, the scheme was specifically intended to assist women re-entering the paid workforce and women locked into low-skilled jobs. However, it was designed and first implemented at a time when unemployment was just beginning to rise and it was not capable of coping with the economic crisis that has since developed. Since the Liberals have come to power, the scope of the NEAT scheme has narrowed and it is ironic that, at a time when the effects of structural and technological change are so much worse, the eligibility criteria for the scheme have been made more restrictive.

However, the numbers of people being trained have gone up. When the Liberals came to power in December 1975 there were about 7000 people being trained. By the end of April 1977 this figure had risen to 17 500, 40 per cent of whom were women. Those eligible at this stage were unemployed people who were unable to find jobs with their current skills, people faced with retrenchment, and women seeking to re-enter the workforce. The government preferred on-the-job training, in which trainees received award wages and the employer received a subsidy. Full- and part-time formal training was also offered, with trainees receiving an allowance higher than the unemployment benefit but lower than a wage. In October 1976 the Special Youth Employment Training Program (SYETP) was introduced, providing on-the-job training for people in the 15-19 age group who were 'disadvantaged' in the labour market. In April 1977, 6426 people were being trained, 52 per cent of whom were women.

From 1979, the NEAT scheme was available only to registered unemployed people - which in itself rules out many women whose skills are not in demand. They can only be trained in skills for which there is a demand or forecast demand. However, given the low demand for labour, even in skilled areas, there are very few training opportunities under the scheme, especially in relation to the number of people unemployed. In September 1979 there were 19 725 people being trained under the NEAT scheme, a number equivalent to about 5 per cent of the official unemployed and 2 to 3 per cent of the total official and hidden unemployed. The majority of these people (54 per cent) were in the SYETP, 26 per cent were in general on-the-job training positions and 20 per cent were doing formal courses. Women made up 45 percent of trainees but were under-represented in courses and adult on-the-job training.

Training has been seen by many people as going a long way to solving the problem of unemployment, especially unemployment resulting from structural change and technological change. But the paradox of the NEAT scheme is that as unemployment increases and the need for training increases, the number of skilled vacancies and therefore the number of openings for training decreases. This shows that unless training is part of an overall strategy to use people's skills by creating jobs, it has no effect other than creating a more competitive and highly skilled pool of unemployed. In an economy heading towards the elimination of the labourforce from the production process it is little more than a red herring.

The effects of unemployment on women

Given the widespread assumptions about the importance of women's domestic role it is not surprising that little concern has been shown about the effects of unemployment on women.

Two research reports, published in 1978 and 1979, dealt with women's unemployment. The first, Adjusting to Change, dealt with the experiences of sixty people retrenched from small clothing factories in the inner and western suburbs of Sydney.31 A high proportion were migrants, all were 'unskilled', the vast majority were women, all had low levels of education and tended to be in the higher age-groups. As such, the sample included particularly disadvantaged education and tended to be in the higher age-groups.

to structural change and unemployment'. However, the report was in no way designed to look at women's employment problems as such. In fact, comments on the role of retraining speak of the worker as 'he', despite the fact that there were only two men in the sample.

Some of the women in the sample had given up looking for work after being retrenched because of problems such as 'sore arms and legs', and 'hopelessness'. One women said she began to get asthma worse than before...so gave up trying'. Another had 'no confidence to go out and look' for a job. Feelings of hopelessness and despair were common because there were no job opportunities. The report states that 'most of the women wanted to work, and some who had given up looking would clearly join the workforce if jobs were available... Work was extremely important to the women for financial and social reasons.' When they first learnt they were going to lose their jobs, most had reacted with 'shock and dismay'. They said they felt 'terrible', 'bad', cried a lot and wondered how they were going to cope. A few said that because their husbands were working it was not so bad, but that they were still pretty upset'.

Financial strain was the most obvious effect of unemployment. Even when their husbands or children were working, the women's income was important. The loss of income led to tension and strain in the family. Some women commented that they had to borrow money. Other women said they couldn't think straight', 'felt like committing suicide', worried about money, had more family arguments, and were 'upset, sad and angry'.

It was clear from the women's comments that they also found the loss of social contact at work hard to cope with. They said that they were bored, lonely, always doing housework or watching television, and had more family squabbles.

There was a general lack of knowledge about retraining possibilities which, together with Englishand literacy problems and, in some cases, age, led to little interest in them. Many commented on the need to learn English and to be educated in their own language first. It was significant that some women commented that they had not been able to learn English in the past because of family commitments. They said they were working and had their job in the house' as well; were too tired when they came home from work and had to cook, look after children and do housework.

Another study, specifically directed towards the effects of unemployment on women, has been carried out by Eva Cox, a long-standing advocate of the right of women to employment and education, job training and child-care facilities. She has been involved in two major surveys of women in New South Wales. The first looked at the employment patterns and preferences of migrant women who were unemployed or out of the paid workforce.32 The second, published in December 1978, looked specifically at the effects of unemployment on women.

It addressed itself to challenges to women's right to employment and women's right to be regarded as unemployed when work is not available:

The residual belief that woman's place is in the home has re-emerged, together with the belief that women at home will not be as badly affected as men at home, and therefore 'Women at home' are seen as being able to occupy them women are better equipped to cope with unemployment. Themselves by providing additional services for the family: they are not seen by society as falling into a vacuum without part employment.

The report stated that if this assumption is correct women, unlike men, do not depend on their work identity and are not under pressure to be providers, and will therefore be less affected by unemployment. The major findings of the study were that over a third of married women and almost two-thirds of sin- this was by no means the only severe effect of unemployment. women found their incomes inadequate. However, this was by no means the only severe effect of unemployment. Adverse changes in family relationships, deteriorating health and emotional stress were reported by considerable numbers of unemployed women. As the report stated:

Women, both with and without dependent children, find notworking a negative experience. Their lives are affected bytheir lack of income and their spending is reduced. Their social life also diminishes; lack of money accounts for some of the cuts - activities such as going to clubs involve expenditure. However, even activities where expenditure is non-existent or minimal, such as visiting friends and relations, also diminish. Only one in ten sees their time out of the workforce as an opportunity to do more.

Very few have taken up new activities. Those without dependants are more likely to enrol in various courses. while those with dependants do community work. Sydney respondents are less likely to take up new activities than those out of Sydney, which could be a factor of size of town or lack of information and resources.

Boredom, depression and loneliness were the main emotions people expressed when asked how they felt about not working. Less than one in ten saw the experience as in any way positive. This negative reaction did not vary significantly with the type of work previously done – those whose jobs may have seemed unpalatable to others were no happier staying at home than those with seemingly more desirable jobs. For those who want work, staying at home is, in itself, a negative experience.

Both of these studies bear out the view that women take themselves seriously as workers, and suffer shock, depression, boredom, social isolation and loss of confidence as well as more tangible financial and family problems when they become unemployed. Reports such as these have helped to show that employment is important to women. However the other side of the coin is that women's labour has been crucial to employers, and is likely to remain so in the 1980s despite the fact that restructuring of the economy is leading to the elimination of large numbers of jobs in manufacturing and tertiary industry, and a lower quality of working life for most women. The argument that women should be at home looking after children is not without emotive appeal, but it should not be allowed to obscure the fact that structural changes – not women – are threatening the right to work of women and men of all ages.

CHAPTER 4

'Recognise your value'

Discrimination

Discrimination against women in the workforce is essential As mentioned in the last chapter, elimination of dis in the process of establishing women's right to work. The granting of equal pay, the extension of the adult minimum wage to women and the introduction of maternity leave were the most concrete advances won by women workers in the 1970s. However, other changes took place that were broader in scope, although harder to pin down. It wasn't simply that women suddenly started to do more about discrimination. What happened was a development in awareness. More women were defining their problem as discrimination and gaining public credibility. As their claims that discrimination was an unacceptable practice found public support, more women were able to challenge specific cases. Individual gripes gradually came to be identified as discrimination and as legitimate and actionable grievances. This represented a change in society's consciousness that was far more important than the rather weak legislation and procedures that were eventually introduced by the Federal and some State governments.

Government provisions In June 1973 the Whitlam government ratified the International Labour Organisation (ILO) Convention

No. 111 on discrimination. Australia committed to eliminating was then... any distinction, exclusion or preference made on the basis of race, colour, sex, political opinion, national extraction or social origin, which has the effect of nullifying or impairing equality of opportunity or treatment in employment and occupation.[1]

To carry out this massive task, a national committee and six State committees were established. The National Committee Discrimination in Employment and Occupation consisted of a chairman and nominees from the State and Federal governments, the ACTU, the Australian Council of Employers' Federations, and three people with specialist knowledge of the problems of Aboriginals, women and migrants, the three groups considered to be most affected by discrimination. The six State committees had a chairman, usually with a legal background, and four members, representing State and Federal government, unions and employers, but no specialists or representatives of particular groups. When the committees were set up in 1973, Gail Wilenski, the member of the national committee with special knowledge of discrimination against women, was the only woman among the forty State and national committee members until Pat Giles, a union official, became chairman (sic) of the WA committee un May 1974. By 1976-77 more women had been intely. who are concentrated in jobs with poor working conditions and other problems. The discrimination they face is not so much individual as built into the social system.

Another committee member drew attention to the ineffectiveness that resulted from the committee's lack of legal power. Nick Padanyi, of the Victorian committee, said that only 25 per cent of people coming to the committee had received any help. In particular, he claimed the committee was powerless to help hundreds of women who had made complaints about not receiving equal pay.

Another Victorian member, Leonie Green, said that employers still discriminated on the grounds of sex, race and national extraction. She had found that a high proportion of complaints came from government or semi-government employees, probably because they had greater job security than employees in private industry, many of whom did not complain for fear of being dismissed. She went on to say that 'their fear is irrational, but it is hard to explain that, especially to migrants and semi and unskilled workers with limited alternative job prospects'. This is an extraordinary statement for her to make, considering that many of the problems the committee deals with concern dis- missal, especially from 'retrenched migrants who believe they've been unfairly singled out', and that the committee can in no way protect people's jobs or prevent victimisation.

These comments all suggest a large area of complaints which fall outside the scope or power of the committees - hundreds of migrants who haven't been unfairly singled out' (they've just been sacked), hundreds of women who are not receiving equal pay, and countless other people who for whatever reason have not come forward and have derived no benefit from the committees.

Although some critics of the committee system have suggested that introducing legislation would be more effective, there have been constitutional as well as political problems. Three States have brought in their own legislation; South Australia in 1976, new South Wales in 1977, Victoria in 1978 (Tasmania proposes to) but in their scope is different from that of national and state committees. At a Federal level, the Racial Discrimination Act became operative in 1975 just before the Whitlam government was dismissed. Since then, the Fraser government has made a few scattered attempts to consolidate. Sex discrimination legislation was announced in 1977 but rights legislation was revived by the Liberals in 1977, but was opposed by the

State committees, but the ACTU and employers opposed this move, saying that the committees had satisfactory dealt wth some 3000 complaints and that the system of investigation by a joint committee worked better than would a system of civil litigation.

The Women's Electoral Lobby argued strongly for legislation as well as persuasion and public education to eliminate discrimination. Joan Bielski of WEL argued that legislation was society's way of expressing disapproval of Anti-Social behavior, that it would give women who experience discrimination in isolation and are powerless to do anything about a means of redress.

Now that three States have introduced legislation (Tasmania proposing to do so and Queensland and Western Australian governments opposing Federal Anti-Discrimination measures and refusing to bring in their own) some assessment can be made of it.

South Australia

South Australia South Australia was characteristically first to bring in legislation, its Sex Discrimination Act becoming operative in 1976. It prohibits discrimination on the grounds of sex and marital status in the areas of employment, education, accommodation and provision of goods and services.

Most studies of discrimination identify two types[1] direct or individual discrimination and indirect or systemic discrimination. The first type is easy to identify: for instance, refusing to hire a well-qualified woman in preference to a man; not training a female employee because women lack ambition' or because of some other stereotyped attitude. The second type is less obvious but more widespread: for instance, using employment practices which appear neutral but in fact result in one sex being disadvantaged; placing a requirement on employees which, while not relevant to specific job qualifications, disqualifies a high proportion of one sex; or penalising an employee for lacking something denied to him or her in the past, such as seniority. As one employee of Victoria's former Anti-Discrimination Bureau has said, ... most discrimination is in-built, institutional and attitudinal discrimination'. The bureau's functions are now carried out by the Office of Equal Opportunity.

The South Australian definition of discrimination is the only one in Australia that begins to deal with the problem of indirect discrimination. Under that Act, one person sex discrimination includes: treating favourably than another (real or hypothetical) of the opposite sex; treating a person less favourably on the basis of a characteristic king any pertaining to unreasonable or imputed to one sex; and of each sex cannot comply with.

This recognises that, firstly, women can suffer discrimination even though there is no man on hand for direct comparison. This is especially important since most of the workforce is segregated by sex, and few 1969 'equal pay for equal work' case, 85 per cent of women are in the same work situation as men. In the women were not affected because they were not doing exactly the same work as men. It means secondly that an employer may no longer discriminate on the basis of stereotyped attitudes such as women don't take their work seriously' or 'single people are unreliable. And thirdly, it means that employers may not exclude more women than men by stipulating a requirement. such as being over a certain height, unless it directly affects job performance.

Despite the relatively wide terms of reference in South Australia there have been few formal complaints. In 1977-78 there were only 132 formal complaints along with many telephone calls from people who did not proceed with complaints. Women filed 80 percent of the complaints, with sex rather than marital status being the most frequent ground. The Commissioner for Equal Opportunity, Joan Colley, in her second annual report, stated that 'a large majority of people have at best a hazy awareness of their rights under the Sex Discrimination Act', and that her office had had very little public exposure. 15 She also commented that her work was hampered by women fearing the sack, especially if they were pregnant. While the 1979 maternity leave provisions give some insurance against this, fear of dismissal is still obviously a major obstacle in the way of getting more actionable complaints. Cases that were pursued included that of a woman who was refused a job as a receptionist because she was married and therefore did not have the image of being sexually available; and another of a woman who was refused work as a night nurse because the employer thought she should be at home with her husband and children. A third case illustrates the difficulty of proceeding:

A company manufacturing household appliances experienced a temporary shortfall in orders. Management decided to lay off all workers engaged in direct production, keeping on only those staff in supervisory capacities or whose qualifications made them useful for routine machinery maintenance. Because of the sex-segregation of the workforce, it just happened that all those stood down were women, all those kept on were men.

This is indirect discrimination, which falls within the scope of the South Australian Act. However, the outcome of the case was that one woman complained and was victimised by the other women who thought she was spoiling their chances of being re-employed, so she dropped the case.

Joan Colley commented on her own lack of real power to deal with the basic situation. However, she describes the root of the problem as 'persistence of sex-typing of jobs by employers, schools, the media and the workforce generally' rather than discriminatory hiring, training or promotion. Certainly this ex- plains why women were the ones to be sacked, but it doesn't deal with the issue of dismissals as such which would surely still be a problem even if both been better industrial organisation among the women a demand for reinstatement supported by their union, and they had put in a complaint jointly, together with the matter would have had a better outcome.

At the time of writing, the South Australian legislation was facing a constitutional challenge. was dismissed. The company maintains that since the complaint to the Sex Discrimination Board when she woman employed by the Dalgety company made Award, a Federal award which has provisions for dis. woman was employed under the Metal Industry missal, the board has no jurisdiction. The case is going to the Supreme Court for an appeal. Its outcome will be significant because questions of the employers' right to sack as well as the power of the State legislation will be decided.

Women at Work not come forward and have derived no benefit from the committees. More suggested that introducing legislation would be political problems. Three States have brought in their effective, there have been constitutional as well own legislation: South Australia in 1976, New South that of the national and State committees. At a Federal-to), but in each case their scope is different from Wales in 1977, Victoria in 1978 (Tasmania proposes op the Racial Discrimination Act became was dismissed. Since then, the Fraser government has erative in 1975 just before the Whitlam government made a few scattered attempts to consolidate. Sex discrimination legislation was announced in 1977 but rights' legislation was revived by the Liberals also in has not been heard of since. The concept of 'human into Parliament in 1979. At that stage, the government 1977, but was opposed by the States and reintroduced intended to put job discrimination under the proposed Human Rights Commission, instead of the national and State committees, but the ACTU and employers opposed this move, saying that the committees had satisfactorily dealt with some 3000 complaints and that the system of investigation by a joint committee worked better than would a system of civil litigation.

New South Wales

New South Wales initially proposed to introduce anti-discrimination legislation which would have made it It one of the most far-reaching acts in the world', would have covered discrimination on the grounds of age, political or religious conviction, physical handicap or mental disability, homosexuality and membership or non-membership of trade unions, as well as sex, race and marital status. Only the last three grounds survived an onslaught of political opposition. Protests came from the Catholic Church (about education provisions), the Real Estate Institute and the Chamber of Commerce. Over a period of eighteen months, from mid-1975 to the end of 1976, the Bill was fought and almost abandoned in the face of hostility from an Opposition-controlled Upper House. Premier Neville Wran announced exemptions for private schools, but further amendments were demanded. The Bill was finally passed in March 1977 after the government had agreed to sixty-four amendments. Protests were still being received by employers about their right to choose staff'.

The Act now covers discrimination in the areas of employment, accommodation, provision of goods and services and access to public places and vehicles on the grounds of sex, race and marital status.

The board is investigating discrimination on the other grounds but cannot take action on them.

Like the South Australian legislation the New South Wales definition of sex discrimination allows a comparison to be made with a real or hypothetical person of the opposite sex, and includes unfavourable treatment on the basis of characteristics imputed to one sex, in other words, stereotyped attitudes.

In the first year of operation, the New South Wales Anti-Discrimination Board dealt with 220 formal complaints and 3500 telephone calls.[21] Discrimination on the grounds of sex and race each made up 42 percent of complaints, with marital status making up a further 16 per cent. The majority (55 per cent) of complaints were lodged by women, who made 78 percent of the complaints on the basis of sex, 59 percent of those on the basis of marital status, but only 25 percent on the basis of race. Employment accounted for 46 percent of all complaints, 63 percent in the private sector and 37 percent from government departments, public authorities and local government bodies. All substantiated complaints were resolved by conciliation, without any having to go to the board.

As well as investigating complaints, the board undertook research and recommended reviews of all on legislation, industrial awards, and government policies and practices. The Annual Report comments that: the grounds of race, sex and marital status, resulting in the many personnel policies and practices do discriminate Government employment, and the concentration of women under-representation of aborigines in New South Wales and migrants in a limited range of occupations. Much of this discrimination is direct and unintentional.

The Board's general recommendations about women in the workforce are that an applicant's sex should not be relevant to recruitment decisions; the concentration of women in temporary positions should be broken down; and that work structures should be more compatible with the career patterns normally pursued by women, including the establishment of permanent part-time work, increased of unpaid leave and use of personal leave to care for dependants.

The only jarring note is the last point: increased use of personal leave to care for dependants. At present, women have difficulty when their children are sick because there is no provision for leave to care for dependants. Most women use their own sick leave when their children are sick, and as a result have no leave left (or are unwilling to use it) when they are sick themselves. So strong is the fear of having sick children who are unable to attend school or their normal child-care centre and have no one to look after them, that many women sacrifice their own health. When they come to work unwell, they suffer increasing fatigue and stress, and become susceptible to accidents.

In late 1979, the New South Wales Anti-Discrimination Board released a report on discrimination against women in the teaching service. The report is significant because it examines indirect discrimination and shows what is possible if a board report is significant because it examines indirect initiates research and policy recommendations instead of just responding to individual complaints.

Indirect discrimination is mainly responsible for the reduction of female principals from 22 per cent of all high schools principals in 1961 to only 10 per cent today. The existing system of promotion has failed to ensure true equal opportunity. While women were 43 per cent of the teaching staff, the fact that they were only 10 per cent of principals was attributed to the department's policies and practices. Numerous recommendations about the promotional system were put forward to create a system free from discrimination. As one editorial commented:... these statistics do not lie and can only be interpreted as showing enormous discrimination against women teachers'.

The report said that women generally are unable to travel to take up promotions, whereas men take a country promotion and then transfer to a more desirable location after a qualifying period. Another impediment was the loss of accreditation on re-entry into the teaching service after childbearing. In short, the requirements for permanency and promotion take no account of women's typical life patterns', the report said.

Another problem was that 'almost no women are represented in the upper echelons of the Department of Education, particularly at the policy level. They have no say in decisions which profoundly affect them.'

In the New South Wales Act's second year, a case came up in which conciliation failed, and a complaint had to be taken to the board. The case has been discussed by Margaret Thornton, a lawyer carrying research into anti-discrimination legislation. A teacher within the Technical and Further Education Department alleged discrimination when she was not put on the promotion list. Her qualifications were excellent, and she alleged that she had been rejected because she did not conform to the female stereotype. The employer on the other hand alleged that she was not suitable because of her personality. The board found the complaint substantiated. The case took six months and revealed some of the problems of the board's operation. The employer did not question her competence, but directed evidence towards her alleged 'personality defects'. For six months the complainant of legal character assassination. Many trivial incidents were raked up and later discounted by the board as attempts by the employer to discredit her. The costs of the proceedings were high - about \$10 000 to the complainant – but there was no provision for legal aid, and the personal stress for the complainant- But there was no provision for legal aid, and the personal stress for the complainant was great. Margaret Thornton remarked on the futility of complaint-based legislation as a means of remedying systemic discrimination against women in the workforce'.

Victoria

In Victoria, legislation was proposed following a recommendation from the Status of Women Committee in 1976. The Bill was criticised for reflecting the 'mildly trendy conservatism' of the Hamer government. 25 It had many limitations: employers with ten or fewer employees, who accounted for 83 per cent of employers, were exempted; discrimination had to be shown by comparison with a person of the opposite sex ignorance of the law was to be a defence; and the in the same situation; sexist advertising was allowed; maximum penalty was \$500. However, amendments were introduced to strengthen the Bill: penalties were doubled; the board was allowed to carry out its own investigations as well as just responding to complaints; exemptions were made for employers with five or fewer employers, instead of ten; and discrimination could be established by comparison of a real or hypothetical person in the same relevant circumstances. However, superannuation and sporting clubs were still exempted.

The Victorian definition of discrimination is narrow because it does not include discrimination on the basis of stereotyped attitudes or characteristics pertaining to one sex. Nor does it take any acccount of indirect discrimination.

Although it covers only the first three months of the Victorian Act's operation, the First Annual Report of the Commissioner for

Equal Opportunity gives an impression of the pattern of complaints as well as some of the shortcomings of the system being used.

As with other States, a high proportion of complaints (60 per cent) were made by women, 64 per cent of them being in the area of employment. However, the number of apparently actionable complaints not proceeded with because the complainant withdrew exceeded the number pursued. More women than men dropped complaints, with a greater proportion of women having complaints in the workplace itself where victimisation becomes relevant'.

The commissioner went on to say that 'the problems of discrimination at work are very different for men and women and of a more serious nature for the latter'. They included refusal by employers to consider job applications, different fringe benefits, lack promotion, dismissal on pregnancy for women, against dress requirements for men.

She also pointed out that employment agencies they did so rather than lose the were the largest group of respondents discriminating on the basis of sex custom of an employer who wanted employees of one sex only. Approaches were made to the Employers' Federation and to 180 employment agencies. However, in 1980, some eighteen months later, this was still a problem.

Another deficiency in the operation of the legislation is that it has not reached those people who, presumably, need it most. The First Annual Report notes that employment complaints were under-used by people in manual, unskilled and process work and that there was a complete absence of complaints from a largely working-class, the western suburbs industrial area, with many migrants, many women in the workforce, a high rate of unemployment and, as the work of the Western Region Centre for Working Women shows, widespread discrimination. The commissioner concludes that:

Migrant women in factory employment, therefore, who have been identified in various studies as a particularly disadvantaged group in many respects have been completely unaffected by the legislation.

Despite this damning conclusion, no recommendations are included on how to make the Act more accessible or relevant to non-English speakers, migrant women in particular, nor on how effectively to contact people where the problem is most severe in the workplace.

As in New South Wales, in Victoria only one case has gone to the board for a judicial decision - that of Deborah Wardley vs Ansett.28 Ms Wardley went to the Equal Opportunity Board when Ansett Airlines refused on the grounds of sex to employ her as a trainee pilot. As in South Australia the case has led toa constitutional challenge to the legislation.

The Wardley-Ansett battle has received a lot of publicity, nearly all of it favourable, because of Deborah Wardley's impeccable qualifications, the blatant nature of the discrimination, the support she received from women's organisations and the personal fame of Sir Reginald Ansett in Australia. The case lasted over a year, starting in August 1978 and reaching a conclusion in 1980. Although Ansett Transport Industries employed Deborah Wardley in November 1979, it was a long and extremely costly process for her as she had to survive the stress of a hearing by the Equal Opportunity Board, intervention by the Supreme Court, a second hearing by the board, an appeal by Ansett to the Supreme Court followed by an appeal to the High Court. Sir Reginald Ansett remained steadfastly opposed to the employment of women as pilots, stating publicly that although the Supreme Court had ordered him to accept Deborah Wardley as a trainee pilot, he would sack her immediately.

Ansett appealed against the order to the High Court on the grounds that the Airline Pilot's Agreement, which gives the employer the right to dismiss an employee, is a Federal law and takes precedence over over a State law which denies the employer that right.

The High Court found that there was no inconsistency between the Airline Pilot's Agreement and considerations, discrimination on the basis of sex was the contract of employment dealt with industrial the Equal Opportunity Act, reasoning that while contract of employment dealt with industrial consideration, discrimination on the basis of sex was quite unrelated to these. The Supreme Court decision ordering Ansett to employ Deborah Wadrley was therefore to stand.

In fact, Deborah Wardley was employed after Rupert Murdoch succeeded Sir Reginald Ansett as Chairman of Ansett Transport Industries, and chose not to pursue his predecessor's policy about women pilots.

Direct Discrimination

Job discrimination takes four main forms: refusal to hire, dismissal, unfavourable working conditions, and limited opportunities when employed. Although the perpetrator of the act of discrimination is usually an employer, examples can be found of discrimination by unions, by a person's fellow-workers, and in the terms of employment regulations and awards.

Since the ACTU adopted the Charter for Working Women in 1977, Australian unions have been opposed to sex discrimination. The charter includes several references to discrimination and equal opportunity.

Firstly, in relation to entry into the workforce, it states that there should be equal opportunity and access to all areas and levels of education and training and retraining'. The charter adds that to achieve this aim women should be made fully aware of all jobs and courses open to them, sex bias in all aspects of the education system should be eradicated, retraining and refresher courses should be made I available to women in view of their pattern of interrupted employment, and active encouragement should be given by unions to women who wish to enter areas of training, employment and apprenticeships which traditionally have been regarded as male preserves.

On the controversial subject of 'protective' or restrictive legislation, the charter says that:

All pseudo-protective laws related to women's employment should be urgently reviewed by unions. Discriminatory clauses, which restrict entry, should be deleted from awards so that the range of occupations open to female workers is expanded.

It is important to note that the charter follows this by saying that 'protective legislation should be reviewed with the aim of protecting both male and female workers' health. There should be no deterioration of working conditions in the equalising process.' 'Equality' can be a misleading term - it is often misinterpreted to imply making women more like men. However, in this case, it means improving men's working conditions and giving higher priority to health and safety because of the importance women workers attach to them.

However, action by individual unions to remove discriminatory clauses from awards or to insert provisions protecting women against discrimination is slow.

Most of the examples of discrimination discussed below are from press reports and from cases taken to the various anti-discrimination bodies. They are therefore biased towards individual discrimination concerning people who are either newsworthy or willing to risk coming forward. Systematic research is needed to find the nature and extent of discrimination in the workplace and to identify the barriers to equal opportunity.

Refusal to hire

Deborah Wardley's legal battle and the extensive publicity attracted have done more than anything to put anti-discrimination provisions on the map. The transport industry has had large share of such cases, women having long battles to become drivers of trains, buses, and trams for State public transport authorities and drivers postal courier vans. The head of the Federal Department of Transport was so concerned that he instigated study if women in the department which resulted in a special effort to recruit women into positions which had previously been male preserves, such as air-traffic controlling.

Before the introduction of anti-discrimination legislation women became drivers within the various public transport authorities only after conflict with the authority itself and with the union concerned, and often after one particular woman had fought for the right to be employed. The attempt by NSW railway employee, Janet Oakden, to become a train driver was opposed by the New South Wales Public Transport Commission and by the union, the Australian Federated Union of Locomotive Enginemen (AFULE).

Not until November 1976, after a change of policy by the New South Wales government and after extensive negotiations' with the union, were women allowed to drive trains in New South Wales. In Victoria it wasn't until 1975 that Melbourne's tramway workers voted to lift their union's nineteen-year ban on women tram drivers. Even then, the Essendon depot continued to refuse to work with a female trainee driver. Then again it was a union – the New South Wales branch of the Postal Workers' Union - that would not agree to women driving vans in a new courier service being introduced by Australia Post in 1975.32 Such blatant examples are less common now.

Other industries in which similar battles have been fought are those where women have either been totally excluded, or, if employed, limited to certain jobs.

In the meat industry, there have been disputes over the seniority system, over the right of married women to work, and over the hiring of women as slicers, a job usually done by men. In 1977 in Cootamundra, New South Wales, the male unionists went on strike when the 50 women working there were granted seniority on the same basis as men. However, the majority of the 500 workers at the abattoirs voted to uphold the principal of equal opportunity, despite the objections of a few men. The managing director was reported by the Daily Telegraph as describing the women as invaluable for the ancillary tasks.

In Townsville's Ross River Meatworks slicers walked off the job refusing to work with a woman. They refused to go back to work even after a meeting of all the workers in the meatworks had decided to and the union recommended a return.

Mining is another industry with an aggressively masculine image and tradition. In 1975 the Sydney Morning Herald claimed 'Mines Ban on Women to be lifted'.The article reported that women would beallowed to work underground in New South Wales 'but the work will be for welfare, managerial and training purposes only'. The premier, Sir Eric Willis, said that the government would not alter the ban on prevalent in the women doing mining work, which was enacted to stop nineteenth century'. If exploitation and nineteenth-century conditions still prevail in mining, it is about time some improvements were made.

Even with formal barriers removed, it is difficult for NSW Miners' Federation, Mr Evan Phillips, said, the women to enter a new field. As the president of the amendments by the government would not change the almost entirely male dominance of the industry. This is especially so when jobs are scarce. The Cleveland Tin NL mine at Luina planned to employ women when male labour was scarce, but the company had an agreement with the Australian Workers' Union that in the event of men being retrenched from other industries it would look to the male in preference to had therefore been the female. Although men 'the was employed, the company had approved the construction of facilities for women in case they were needed. Such an agreement, which blatantly discriminates on the basis of sex, would now be illegal in some Australian States. Some branches of the Miners' Federation have passed resolutions in favour of women working in the industry. The Peak Downs branch in Queensland carried a resolution that this union bars no person from entering the industry on the grounds of sex, colour or creed and that the executive approach the Mines Department for the elimination of the rule discriminating against women'.

Dismissal

The examples given so far have all been of outright refusal to hire women in industries or occupations that have been male dominated. Discrimination against women has also taken the form of discriminatory dismissal for various reasons. For instance, in the absence of any right to work protection against dismissal depends on the strength of the union and the shop-floor organisation. Shop stewards and other activists are a prime target for the sack if the rest of the workforce is not organised enough to protest. In Perth, a clothing worker was sacked by Mitex International (Aust'asia) Pty Ltd, after a union official approached the management to get four days leave for her to attend a course at the Trade Union Training Authority (TUTA). Ruth Geneffe, the secretary of the union, and Peter Cook, the secretary of the Trades and Labour Council, went to the factory to try to persuade Mitex to reinstall the woman, but they were unsuccessful and a further four women, including an office worker who spoke to the union officials, were sacked. The union took the case before the Industrial Commission for wrongful dismissal and the company was ordered to reinstate the women. The industrial officer who took the case, David Parker, said that at a time when governments, employer organisations, unions and women's groups calling for more involvement of women as a matter of urgency, here is an employer who sacks a woman for even showing an interest...

This case is a good illustration of the problems of anti-discrimination legislation. The woman who was sacked was clearly victimised for showing an interest in union issues, not because she was a woman. However, taking a broad view of discrimination, this was an example of indirect discrimination because women are disadvantaged by their disproportionate involvement in unions and lack of knowledge of their entitlements at work. Senator J.A. Mulvihill has claimed that thousands of female employees could be exploited because of their lack of knowledge of awards. Glaring cases of underpayment - especially of Preventing migrant and women workers - have brought this form of discrimination to his attention. the consequence of perpetuating this situation and is women from attending a TUTA course, therefore, has the consequence of perpetuating this situation and is discriminatory. Furthermore, not all industries or awards provide remedies such as going to the Industrial Commission for wrongful dismissal.

In a similar case in Melbourne, a shop steward in the clothing industry was sacked when she 'caught' by the boss during the lunch break telephoning the union about forming a shop committee. Such was the state of organization in the factory that no industrial action was taken. However, the union was able to negotiate two weeks' pay in lieu of notice and back-pay for the sacked steward and other women who had all been underpaid. The company decided it would rather pay up than go to court.

When shop steward Edy Turnevitch was sacked from Everhot, a Melbourne whitegoods manufacturer, in late 1974, she felt it was because she was 'a union official and a woman'. 38 While the union tried to pursue the dispute as a case of discrimination some women felt that this tactic just allowed the employer to play on the hostilities of the men, and so divided workers who could have fought the sacking as an industrial issue.

Discriminatory sackings may have many purposes: to get rid of a union member or activist, to create a smokescreen for other motives for dismissal, or simply to provide a 'reason' when retrenchments are being considered, and to divide workers who might otherwise unite to resist all retrenchments. Often in such cases the discrimination is not direct - women are not being dismissed solely because they are women, but the impact of retrenchment or dismissal is falling more heavily upon women.

Another common form of discriminatory sacking in the past has been the dismissal of women when they This rule was only eliminated from the Commonwealth Public Service in 1965. More recently it has continued to be the practice of many municipal councils the most notorious case being that of Rockhampton, discussed in Chapter 3. Many other councils followed the same practice and others, while not automatically sacking women on marriage, have considered introducing a policy of discrimination against married women in response to unemployment.

The Preston Council (Victoria) called for an investigation of the number of married women which it employed. The Town Clerk agreed to provide the council with aggregate numbers but said he would not give details of individuals. After considerable controversy in the local area about single girls on the dole and the right of married women to work, the matter was dropped. A similar controversy was reported in the local press when Springvale councilor Dorothy Bell called on employers to 'sack the mums!' (all of them).And in Devonport, Tasmania, in April 1977 a motion to ban all married women from working for the council lapsed for want of a seconder. The council did, however, decide to give preference to a married man to fill a vacancy as a 'meter maid'.

The decision by the Arbitration Commission in the Rockhampton case that dismissal of women on marriage was a form of sex discrimination that was both unacceptable to the community, and an industrial issue that could be prohibited in awards – shows the 1970s. The change has come mainly from the left women, community attitudes have changed during that despite the recent backlash against married (broadly speaking) of Australian politics but there I have been exceptions: the Minister for Productivity, Mr Macphee, described as pernicious, misleading and mischievous' statements which attributed Australia's economic problems to equal pay and the employment Mr Viner, from claiming that 'equal pay was significant factor in the downturn of Australia's Economy or other ministers from blaming youth unemployment on married women.

Unfavourable working conditions

Publicised examples of discrimination in the form of unfavourable working conditions are hard to find, are influenced more by the extent of industrial organisation of workers than by the existence of regulations. Neither awards nor labour and industry acts ensure standards are observed unless workers are aware of these provisions and able to have them enforced. So if certain conditions are observed for male employees but not for female, there are likely to be tensions in the workplace, fears that if the women protest they will be victimised, and fears that if the men support equality, they will lose benefits rather than having them extended to women. It is also likely that the women will be less aware of their entitlements and in a weaker position in relation to the union. Even so, many women would be reluctant to go to an anti-discrimination board over a 'union' matter.

Secondly, even if action through anti-discrimination probably for three reasons. legislation is possible to redress unfavourable working conditions, it is less likely to occur than in the I case of dismissal or refusal to hire, simply because a person who is currently employed will be reluctant to act as he or she has more to lose. And a higher proportion of women than men choose not to pursue complaints since the greater volume of inquiries from women is in the workplace itself where victimization becomes relevant'.

The Victorian Committee on Discrimination in Employment and Occupation has said that many workers, especially women and migrants, would not make a complaint until they had left work or were assured of another job. Given the difficulty of finding another job it is likely that many people are keeping quiet about discriminatory treatment for fear either of further singling out or dismissal.

The third reason is that, because the workforce is so clearly segmented by sex, women have taken for granted the fact that they do different jobs and experience different conditions from men. While they are aware of the differences, they are less aware that these differences constitute discrimination. Furthermore, if anti-discrimination provisions are narrow and technical, they may require that a woman's conditions of work be compared to those of men doing *the same work*, or in the same situation. Yet few women are doing exactly the same work as men. This in itself seems discriminatory, but makes it difficult to distinguish between the case of a woman and a man in the same job being treated differently in a way that discriminates and the case of a woman and a man in different jobs being treated in a lawfully different way. The Victorian legislation requires that a woman be treated differently from a man 'where the relevant circumstances are the same', before discrimination is established.

For example, if a female process worker has to for the laundering of her uniform while a male forklift expense, this is discrimination because even though driver has his uniform laundered at the company's are the same. But if only one is provided with the jobs are quite different the relevant circumstances earmuffs, this would not be discrimination, assuming only one is exposed to noise.

The Women's Trade Union Commission (NSW) has given several examples of unfavourable treatment at work:

On the factory floor women are more jobs that have disadvantages, like an ear-shattering noise which men would not be expected to tolerate. Women are and workshops is installed for the sake of the product and very concious of the fact that air conditioning in factories not the personnel. No consideration is given to the positioning of the employees in relation to the air conditioning units: here again women are expected to tolerate conditions that men would not.

Similarly, in relation to assembly line work:

A worker is chosen for what is known as 'tag relief that is one who takes the place of an operator who temporarily leaves the floor. This classification was paid about $5 a week more than the line workers. According to the women this is always given to a man.

Another form of unfavourable treatment which is often mentioned is when women may be asked to relieve or fill in on a job normally done by men if a line is short-handed. Although the men's jobs are usually higher paid, the women filling in for them do I not get paid extra and traditionally, too, they have I not been eligible to do such work as their regular job.

Limited opportunities

In banking and clerical work, in particular, there have been accusations that women have been denied opportunities for training, advancement and promotion. However, increased involvement by women in white-collar unions has done much to challenge this situation, although not to eliminate it entirely. The dropping of sex from job classifications was said to provide women with access to all jobs in banking. But Victoria's Commissioner for Equal Opportunity has still received complaints from women employed in banks who were not receiving the same health and credit benefits as male workers. These women expressed fears of their employer's reaction to them if the complaint proceeded. Ironically, as researchers Pringle and Game have pointed out, equal opportunity has been won just as technological change is radically altering the nature of employment in the banking industry.

Discrimination has also been instanced in the retail trade: 'Where women are acting as branch or section managers they sometimes do not receive the full rate for the job because their appointment, has not been "confirmed" While benefits may only be given to 'confirmed' appointees, the discrimination occurs when women are persistently denied this status.

Some unions, such as the Shop Assistants' Union (the SDAEA), are particularly concerned with women's opportunities for promotion into management positions. In 1979 the union organised 'a meeting with personnel managers from top retail firms as well as top-level executives to discuss the situation of women in management. A similar conference was organised by the Equal Opportunity Advisory Council and the Australian Institute of women in executive or management positions

However, these initiatives have in a sense given impression that the issue is relevant only to a small, anti-discrimination a bad name with the misleading elite number of women aspiring to high positions, However, discrimination is as rife on the factory floor while doing nothing for ordinary working women. as it is in the executive suite, although it may be harder to detect, publicise and deal with through legal procedures.

In Victoria, the Commissioner for Equal Opportunity has found that:

…in the promotion issues which were discussed with me complainants were reluctant to pursue their suspicions because while they were dubious about the success of the for their relationship with their employer... In none of investigations, they could see certain inevitable outcomes were the women prepared to risk any deterioration in their present working relationships.

Indirect discrimination

The segmentation of the labour market migrants working in unskilled jobs in manufacturing industry, women working in routine clerical and service jobs, Aboriginals working in casual rural and domestic jobs, or being unemployed - is only partly due to preferential or discriminatory treatment of individuals by employers. It is also due to indirect or systematic discrimination, which is more widespread and significant. However, some critics of the Australian committee system and State legislation have commented that they are not equipped to deal with such discrimination. For example, in their paper to an ANZAAS Congress, Entrekin and others have pointed out that in the United States the aim of anti-discrimination legislation has been to ensure equal opportunity in employment by focusing on employment practices which result in discrimination against whole classes of people. For instance, low-income groups, who characteristically suffer insecurity at work, have an unstable employment history and have a past experience of failure, are disadvantaged by various employment practices such as requiring prior experience references, certain educational levels and completion of tests, which are often not related to specific job performance. Employment practices can also perpetuate past discrimination against minorities or whole groups of people, such as women. For example, age limits on apprenticeships prevent women from making up their past lack of training. Entrekin and others say the Australian system is not geared to seek out cases of discrimination or to act at a policy level, only reacting to complaints:

...in the United States the Equal Employment Opportunity Commission has concluded that systematic discrimination based on normal, often unintentional and seemingly neutral practices, is the most pervasive form of discrimination today. [However] the Australian system is geared to deal with individual discrimination and does not possess the resources or the investigatory powers necessary to compile comprehensive statistical evidence that is necessary to reveal or deal with class discrimination.

In addition, they comment that the Australian system does not guide social change.

Possibly the NSW Anti-Discrimination Board answers some of these criticisms, especially in its attempts to conduct research into indirect discrimination, recommended policy changes to counteract it, and to publicise extensively the issue.

There are several studies of specific occupations and or systemic discrimination is widespread. Apart from employers that bear out the contention that indirect the report on the teaching service, discussed above, there have also been studies of the NSW Public Service, the Australian Broadcasting Commission, the Australian Public Service, the Commonwealth De-institutions. Generally speaking, they all have similar findings: that women are concentrated in the under-represented in many positions; that women are more often found in temporary positions, or positions with fewer fringe benefits; that they are not promoted as quickly as men; that they are found in fewer management or senior positions than men; and are discouraged by the male image of many jobs even when formal barriers are removed.

Many articles equate 'discrimination' with under-representation of women in particular industries, occupations and positions. If the concentration of women in a narrow range of low-status jobs is the problem-and most writers agree that it is then legislation to prevent specific acts of individual discrimination in hiring, training, promotion and firing is not going to make much difference for the causes of the concentration are far more subtle and indirect. They include social conditioning of girls, their channelling into non-technical education, community attitudes and expectations, the self-image that girls acquire and the opportunities they have for developing vocational skills-issues which were also mentioned regarding women's right to work.

Ann Calvert, a Victorian education researcher, has done a study of apprenticeships for girls.52 She found, predictably, that apprenticeships were associated with boys. Only 5 per cent of apprenticeships in Victoria were held by girls, and fewer than 1 per cent if hair- was excluded. Some girls had apprentice- dressing ships in cooking, printing, horticulture and jewellery, but in Victoria in 1978 the female apprentices in traditionally male areas consisted of four motor mechanics, two electricians, one carpenter and one boilermaker. Ann Calvert found that girls did not apply for apprenticeships for a combination of reasons, including their own negative attitudes, community attitudes, lack of publicity in schools and career centres, and reluctance of employers to employ girls. She interviewed twenty-five employers and found that most of them were reluctant to give outright reasons for not employing girls; they were acting on the basis of stereotyped attitudes and falling back on excuses such as lack of toilet facilities.

Unpublished figures provided by the Industrial Training Commission show that in March 1980 there were 2014 female apprentices in Victoria, working in trades. Over two-thirds of female apprentices worked in ladies' hairdressing, a further 13 per cent in men's hairdressing and cooking, and fewer than 5 per cent in the various printing trades. The rest were sprinkled in very small numbers throughout the less traditional occupations, including eleven in which there had been no women prior to 1979.

Since International Women's Year in 1975 there has been a steady trickle of newspaper articles about women in non-traditional jobs, possibly giving the impression that barriers against women have broken down. The West Australian claimed 'Job Discrimination pression that barriers against women have broken male road-traffic patrol officer, a mounted policewoman and a female bus driver were announced. It is probably true that prejudice is not as strong, but the segmentation of the workforce is as strong as ever, only a handful of individuals having moved into so called 'men's jobs'. In fact the articles themselves confirm this by regarding female 'firsts' as newsworthy.

Encouraging girls to enter non-traditional jobs, especially technical ones, has become a popular cause offices and with organisations concerned with counter- with some State employees of equal opportunity sexism in education. In South Australia and Victoria, kits showing women in a wide range of jobs have been produced and widely distributed as part of a long-term aim of community education on this subject.

These projects concentrate on broadening girls' horizons as well as influencing teachers and employers to encourage girls to train and apply for a greater variety of jobs. However, their shortcomings are that they still do not come to terms with the processes of the labour market and especially with high unemployment. Indirect discrimination could be more usefully replaced by a concept such as 'systemic social inequalities' whose cumulative effect is a labour market segmented by sex, in which women are found in a smaller number of industries and occupations than men, and mostly offering lower paid, low-status, routine work with few prospects.

Chris Ronalds, in her book about discrimination, makes a comment about the Australian labour market: The position of various groups in the Australian labour market illustrates the existing nature of discrimination in employment. At the bottom of the employment ladder in the low-paid, most unpleasant jobs are aboriginal women; above them are aboriginal men; then non-English speaking migrant women.

She adds that the aim of any anti-discrimination legislation in the area of employment is to ensure equal access to all types of employment for those who want to work'.

Perhaps she means that the aim of anti-discrimination laws should be to do this. The politics surrounding Australia's tentative ventures into conciliation and legislation reveal far more limited aims. Furthermore, anti-discrimination laws are an appropriate response to the problem only if the labour market conditions and the hierarchy of jobs and workers directly result from discriminatory employment practices and not other social or structural conditions.

Every so often, a newspaper will report a member of an anti-discrimination board or committee as saying that discrimination - especially sex discrimination at work is dying out. For instance, because discrimination at work was 'dying off to a great extent', the Queensland committee was reputedly concentrating on sport. And the South Australian Equal Opportunity Commission has been directing a lot of its energy towards equality for women in sport, in the belief that discrimination at work is less prevalent.

It is hard to be anything but sceptical about these judgments. They are probably the dangerous result of the shortcomings of the system that emphasises direct discrimination, requires women to know about anti-discrimination provisions and come forward to make complaints, while offering little protection against either dismissal or more subtle forms of victimisation in the workplace. Furthermore, little research is done and there is virtually no direct contact with women in their workplace so it is inevitable that the committees, boards and bureaus should be out of touch with the problems of discrimination in the office, shop or factory floor.

It is likely that, even though direct discrimination (especially in the form of rules and practices which totally exclude women) has lessened, indirect discrimination is worse than before the committee system and the State legislation were introduced.

Economic recession has created a social climate less favourable to women entering non-traditional jobs and has increased the tensions between different groups in the workforce - young, old, married, single, men, women, migrant and Australian-born and so on. Job applicants vastly outnumber the number of cavancies, giving employers the ability to choose between different people. The basis of their choice may be discriminatory, but this is so much harder to prove. Given such competition for jobs, employers can use indirectly discriminatory criteria to select one applicant from several who are clearly qualified.

As early as mid-1975, Hilary McPhee, in an article about women in the workforce, was voicing fears about the success of reforms in the face of economic about the success of reforms in the face of economic downturn.[57] She felt that if anti-discrimination legislation and other reforms benefiting women in the workforce had been introduced in the 1960s they would have been sufficiently entrenched to withstand economic changes.

However, with practices and attitudes just beginning to change in favour of equal opportunity for women in the workforce, the gains are rather fragile. If men's jobs are at stake, women's demands are presented as inflationary, selfish and impracticable. Cutbacks in government spending, especially in child care, increase the inequality between women and men at work. Unions become less willing to take industrial action for a 'women's issue' because of the generally greater job insecurity. Government responses to unemployment can also be discriminatory in effect. For example, Sue Edmonds, a Tasmanian community worker, has given the example of a Launceston textile mill which closed down, putting 240 women out of work. The government response was to put money into a local housing scheme which was providing jobs mainly for men.[58]

Hilary McPhee also comments that, despite positive government initiatives such as the NEAT scheme, the ratification of the ILO Convention and equal pay, 'out there in the workforce nothing much has changed'. She goes on to say that 'girls are still leaving school with limited aspirations, and equipped in the main for "womens at work" - jobs which frequently have no male equivalent and where only a subjective assessment can rate their "equal value".' Another problem is that career counselling is conservative and unimaginative, and that apprenticeships, although they are starting to be sought by more girls, still depend on available employment.

Writers within the women's movement have often expressed, firstly, the feat that as economic conditions worsen the situation of women and reforms designed to improve it will go down the drain; and secondly, the belief that if awareness and organisation amongst women is strong enough, those gains have a chance of being protected. Sara Dowse, who witnessed the downgrading of women's affairs at Federal government policy level, stated after her resignation from the position of head of the Women's Affairs section within the Federal government: 'Equality of opportunity has a hollow ring indeed if it is meant to apply only when times are good'.[59]

Perhaps that hollow ring is all too realistic. Although equal opportunity has been officially espoused by most of the population, both Labor and Liberal Federal governments, the majority of State governments, employer organisations and unions, there has been a noticeable lack of thought given to the social policy goals and implications of anti-discrimination provisions. What would society be like if equal opportunity became a reality? Would it have a larger sprinkling of women in the lite, high-status jobs? Would it mean that instead of the concentration of women and non-Anglo-Saxons in low-status jobs, there would be a representative sample of the population in each occupation?

It is one of the strong prevailing myths of our society that the 'bad' jobs are inevitable. This is not so. If equal opportunity were to become a reality, perhaps two changes would have to occur.

First, inherent working conditions would have to improve with jobs becoming less dangerous, less physically unpleasant, less stressful, and more fulfilling. Second, jobs which necessarily retained elements of danger, difficult physical conditions and so on, would have to be more highly rewarded to compensate. The first change, although it would entail different priorities as well as practical reorganisation, is relatively easy to envisage: it would involve automation of some processes, rearrangement of others, introduction of more rigorous health and safety standards.

The second seems much further away, as it entails a fundamental reorientation of values that could only emerge from a period of conflict and crisis.

Unemployment and technological change - both forces which in the short term pose a threat to women's chances of gaining equal opportunity in employment - are likely to produce such a period of conflict and crisis in Australian society.

Equal opportunity is ambiguous. It could mean equally massive unemployment, equally unhealthy working conditions, equally unfulfilling work and equally non-existent prospects for men and women workers. However, the movement of women workers that has seen the introduction of anti-discrimination laws and the Charter for Working Women has also emphasised improving health and safety for all workers, establishing a right to work for all workers which has never been achieved for men, and changing the quality of working life. There is a cartoon which has been circulating in the women's movement for some years. A man is saying derisively 'Surely you don't expect to be equal to me!', and a woman is replying 'Actually I was thinking of something rather better'.

If the equal opportunity lobby can remain active throughout the confusion of the 1980s, and relate its goal of equality to changes in employment and social values over that period, then the short-term threats to women's status in the workforce may be overcome.

CHAPTER 5

'I sew up shirts and trousers'

Migrant Women

Since 1947 over three million migrants have entered Australia and played a crucial role in providing labour for the expansion of Australia's manufacturing industry in the 1950s and 1960s.[1] Consequently Australia's workforce now is vastly different from that of a generation ago. Whereas Anglo-Saxons predominated formerly, in February 1980 people born outside Australia constituted 24.5 per cent of the total workforce.[2] These facts were ignored for many years until migrants themselves, together with other community organisations, began drawing attention to Australia's multicultural society and workforce, and calling for recognition of the needs of migrants.

Over the same period, the participation of women in the labourforce increased from 24.9 per cent in 1947[3] to 45.3 per cent in March 1980.[4] Migrant women have joined the paid workforce at a higher rate than Australian-born women, prompted largely by economic necessity.

Migrants came firstly from the United Kingdom and later from Italy, Greece, Yugoslavia and other European countries. More recently large numbers of Turkish, Lebanese and South American migrants have entered Australia, the women also joining the industrial workforce. The 1976 census showed that, of the total of 2 070 534 women employed in Australia, 9.5 per cent were born in the United Kingdom and Eire, and 15.2 per cent were born in other overseas countries.5 In other words, a quarter of Australia's women in the paid workforce were born overseas. In February 1980, 46.7 per cent of overseas-born women were in the paid workforce, compared to 44.7 per cent of Australian-born women. For some groups, however, the proportion was higher, for instance, 49.1 per cent of Yugoslav-born women and 54.4 per cent of Greek-born women were in the paid workforce.

The occupations of these migrant women workers varied considerably between ethnic groups. In particular, the occupational profile of women from the United Kingdom and western Europe was very similar to that of Australian-born women, while that of women born in non-English-speaking countries - especially Italy, Greece, Yugoslavia and Turkey - was strikingly different.

Migrant women from non-English-speaking countries are under-represented in five of the seven major urban occupational categories. In the 1976 census, although they were 15.2 per cent of the female workforce, they were only 7.3 per cent of transport and communication workers, 10.1 per cent of clerical workers, 11.3 per cent of professional and technical workers, 12.7 per cent of sales workers and 14.3 per cent of administrative or executive workers. They were concentrated in the two remaining occupational categories, making up 21.1 per cent of service industry workers and 42.1 per cent of industrial workers - process workers, machinists, packers, factory hands and so on. Migrant women from the United Kingdom and Eire were far more evenly distributed throughout the occupational range. They constituted 10.4 per cent of industrial process workers. All migrant women together constituted 52 per cent of industrial workers.7

Des Storer, former research officer at the Centre for Urban Research and Action (CURA), has written extensively about migrants in the Australian workforce. As he has pointed out, migration is linked to industrial development.8 Whatever reason individuals might have for migrating, governments agree to mass-migration programs for largely economic reasons. The source country, with a large supply of labour but little industrial development, encourages emigration to relieve the tensions caused by unemployment. The host country, able to attract investment in industrial development, imports a ready-made labourforce for its rapidly expanding industry.

In this context, women from rural areas, women with little or no formal education or training for urban industrial work, speaking no English and used to different family and social customs, arrive in Australia to enter the unskilled and semi-skilled industrial workforce. They are limited to the low-skilled, poorly paid jobs that provide a poor working environment and some danger to their mental and physical health.

When discussing the situation of migrant women in industry, it is important to realise that while problems are compounded by the social circumstances of migration, language and cultural differences, racial prejudice and discrimination, many are inherent in the work, and are shared by the Australian-born women who do the same work. It is also important to remember that while migrant women are heavily concentrated in industrial occupations, almost half of their fellow workers are Australian-born. In fact, Australian-born women together with British migrants form a majority. Similarly, migrant women from non-English-speaking countries are found as substantial minorities - on average about 10 per cent - in other occupations.

General problems

The Jackson Committee, in its Green Paper on manufacturing industry, said migrant women workers were 'trebly disadvantaged' because of their ethnicity, sex and class.9

Helen Hurwitz has written a sensitive account of the scope of those problems based on interviews with migrant women in a car-manufacturing plant where she was employed as a social worker.10 She says that migrant women shared with men 'the language barrier, difficult working conditions, and the stress of adjusting to a new culture, but also had an additional mass of other problems, simply because they were women'.

Although conditions vary enormously from workplace to workplace, 'the concerns of women workers are always the same, extending beyond the factory and into their wider lives', she claims. The greatest of these concerns is child care. Others which come out in Hurwitz's interviews are fear of dismissal or punishment for speaking out, theri resentment of familiarity or sexual harassment from the men, especially supervisors, and inability to communicate about these matters with union representatives.

The National Women's Advisory Council has pinpointed several key problems of migrant women in Australia's workforce. There are: lack of fluency in English; lack of introductory knowledge of rights, entitlements and procedures related to employment; exposure to unsafe working conditions; exhausting, monotonous work; inability to communicate with supervisors; inability to participate in trade unions, or communicate with union delegates; lack of training and promotion opportunities; lack of adequate child care; and the pressure of the 'double shift' of paid work and domestic responsibilities. They add that many migrant women have been employed in declining industries such as footwear, clothing and textiles, and are vulnerable to retrenchment and hard placed to find alternative employment. They draw attention to 'the apparent ease with which firms can open, close and re-open and not pay employees' wages and their other entitlements simply by going into voluntary liquidation', and comment on the 'inability of the Commonwealth Employment Service and other employment bodies to help disadvantaged migrant workers'.11

The council, in its report on consultations with migrant women, lays particular stress on language and other 'social survival skill' training for migrant women:

. . . many of the problems migrant women confront in adapting to Australian society can, in part, be diminished if positive action can be taken to ensure the provision of education and induction programs at the time of arrival in Australia.12

The council is aware of the impediments to this becoming a reality, for example, difficulty with child care, and the low priority placed on migrant women's education in their own communities. It is also aware that for many women, 'induction' programs are twenty years too late. They have been required by their families and by their new society to work in, participate in and have knowledge of the broader community, and yet they have been constrained by their limited English and access to information, and effectively denied the opportunities they sought.

The council believes that lack of fluency in English contributes substantially to personal loneliness and isolation, limited employment opportunities, exploitation in the workforce, and other difficulties of coping with social and family needs. Many migrant women have been 'completely bypassed' by all available English programs. Whether they are at home or in the paid workforce, child care is a problem, husbands resent their wives going out to classes at night, and there are not enough home tutors to meet the need.

Daughters of migrant women face further problems:

Many migrant girls face serious difficulties in gaining paid employment because of educational disadvantages, added to a lack of suitable vocational counselling and restrictions placed on them by their families.13

Migrant women in the workforce

The particular problems of migrant women in the workforce were first raised in 1976, when the report of the Centre of Urban Research and Action's study was published.14

The CURA study aimed to contact migrant women in their workplaces, and to convene women in their various language groups to provide a forum for them to speak to the researchers and to each other about their work and the problems it entailed. The study covered metal, electrical, footwear, meat, food and clothing industries because of the high proportions of migrant women they employ. It is still a major source of information on the situation of migrant women in factories, and remains the only substantial study actually undertaken in the workplace. Little change has occurred since the study was done. Unemployment, due to declining manufacturing industry, has worsened, and more refugees have joined the workforce, while initial settlement programs have made little impact on the workplace.

The work environment

General work environments were described by the research team and give a memorable picture of situations in which thousands of women work from day to day:

The work area in this factory was very hot, cramped and stuffy. There was little ventilation and pungent odours from chemicals used in the production process caused women to cough and splutter while working. Toilets were filthy and unhygienic. A canteen area was provided but women tended to eat at their work benches.

Canteen facilities in most factories were quite good although in two cases provisions were very crumpled. In one case, the canteen was very old. Work areas were also reasonable with two exceptions. These were dark and cramped conditions in one factory, and in another, concrete floors with no mats as well as very dirty and dusty conditions due to the type of paper used in the manufacture of car filters.

Work areas in all factories visited in this industry were subject to extremes of temperature, damp, noise and poor ventilation.

In most cases women worked on concrete floors causing varicose veins, swollen ankles and problems with leg muscles. Factories were almost wholly mechanised causing constant, high levels of noise. Work areas were large, open and draughty, with no cooling facilities provided in summer or heating in winter. in one potato chip factory, the heat in summer was stifling despite the large number of fans installed by management. Large volumes of steam were emitted from the vats in one tinned food factory which resulted in bitterly cold, damp and humid conditions, necessitating areas for workers. In one of these, women were forced to eat either outside or in the work area which was noisy, very cramped, poorly ventilated and very dusty due to the use of flour in production. In the other case, women had to use one room of an old house in front of the factory, both as a changeroom and eating area.

The room had some benches and trestles, no sink or tap and one old stove for women to cook on. Most women ate their meals in the street outside. In the work area, the smell was offensive and concrete floors were wet, slippery and cold. Women had to work with boiling water which often spilt on to the floor where they were working. Canteens in other factories were clean and provided a wide range of foods, but in all cases were either too small, cold, poorly ventilated or too draughty. Toilets were mostly quite clean with soap and towel provided.

In the meat industry, factories were large, sprawling complexes surrounded by high fences with usually only one entrance, giving a prison-like appearance. With one exception, buildings were very old and run-down. All had concrete floors throughout, in most cases made up of uneven slabs which were very slippery due to spilt blood and water used to hose down the work area. Some factories were poorly lit and all were cold and draughty, especially in winter when women had to wear several layers of clothing to combat extreme cold, as meat had to be packed in rooms kept at a constant 47°F.

Meat hooks hanging up throughout the work area added to the accident risk. Canteen facilities in some of these factories were quite good with one providing airconditioning, a stove, heater, and refrigerator. In contrast, the eating area of one factory was stark, old and dirty with primitive, barn-like conditions and inadequate changing rooms. Another factory provided a small and crowded lunch room although some urns and washing facilities were available.

And in another industry:

Canteens were inadequate in all but one of the seven factories visited. Two factories provided no eating area at all (one without access to water) and women had to eat either at the work-bench or in the street outside. Of the other canteens, one provided no chairs, another was very cramped and surrounded by lockers and the third was situated close to toilets and consisted of a few tables set up amidst rows of hanging dresses. Working areas in general were not well ventilated with few or no open windows. Often we noticed heavy dust present which women complained about, stating it had caused asthma and bronchitis in many.

In many cases, women had to work in cramped conditions with clothes hanging all around them, or machines situated very close together. In one factory, large amounts of materials were stacked around machinists while they worked. Some factories were well lit and some provided heating, although in one case this consisted of only one heater in the front of a large area. Some factories were crowded, dusty and very hot in summer. In many cases, toilets lacked towel dispensers and were cleaned inadequately or not often enough (e.g., once per week).

Work processes

The work itself was described as hard, boring and repetitious. The production process was typically highly regimented and strictly supervised, with women working under constant and heavy pressure to produce quickly. Often this pressure was reinforced by a piece rate or bonus system. Relations between workers and supervisors were generally reported to be bad.

In the metal and electrical industries, CURA found that:

The major problems confronting women in these industries resulted from widespread use of highly regulated production lines. Workers were required to perform one operation again and again throughout their work period at very short intervals. The complete absence of any variation meant that women gained no satisfaction from their particular tasks, which they found boring and monotonous. Added to this was the pressure of work at a fast and constant rate, created by the speed of machinery, the need to keep up with other workers in the line and employer incentives - both positive and negative. Negative incentives were especially effective due to the high level of unemployment, enabling employers to take an attitude: 'If you don't want to work faster, we can find others who will'.

Women described their jobs, nearly all on process lines, as boring, frustrating, and an insult to their intelligence. Most women in the factory worked on a production line system and found their job tedious and routine.

Workers were rotated among various jobs in only on small factory, and women employed there stated they were happy with scheme. They were able to become skilled in a variety of tasks as well as escaping the frustration and unhappiness of constant repetition. According to our researchers, interest in the job was much higher than in most factories.

In the meat factories the research team found that:

The second major problem [in another group of factories] arose out of the nature of the job itself. Women were mostly employed in packing meat which they described as very heavy, hard, boring and laborious work. Other tasks normally undertaken by women were scraping, cleaning, working with intestines and cutting off bones left by the slicers. Women working in the packing section stated they were sometimes required to lift meat weighing more than the award maximum [of almost sixteen kilograms], causing severe and constant backaches and pains in the legs as well as sore and swollen hands. Women told us that in order to offset sore arms you had to learn to 'pace yourself'.

Payment by results

Piecework and bonus systems create enormous pressure to work quickly, which produces nervous tension and strain in the worker. They also lead to a high incidence of 'repetition injuries', tenosynovitis and similar diseases, which are caused by repeated, small movements of the hands and wrists.

Interviews encountered a very hostile response to the bonus system from the women, who felt that their union should be 'doing something about stopping it and getting us a better salary'. They complained that the bonus system put them under constant pressure to produce, causing severe nervous tension:

The piecework system was characteristic of the clothing industry. Under this system workers were not paid a general wage but received a minimum amount for each piece of work they completed. For example, a woman machinist employed to make pockets might receive 10 cents to 15 cents per finished pocket and she would have to complete about 250 of these pockets per day to make a reasonable wage. Speed of operation was therefore paramount, not only because the amount earned depended entirely on the number of items finished, but also because employers often imposed minimum requirements which had to be completed each day. Another common system for payment which was closely allied to the piecework system was the bonus system. This involved workers having to complete a set quota of work for a minimum wage and then receiving a bonus calculated per item for work over the quota.

In one factory which used the bonus method of payment, women claimed that unless they completed 6000 buttons per day, they were called to the office to explain why they hadn't completed more. As a result, women in a substantial number of factories were found to be still working well after the lunch bell, taking five to ten minutes for lunch or working throughout the half-hour lunch break.

In the meat industry, the system of daily hire increased the pressure:

When the daily production tally was high, workers had to work at a very fast rate to achieve the amount required, knowing that if they failed to produce the amount they might not have a job to come back to the following day.

Supervision

Added to the pressure of the 'payment by result' systems and regimented production processes, supervision was usually heavy handed and ever present. It was backed up by sanctions such as transfer to less desirable jobs or by dismissal.

The pressure to maximise production meant that constant surveillance in some cases included timing visits to the toilet and abusing those women who stayed longer than a few minutes.

Attitudes to work

The women surveyed in the CURA study were asked what they liked and disliked about their jobs. Although there were positive as well as negative comments, the negative ones predominated, reflecting the physical environment and work systems described above.

One-fifth of the positive comments mentioned wages, with fewer than 10 per cent of women saying they liked their job for its intrinsic interest, friendships at work, good working conditions or management attitudes.

More detailed comments were made about what women disliked about their jobs. The most unpopular aspects were bosses' attitudes and actions, physical working conditions, hard physical work, repetitious, boring work, piecework and bonus systems and discrimination against migrants, in that order.

Only a small number of women (twenty-four) mentioned that the 'positive attitude of management' was something they liked about their job, whereas twice as many said that they disliked the attitudes and actions of their bosses. A strong feeling of dissatisfaction came through at all stages of the study about the way that middle management and supervisors treated migrant women workers. Women said they were treated like 'second-class citizens', 'numbers', 'animals', 'horses' and subjected to undignified and dehumanising routines such as verbal abuse and name-calling, regimentation, timing in toilets, calling by whistle and so on. While not all factories were as bad as this, many women had strong feelings about the lack of respect shown to them at work.

Relations with management in the five industries studied were described by the research team. In one industry direct contact between workers and higher levels of management took place mainly in smaller factories with control by supervisors, foreladies and foremen predominating in larger factories. Except in a few small factories, where a 'family atmosphere' were characterised by constant observation, fear, abuse, dislike, distrust and suspicion. Fear of management prompted by the pressure of piecework meant that in some factories women were afraid to lift their heads from their work or even go to the toilet. In one factory women were so afraid of an English-speaking foreman that they were reluctant to talk with interviewers even during their lunch break. As well, the factory manager moved constantly around the work area checking on the work output of the women.

In another industry it was found that attitudes of migrant women towards management in one factory were completely negative, with women complaining that employers treated them like animals and not human beings.

In a third industry, all women interviewed in all factories were very hostile towards management. they complained of inhuman treatment and that they were watched constantly by supervisors, managers, and people employed to carry out time-and-motion studies. In one factory frustration and resentment had reached such a high level that on many occasions both Australian and overseas-born women had deliberately smashed large quantities of the light globes they were producing.

In most factories visited, control over workers was emphasised by foreladies and supervisors and there was little contact with higher levels of management. However, with two exceptions, women were hostile to managers, whom they blamed for bad working conditions. Worker-management relations were happier in one factory where neither lunch breaks nor visits to the toilet were strictly timed, and in another where women were rotated among a number of various jobs.

The main feature of relations between workers and management in factories in the meat industry was fear of dismissal. Most women were under the control of foreladies, supervisors and tallymen. Many of them used the practice of employment on a daily basis as a threat against workers. Typical comments by supervisors in one factory were 'You are slowing down', and 'There is a lot of meat piling up here'. Constant observation and a high proportion of English-speaking people holding positions of responsibility contributed to the overall sense of fear amongst migrant women in the industry.

Those who disliked the management's treatment of them complained in particular of the extensive surveillance of workers by supervisors, abusiveness and discrimination against migrants. For instance, the following selection of comments is typical.

We are all women workers and most exploited. We are already the slaves of men. Here they work us like horses without compassion. We are all afraid of the boss - he screams at us.

Bosses should be more fair to migrant women. I think both employers and employees should have more respect for each other - maybe then we can overcome some of our problems.

I have worked in a factory for over ten years. Management forced me to look after three machines - this was done by two persons before. I obviously could not cope so they sacked me. What's worse, I lost my long-service leave which was the intention of management to save on three months' wages - the union didn't care.

Management treats us as inferior and gives workers of other nationalities easier jobs than us.

The more work we do, the more they like it and since we are migrants then we get the worst job.

I think delegates from government and unions should try to get into these factories and see with their own eyes problems that workers are faced with. Workers are frightened to speak up because they are fired.

Questionnaires such as these should be given to workers frequently because they can give information without fear.

Some women made the point that although their families were dependent upon the money they earned, 'that is no reason why we should have to put up with inhuman conditions'.

Australian and British-born women strongly supported strike action over the issue of abusive treatment, indicating that adverse management attitudes were not directed solely towards migrant women, and probably also that the English-speaking women had greater confidence in their own rights. Amongst non-English-speaking groups, Greek, Maltese, Turkish and Yugoslav women were more reluctant to consider strike action, but nevertheless a majority of them supported the idea of some form of union action to control supervisors' behaviour. Spanish-speaking and Italian women were more strongly in favour of both approaches.

In short, the dissatisfaction voiced by workers concerning their employers centred around two main issues: the fact that the behaviour of bosses implied that they saw workers as belonging to a social class which could be treated in a degrading way; and the fact that the role of supervisory staff in the production process was objectionable.

The work itself was described as physically demanding, boring, demeaning, and creating emotional tensions.

Work systems also came in for criticism:

I don't like the bonus system. It is degrading and makes us nervous.

I hate the monotony, the speed of the line, the bonus system.

The rate of production is too high, the bonus system is bad because some of the women don't even go to the toilet - just to keep production up.

It is too hard, and too much work. It is hard on my arms, legs, eyes and I get headaches.

Other comments were directed against the physical working conditions:

I hate the noise and smell and concrete floors.

It is very hard on the eyes and gives me headaches.

Very cold and damp.

The treatment here is harsh and conditions unhealthy.

The factory is too hot, cramped and stuffy and we have to stand on concrete all day.

It is very cold and draughty which gives me continuous headaches.

It is very dangerous here and makes me nervous.

It is not hygienic with respect to toilets; there is not enough room here and is very unclean.

The steam makes work unpleasant.

Language problems

Although the largest non-English-speaking ethnic groups in the Australian workforce are still Italians, Greeks and Yugoslavs, some factories also have sizeable Maltese, Turkish, Lebanese, Spanish-speaking South American, and Indo-Chinese groups in their workforce. As well as these, there may be smaller numbers of people from a wide variety of other countries. It means that communication between migrant workers and the predominantly English-speaking managers, supervisors, union officials and Australian-born workers is limited and usually surrounded by mistrust and some hostility. It also means that migrant workers - who tend to be labelled as a uniform group by English speakers - cannot talk amongst themselves. Not surprisingly CURA found women sitting together in language groups at lunch time and in some factories being grouped together at work by their employers.

The majority, nearly four out of five, of the migrant women had never received any instruction in English. However, the same proportion also thought that learning English was important, with many saying that they would learn English if classes were provided during working hours without loss of pay.

It has generally been recognised since the CURA study stressed this point so strongly, that migrant women do not have access to English classes because of work, child-care problems, domestic responsibilities and sometimes their husbands' attitudes. Classes in working hours seems to be the only viable solution for women in the paid workforce.

Employers generally estimated that most of their migrant women employees could not read or write English, or could do so only minimally, and that most were able to speak some English. However, they were divided on whether language was a problem. Some agreed that migrant women did not need to speak English in order to do their jobs properly, and others indicated that although there were language difficulties they were not a problem because factory personnel and sometimes individual women acted as interpreters.

One employer felt threatened by this process:

When I do have to get my point across and I can't speak to them then I use supervisors to get it across. It leaves me cold at times, their conversation in Greek. You don't know what they are saying.

Employers did not mention that using supervisors to 'get their message across' was a one-way communication process. Women were less able to initiate communication to their employer via a supervisor, or to get information that they were seeking for their own benefit.

Another common occurrence is for workers to be taught their jobs by demonstration and sign language. This can be dangerous, especially when workers are operating machinery that they do not understand using procedures that have not been fully explained to them. However, some employers insisted on a certain level of English ability before employing machine operators.

Given that most employers felt they had successfully tackled any language problems, it was not surprising that they responded negatively to the suggestion of on-the-job English classes. Some employers argued that classes in factories were unnecessary because free classes were available outside the workplace. Others felt that the women would not use classes either after work or at lunch time, but they nevertheless rejected time off during working hours.

Generally speaking, union officials were far more aware than employers of language problems and the difficulties of communicating with a multilingual workforce. In fact, the majority of union officials saw communication as a very real barrier to involving migrant women effectively in industrial action. It was significant that in the CURA study a wide variety of problems emerged from unionists' comments, rather than a consensus view on a small number of difficulties:

First, some union officials expressed frustration and annoyance at not being able to tell whether they were effectively communicating with employees.

'It's much easier for us when there's one nationality in the majority, for example, at [factory A] workers are mostly Greek but [factory B] is a bad one: there are six or seven nationalities - it's a bloody nuisance. It's a real problem to get things across.'

'If I'm explaining something to English-speaking people I can tell by the look on their face whether they understand. I might have to say it twice, but I can tell. But with others I wonder when I go away whether they have understood or not. It's very frustrating.'

This feeling of uncertainty was more significant to these unionists than simply knowing they were not 'getting the message across'. In once case, a union official was reluctant to use workers as interpreters because he could not be certain whether they were altering his words to suit their political views.

Second, some union officials felt that language barriers prevented migrant women from understanding the purpose of unions or details of particular union disputes. They stressed that the problem remained unsolved: 'The problem of communication and of raising the consciousness of the women is a universal problem for unions. We don't do anything about it.'

It extended past language to the communication of ideas; 'It's not just a language barrier alone but a lack of understanding of the unions' way of thinking'.

As a result, women tended to participate in industrial action without understanding why they are doing so. Added one steward, this lack of understanding meant that the benefits of unionism were not apparent, with understandable effects on the level of that makes it so hard to get money from anyone.'

Third, it was argued that language difficulties made it very hard to attract migrants into the union when officials visited a new workplace:

We spent quite some time in one place recently and only joined up twenty, then they got upset at the others not joining. It was complete balls-up but it was mostly English-speaking people who joined up.

This view not only noted the difficulties involved in explaining the benefits of unionism to non-English-speaking employees,, but also the tendency of migrants to 'go with the strength'.

Fourth union officials argued that the lack of understanding resulting from language problems led to fear of participation in union meetings. The implication was that while voting was ordinarily nothing to be afraid of , migrant women felt it was safer not to risk acting on an issue which they did not fully understand:

This is no union communication with migrant women. The majority of women here are Greeks and they just don't understand. At meetings, three-quarters of them are not gam to put up their hands at all. There are no interpreters - the first we have had here came with a group from your people [CURA].

Fifth, one English-speaking shop steward felt that the language barrier contributed to difficulties in worker-to-union communication by making migrant women reluctant to bring forward their problems.

Sixth, an organiser argued that, while migrants understood workers' compensation, union efforts to pursue workers' compensation claims were more difficult when those involved did not have a good command of English.

Finally, some union officials claimed migrants were more vulnerable to exploitation by employers because of their problems in using English. Many were either not aware of their rights or did not feel capable of defending themselves in verbal battles with employers. A number of union officials stressed the importance of attempts at improved communication in gaining the respect and support of migrant women workers. They believed that efforts to overcome language barriers were an important means of obtaining respect, feedback, support for industrial action and confidence in the ability of unions to act for employees.

Relatively few union officials commented on the importance and practicability of obtaining on-the-job English classes for migrant employees. One union official admitted that while migrant women would use such classes, 'I've never asked about it'. Another saw the issue as requiring a lot of union pressure, since 'management won't fall over trying to provide classes', but did not indicate that he intended to initiate any action. One union was reportedly 'taking up demands for English classes on the job', and another union had been partially successful:

We have asked for English classes. A couple of companies have agreed. Some have even agreed to paid time off but they didn't get a high migrant response, e.g. [factory C]. I don't know whether any of them are still going or not.

The above statement deserves two comments. First, the official obviously regarded paid time off as a bonus granted by the employer rather than as a reasonable service and right required by the union. Second, the absence of enthusiasm on the part of migrant women tended to weaken the union case. As another union official commented: 'If migrant women took up the issue of English-speaking classes on the job, we could get it.'

On the other hand, some union officials claimed that migrant women did not need to use English on the job; that those who needed to understand complex requirements for machine operation were long-term, experienced workers who had learnt from other employees or could understand English; and that while many employees could not speak English, they could understand enough to get a rough idea of union activities.

Employers were on the whole unwilling to do anything about providing English lessons, unions were not very enthusiastic in practice, but strong support for the idea was expressed by the women themselves. Unions now point out that English lessons during working hours is a far less winnable demand due to the worsening employment situation. However, most of them are now distributing far more multilingual written information.

Prejudice in the workplace

It's hard to assess how much tension, hostility and prejudice exists between ethnic groups in the workplace.

The CURA study suggested that tensions between Australian-born and overseas-born workers was greater than between different migrant groups. Prejudice of English-speakers towards migrants was greatest, or expressed most openly, when there was a large

Anglo-Saxon group. Hostility was particularly noticeable in one factory where migrant women were in a minority. The attitudes of Australian and British workers emerged in such comments as, 'You are in our country and therefore you should learn English'; 'You don't learn English because you are so ignorant'; and 'You have come to our country, you should change and become like us'. These sorts of views are often followed by the inconsistent opinion that 'Migrant women are cunning, they know more English than they let on'.

Two factors contributed to the high level of antagonism between English-speaking and non-English-speaking groups. Migrant women in most factories tended to sit in their own ethnic groups during lunch and other breaks, evoking such comment as 'Look, they're sitting in groups and won't mix'. However, English-speaking workers made little attempt to socialise outside their own group. the second divisive factor was the common practice of limiting leading-hand positions to Australian and British workers. This gave non-English-speaking migrants cause to fear discrimination and made communication on the job difficult.

In small factories where nearly all workers were non-English-speaking, employees congregated in their own language groups but there was little or no reported friction. In larger factories, where there was a mix on non-English- and English-speaking workers, animosity and lack of communication were common. The tendency for workers to remain in language groups was even more marked with even British and Australian-born workers remaining in separate groups during lunch and other breaks. In some factories name calling was mutual - the term 'wog' being answered by 'kangaroos'. It was also the common belief of many English-speaking workers that non-English-speaking workers could learn English but didn't want to because they were too ignorant.

In one factory with mostly English-speaking workers, European-born women in general were very subdued, although Greek women were hostile towards English-speaking workers. The turnover rate amongst non-English-speaking workers was extremely high. In another factory, English-speaking workers believed that 'Everything is being done for migrants, but nothing for us'. European-born women felt comments were made behind their backs but felt more secure because English-speaking workers were in a minority.

Some migrant women commented about the hostility that they felt directed towards them by Australian-born workers:

When I speak to an Australian woman, she doesn't understand what I am trying to say and she becomes angry.

I don't like my work mates because I don't understand English. They act as if they are the boss and this is very degrading.

Employers' comments

Employers' comments about migrant women revealed a double standard: 'The factory is terrific, the women here don't have any reason to complain about the work, but I wouldn't want my wife to work here'. Remarks like this show that many employers have a stereotyped image of what migrant women are life, and reinforce the statements made by the women themselves who felt that they were treated as inferior beings, without the dignity and respect due to them.

Some employers had stereotypes about women in general:

A woman is more capable of washing cheesecloths, and packaging is a light job. Women are sometimes more dextrous.

On the fiddling jobs with brittle, small bearings, the woman does the job better and faster.

They are temperamental and play on the fact that they are women.

Other employers distinguished between Australian-born and migrant workers, regarding the migrants as more hardworking because they were more desperate and less secure.

Another strong theme in employers' comments was that migrant women were 'primitive' or 'peasant' people - terms always used in a derogatory sense:

They are not like Australians. They will save money rather than spend it and then buy something of value with it. not something of value to us, but something they haven't had which is important to them. It is a problem of bringing a primitive society into a highly industrialised society. It's like bringing Abos from Arnhemland to the city - but they won't make it, whereas these people will succeed.

A large number of employers said that work was easy, and stressed that the women were not dissatisfied. However, this usually meant that few actual complaints had been received. Furthermore, many employers using a double standard, and explained that although other people might find the work tiring, unattractive or monotonous, migrant women or women in general were 'suited' to it. The following example illustrates this view:

The women are suited to these jobs because they can sit at the machine all day doing the same thing. If they were more intelligent or better educated they would become bored or go round the bend. But this class of person is united to the job. These women come from peasant-type backgrounds.

I wouldn't like my wife to work here. It's a hard job wrapping tape around wires, bundle after bundle. It's the same thing all the time. But they seem to like that sort of work. They get down there - yap, yap, yap all day - we don't mind them talking as long as the work is done. Some tell you the work is easy but in my opinion it is hard . . . but the money is good.

When asked about the pressure on women to work very fast, performing the same operation over and over again for long periods, most employers claimed that such pressure was self-imposed and resulted from a worker's strong desire to earn a lot of money in a short time. Bonuses were mentioned to justify any unpleasant features of high production work:

It's hard to work at a monotonous job. But it's piecework and there is incentive to keep going so I suppose that keeps up their interest. It would drive me mad. But I've never heard them say it's boring.

Employers' attitudes to migrant women's problems ranged from benevolent paternalism to downright hostility, as the following comments show:

Migrant women are like sheep. They are led by their husbands. Because they are loath to make decisions for themselves it is very easy for a man to convince them to do what he wants.

If you see them in the street and recognise them - well it's a recognition that they don't get otherwise and their faces light up.

Migrant women are emotionally more reserved. In many cases they don't come out with their problems. I encourage the foremen and supervisors to tackle 'people' problems. Sometimes I bend over backwards to help and still get abused. I wonder if it's worth it at times . . . Even shop stewards say it's hard to get these people to express an opinion. We are not getting to the migrant people . . . They are slow in coming forward . . . I don't know how to overcome it . . .

I don't get involved in the nitty-gritty of the women's problems. Thank goodness for that - I don't want no bloody squawking women on my doorstep.

Migrant women - some comments
by Australian-born women

Many of the Australian-born women to whom I have spoken worked with migrant women and made comments about some of the difficulties they encountered on the job, especially in trying to organise at the shop-floor level. While some Australians were undoubtedly hostile, others had a more sympathetic understanding of the problems, did not blame the migrant women and had positive suggestions for action. Language was, of course, recognised as a huge problem:

Communication was often difficult, and we were often isolated, it was a really good experience for an Australian-speaker to be in that situation. It was pretty horrible, sitting around all the time and everyone else is talking a language that you can't understand. And to think that they have that all the time. That's one of the few instances where they are not subjected to that. It really makes you become more aware.

Often the only English teaching that occurs comes from other workers. most people said that 'Oh well, when I come here they taught me a bit of English'. Yeah. Ask them what sort of things people taught them, it's just the bare essentials, to carry on with the job. You know, what things are called, and so that they can understand what they were told. And often it's mainly other workers on the job who do the teaching anyway.

At the power transformer company, for example, you used to swop lessons at lunch time, and even while we were working actually, because you used to work on a guillotine machine there and we had these large sheet [.9 x .6 metres] of thin steel that you used to push through. One of you would push them through and the other one would pick them up on the other side and put them together, and so those Spanish-speaking people I was working with, and South Americans, would ask me what words were in English and I would write them down on the sheet where it wasn't going to be cut in two, and push it through and they would read it, because it was pretty noisy, and hold it up and everybody would learn it, and then they would put it down and then they would do the same with Spanish words. And at lunch we used to work over their correspondence lessons.

One of the real problems for unions is the cost of employing interpreters and translators, and of producing multilingual material. However, some women pointed out that the bilingual people in the workplace were a great potential resource, not to be used as makeshift interpreters, but to be developed as key people within the shop-floor organisations:

We still have workers, migrant workers on our jobs who can't speak English and certainly can't follow a union meeting because union meetings are far too formal. This time around I said at the shop committee meeting that we were going to have the meeting in groups but, no, it had to be all together. They just will not bend. There is no reason why we couldn't have had our discussion in different language groups, but of course they are frightened of it.

They didn't know what he was saying. He might have been saying the wrong thing and, of course, the Australian workers will yell out. 'What's he telling them?' They are so arrogant.

The union has resources to make available to the members and the members have resources to make available to the union but it seems that never the twain shall meet because you just can't get over their hide-bound attitudes.

Although some English speakers were hostile and suspicious, one Yugoslav women who was working part time had taken on the role of interpreter for her union organiser when a long dispute had arisen in their industry:

Many women don't know nothing and don't trust the union, and they are too frightened to say anything against the boss, and too frightened to complain. Many times I've heard a few migrant women have been working overtime and all and they didn't get paid and they just forgot all about it, never bothered. They're too frightened to go the office and say 'Look, I didn't get paid for it', because they think 'Oh God, you're going to lose the job'. That's why they need someone to enlighten them about the union and the work that they are doing and that they are trying to help them. And of course in their own language because they can't speak much English, and many can't speak at all. I didn't realise that until I went to that meeting. i counted how many women there who just didn't understand one word, nothing; I just can't understand how they can work. I suppose the bosses say, 'You do this' and then they go, and hurry up and do like animals; honestly, it's not fair. They need someone to tell them the union is there to help them.

Some Australian-born women regarded migrants as being more easily intimidated by their employers:

I think that could be why contract cleaners employ so many migrants because they put the fear into them, you know, whereas Australian women can talk more and discuss it more. They won't have as much put over them. Although I believe there was a bit of a stoppage. There were two cleaners there and they were both migrant women. They stuck out for what they should get. They were pretty strong. But even I think migrant men might take on jobs that Australian men, that nobody else would have, you know.

Some were openly hostile about migrant workers' timidity:

Too many new Australians. They're intimidated, you know, they're frightened. But the main thing, too many new Australians in it because new Australians are not very union wise. They'll cut each other's throats for overtime and dob everybody in for what they do to the bosses so they'll get the overtime in preference to the other person. Even if we came in and said stop work for a cause they wouldn't stop work because it's going to cost them money.

Other women had a greater awareness of the pressures on migrant women. As one works delegate commented:

The women are very confined, very subtly oppressed on jobs. Some ethnic groups have got more front than others. For instance the South American women are very outgoing, very fiery, even in the temperament. But the Turkish women in the main are very timid. Not really timid, but as far as being outgoing in the outside world they are very reserved.

Greek workers - well, of course, they are all reserved because there is a lot of racism in the jobs and women have to cope with the racism and sexism as well as being in a very exploitive situation. So it is extremely oppressive. Very, very difficult. They just make their own little niche for themselves on the job so that they are able to cope and find their support amongst their friends on the job.

Not all the Australians regarded migrant women as reserved or subdued:

But especially at [company X] it was really good, the migrant women there, because they were in such a n exploitative situation, and they were so strong, I mean compared to the men there, even the migrant men; the women just had whole lot of energy and strength and they just wouldn't take shit. I mean, if their supervisor put them down they would put him down back, even if it was in their own language so that it was only all the other Yugoslav women laughing; and that was even worse, because the boss didn't know what they said, and that used to really piss them off. Or actually punching into them a couple of times.

Those who did come forward as activists were likely to be exposed to swift reprisals from the employer:

But we had a Turkish lass that became a shop steward just recently and she was very intelligent and showed a lot of potential, but it's a slow process. She would only be able to be effective by working together with other women who gave her a lot of support. But she had a lot of courage. She was a very fine lass but she got the sack on Friday.

As one woman put it, if people, especially migrant women, are to be active on the shop floor, they need support and protection from fellow workers through a structure such as a shop committee, not only to protect them from the sack, but also to overcome the resistance they encounter from the workers at the top of the hierarchy, the Australian-born skilled tradesmen:

We are all workers on the job together as long as the interests of the tradesmen, the elite workers, are the ones that are fostered. Of course, elite workers also go over those workers who have got some control and they are usually the ones that are cultivated by the company. So the general workers are in a very divided, fragmented and oppressed situation. I would love to see women on the job, particularly ethnic women, organising their own child-care centre instead of somebody else doing it and bringing in all the patronising ethics with the way these institutions are organised in our society. The Australian ethic, they are just determined to force it on to everybody. The older European workers on my job, with their years of experience of working on a job like that, they have got a shell around them that thick that no way would you be able to take it off. They will die with it. They have got to speak English. They've ot to be the same as the Australian workers. They have to adopt every value and every ethic. And it's the whole of the bosses' values that dominate on the job. Dog eat dog. We are in a situation where everything is designed to maximise profit and if you are not succeeding it's your fault and the workers just force all that onto the other workers and consequently they don't stick together. The women and the migrants just become the whipping boys. You get a feeling on the job that the workers that are there are just forcing the others out the gate. They can't get rid of them quickly enough. It's shocking. How do you change that? One way to change it, of course, will be various groups to get together and support one another and attack the situation that way.

If anyone has a sense of community the ethnic groups have because they have to have the support of their community or they can't survive; that should be utilised, and developed. The women have to do the same thing. Hopefully, when women do that they will be able to bring much more human values into it. One of our best shop stewards is a young ethnic person who has just come onto the shop committee. We have got some good ethnic people on the shop committee. We have got some good ethnic people on the shop committee now but he's the best because he's a very humane person but he's a fighter too. So he's the one that they are out to destroy. But, of course, you've got to give people a lot of protection.

Several women stressed the importance of shop committees as a way of overcoming the divisions between workers of different language groups:

I think it has a lot to do with the concrete situation that people are in, and if some condition, or some issue of wages, or injustice or unfair sacking comes to a head, it's just really hard. The only way of overcoming those divisions is when people are united around some specific issue, but the problem is that the unity that can be built up there, if you win the case, or if you lost it or whatever, can be dissolved the next day, unless some structure is set up to maintain it. Which is some sort of shop committee or whatever you want to call it, which has representatives on it from not only all the sections, work sections, in the factory, but from migrant sections as well. And that those decisions taken at those shop committees have to be actually put to people. As well as being communicated back in verbal form, they should also be printed in all the languages. We, for example, tried to do that at the power transformer company. When we had union meetings we had some translations of people speaking in the lunch-time meetings that we held just without the union official, and when we printed anything, which might have been a report of negotiations with the boss or resolutions we had carried, we got them printed in the major language groupings of that factory.

Migrant women and the Working Women's Charter Campaign

Migrant women: We call upon the ACTU Congress to campaign actively and support the struggles of migrant workers and their organisations. WE deplore the fact that many migrants cannot communicate with other workers or their union, because of language barriers. English language lessons on the job - without loss of pay - particularly for women, is an essential demand. Unions should also assist to break down barriers by producing multilingual union publications. Migrants suffer some of the worst working conditions in Australia - this needs urgent attention by the trade union movement.15

This was one of the five urgent demands that the Working WOmen's Charter Campaign presented to the ACTU before the 1977 congress. The response was disappointing in that the ACTU charter mentioned migrant women only once.

The Charter Campaign Conference of 1977 raised many issues related to the implications of Australia's multilingual workforce for labour organisation. In particular, the question was raised of whether migrant women workers were more concerned about organising with migrant men or with Australian women.

The FILEF (Federation of Italian Workers and their Families) Women's Group said that migrant women workers had been more actively organising on their behalf but to participate in bringing about change through unions and other pressure groups they needed encouragement 'because in the past our greatest concern or rather fear has been that of losing our job and having very little possibilities of further employment'.16 One of their basic demands, therefore, was for the right to work.

The charter campaign took up the issue of the right to work as an urgent priority, and commented further that:

Migrant women are particularly intimidated by the threat of the sack. This increases the fear and alienation they feel as a result of not speaking English and the sole use of English by the unions and companies.

Conclusion

It is unfortunate, although perhaps typical, that there have been far more recommendations made about the problems of migrant women workers than outcomes.

The CURA study made fourteen recommendations, deliberately limited in scope and intended as an indication of the specific changes which may lead both to some immediate improvement in the work situation of migrant women and also to the development of processes by which migrant women may gain the confidence, experience and organised capacity for assuming greater control over their social situation.

The first recommendation, the establishment of a Migrant Workers' Centre within the union movement, has been put into practice. The centre was established in 1976 with the support of several unions. Multilingual workers were employed to act as links between migrant workers and their unions so that, although few unions employ bilingual organisers, they have been able to print and distribute more multilingual information about wages, conditions, compensation, social welfare and various other matters.

Three other recommendations, for the development of processes for involving migrant women in union activities and in trade union training and the provision of multilingual materials, have been taken up in varying degrees by individual unions. Some trade union education now takes place in major migrant languages. However, no progress has been made to achieve English lessons on the job, within working hours, two issues for which changes were recommended, have probably become worse as the labour market has deteriorated. Retraining has become less readily available as alternative employment for migrant workers discarded from manufacturing industry becomes scarcer.

The National Women's Advisory Council recommended that migrant women should be given courses before they start work, covering employment entitlements, wages, sickness and holiday pay, basic rules and regulations, maternity leave, correct safety procedures, trade union activity and procedures for obtaining workers' compensation. The courses should make use of audiovisual material, written materials and group sessions.

It sounds like quite a course. My own experience at the Western Region Centre for Working Women indicates that to be effective the course would have to continue after the women were employed, and be developed in response to their experiences on the job. Furthermore, it is apparent that Australian-born women have just as much need for this type of community education in the workplace.

The council also recommends that courses be set up to educate supervisors, shop stewards and management about migrant problems and services available to them. Vivi Koutsounadis of South Sydney Community Aid has extended this concept by suggesting that union officials need training in the cultural characteristics, values and modes of living of different ethnic groups so that they can work effectively with them. 'From my observations in some factories many women are quite vocal in their own language and if given the opportunity they express their ideas. They are natural leaders.'17

She goes on to say that these women could be trained to become spokespeople, union delegates or resource people on the shop floor.

Her description of the social situation of migrant workers is familiarly bleak. Although she was referring mostly to women from southern Europe, the same fundamental problems continue to arise with each succeeding wave of migration and refugee intakes from South America, the Middle East and South-East Asia. Although resentment has been expressed within some of the more established migrant communities because refugees have allegedly received better post-arrival treatment than recent migrants, any improvement is undoubtedly due to the pressure of ethnic organisations drawing attention to such problems. However, post-arrival services have not solved the problems of women moving into the lowest stratum of the labour market, and having to cope with financial and family pressures in an alien social environment where prejudice and hostility abound.

In the short to medium term, this situation is likely to persist. Even though immigration policy is moving towards greater selectivity (e.g., in higher and more specific job qualifications and ability to speak

English) and refugee intake is tightly regulated, it will be a long time before past immigration patterns cease.

As Des Storer wrote in 1975, migration movements are caused by unequal development of different societies within capitalism.18 Specifically, there have been mass movements of workers from less developed countries and regions (such as southern Italy, Spain, reece, Turkey, Yugoslavia, Algeria, Morocco, Tunisia, West Indies, India and Pakistan) to more developed countries (such as western Europe and Australia) which have encouraged heavy investment of multinational capital. As Storer says, migrants, women and workers are generally not represented in decision-making processes and are consequently most ignored and exploited, but they do constitute a potentially powerful force because of their central position in the development process.

Unemployment in 'developed' or highly industrialised Western countries could break this pattern. However, if masses of migrant workers are discarded from the labour market, social tensions will arise and ethnic organisations will probably be radicalised.

Another challenge in the longer term to the importance of migrant labour is the increasing international division of labour, whereby large, low-paid, unskilled industrial workforces have been created in port, communications and technology allow corporations to move raw materials, components and finished products around the world, taking advantage of low wages in one country for labour-intensive work, and high levels of skill in another country for capital-intensive work. Thus capital rather than the labourforce is moved around the globe. The implications of these changes are discussed in Chapter 10. One result, however, could be the end of Australia's mass migration program so that at least its residual problems will not be added to by continuous new waves of migrants.

The immediate impact of these structural changes will be large-scale displacement of migrant workers from the sorts of jobs they have characteristically held over the past thirty years. While the jobs themselves have been notoriously unattractive, their loss will constitute a serious problem unless the special needs of migrants are part of our response to issues such as alternative employment, retraining and income distribution.

'When the whistle blows for knock off'

Hours and Work Patterns

'Eight hours' work, eight hours' rest, eight hours' recreation.' This was the historic call of the Australian labour movement which led to the establishment of the eight-hour day, sex-day week in the second half of the nineteenth century.

The length of the working week, the pattern of working hours for full and part-time workers and the associated terms, conditions and benefits of employment have long been a major issue around which labour has been organized.

In 1947, Australian workers won a forty-hour week after several years of renewed lobbying court action and mass campaigning by unions. However, women, whether they are employed 'full' or 'part' time, are still a far cry from working an eight-hour day.

As Linda Rubinstein has pointed out:

. . . the call of the eight hours movement has not yet been achieved by the majority of women. For most women with children theirs is the equivalent of a full working day at home in addition to the time they spend at the machine, the shop or the office.[1]

The resurgence of the women's movement and the entry of women into the paid workforce has led many of them to voice their need for both better employment conditions and more sharing of housework and child care. Establishment of good quality, community-controlled, free child-care services operating twenty-four hours a day to suit the needs of working parents, including shiftworkers, has been one of the key demands of the women's movement.

Although many women have continued in full-time employment while taking major responsibility for housework and child rearing, others have entered the paid workforce as part-timers, juggling their hours of paid work with school hours and times of available child care. Since 1947 there has been a growth in part-time employment, mainly due to these numbers of married women combining paid work with child rearing. This trend, together with the enormous pressures on women doing two full-time jobs, has led to suggestions that there should be more part-time work available for women to ease their pressure. There have also been suggestions that husbands could work part time in order to share housework and child rearing. More recently, part-time work has been seen as a way for people to support themselves while developing 'alternative lifestyles'.

However, this is only part of the story, especially for women. Even part-time employment combined with full-time child rearing and housework can generate Australia's most common occupational health problem – fatigue and emotional stress. Women in part-time employment still need child-care services, flexibility in their working hours and shared responsibility for domestic work.

Support of part-time work by some sections of the women's movement has been based on the need for more job opportunities, and the need to ease the workload most women carry. However, these views have sometimes been expressed without any understanding of the importance of the struggle around working hours within the labour movement.

Work arrangements, far from being a 'trendy' superficial issue, go to the heart of the power of organized labour. There is an issue of job control involved in determining not only how many hours are worked and when that work takes place (e.g., regular or varied shifts, night work, starting and finishing times) but also what the rates of pay shall be (e.g., the number of hours to be worked for the minimum wage, overtime and penalty rates and loadings given to casual workers). The issue is of crucial importance for women workers since, if they are to exercise power through industrial organization they will be faced with three tasks: maintaining some of the historical gains of the labour movement in respect of pay and working hours, bringing in reforms to allow greater flexibility of work arrangements and, lastly, using their emergent power in the paid labourforce to make gains in the general community, such as child-care provisions that lessen the double burden on women workers.

Unions, seeing their achievements in the labour movement as central, have been reluctant to support part-time employment or to organize and protect part-time workers.

There has been no general reduction in working hours for over thirty years, yet the recession, with its high unemployment, has gain drawn attention to how crucial working hours are in negotiations between labour and employers, Faced with the prospect of retrenchments, closing of factories, reduction of working hours and wages and campaigns to remove penalty rates, some unions have responded with a campaign for a thirty-five-hour week. Meanwhile, most unions have shied away from the issues raised by part-time employment which shows, in part, a reluctance to come to grips with the needs of women workers. This is definitely not to say that unions and the women's movement have had irreconcilable differences.

The Working Women's Charter Campaign Conference of 1977 put forward a program that recognized both the historical advances of the labour movement and the needs of women for more suitable working hours.[2] A workshop on this topic called for: union to campaign for a thirty-five-hour week in response to unemployment and Federal government 'attacks on the trade union movement'; the abolition of 'casual' work; and reform in the area of part-time work. Recognising the possibility of exploitation of causal part-time workers, their lack of unionization, and the possibility of casual and part-time workers being used to displace full-time workers, the workshop advocated 'permanent' status for part-time workers, with the same leave and other entitlements as full-time workers, on a pro rata basis; stronger union action on behalf of part-time and casual members; active union efforts to recruit and organize part-timers and casuals; and greater availability of child care.

The proposal was based primarily on the needs off women, given their dual role, for better child-care services, access to more suitable working hours and greater trade union organization.

Another attitude to reviewing working hours has been to assume a set number of jobs, a set amount of wages being divided amongst a larger group of workers, all with reduced hours. In other words, unemployment is to be dealt with by reducing both wages and working hours of employed people to provide jobs at reduced wages to unemployed people.

This approach has been criticized at length by Mike Gallagher, former research officer with the Labour Resource Centre, who argues that it is ludicdrous to reorganize the distribution of time amongst employees without also changing relationships between employers and employees, between production and social goals and many other aspects of employment. He maintains that the reorganization of working hours, as a response to unemployment, is motivated by the desire to reduce the costs of labour, but that it has gained acceptance because it has been presented as and confused with attempts 'to open up broader avenues of access to employment especially for women', and 'to restructure working hours and commitments to allow people more options outside their world of employment'.[3]

The issues raised by his debate are complex, but lead back continually to several fundamental questions. What are the appropriate responses, in terms of the organization of employment, to recession? Are proposed changes in work patterns progressive for workers or do they represent a deterioration in the labour market? How (and to that extent) can workers have control over their conditions and hours of work? How should the tensions between women's dual role be resolved? And finally, what are the implications of changes in women's employment and work patterns for organized labour?

These issues will be discussed after the current working patterns of women and the changes – such as increasing part-time work, shiftwork and outwork – have been reviewed.

Current work patterns

Present work patterns of women cover a great variety of arrangements. The *number* of hours worked (whether part time, full time or overtime), the *terms* of employment (whether regular or casual) and the *shifts* worked (whether day, night or weekend) are all important variables. While there is extensive information available on the numbers of hours worked, there is less on shiftwork and no reliable information on the overall incidence of casual employment.

One third of the women in the Australian paid workforce work part time, defined as less than thirty-five hours a week[4], and a quarter work during the evening or night.[5]

Although the traditional working week has been an eight-hour day within the span of 7 a.m. to 8 p.m., Monday to Friday, many workers are required to depart from this pattern. The labour movement maintains that those who do so should be paid 'penalty rates', or loadings on their wages, to compensate for the social dislocation involved. Another goal of the labour movement has been the establishment of paid leave and sick-pay entitlements. However, union organization to achieve these entitlements has been concentrated on the regular, full-time workforce, with the result that casual and part-time workers have been relatively neglected.

Casual workers do not receive holiday or sick pay or other benefits of regular employment, but they are entitled to a loading on their hours' rate of pay to make up for this. Although no precise figures are available, it is likely that many of the women who work part time are employed on a casual basis. According to the Victorian Liquor and Allied Trades' Union, about three-quarters of all employees in the service industry are casuals.[6] Because of the difficulties in organizing casual workers and the irregularity of their employment, they are very vulnerable to exploitation. The most widespread example of this is disregard by employers of casual loadings. Working hours of casual workers are variable and unpredictable, and in some cases penalty rates are not paid.

In the past, most part-time employment has been casual, giving rise to an association between part-time *hours* of work and poor or exploitative *conditions* of employment. Unions have expressed the fear that acceptance of part-time employment on these terms would lead to an erosion of conditions of full-time workers.

One response to this, especially from organisations favouring part-time work opportunities, WEL for example, has been to advocate the introduction of regular part-time work with the same pro rata entitlements, conditions and benefits as full-time work. To date, this policy has found most acceptance in the public service and the teaching profession. One survey of women and part-time work in the Waverley area of Melbourne found that 53 per cent of regular part-time workers received holiday pay and 43 per cent were entitled to sick pay.[7]

While advocates of part-time work want to see the entitlements extended to all part-time workers, there is growing concern among unions that the increase in part-time work is being sought by some employers who are taking advantage of the deteriorating job market to withhold such entitlements from their part-time employees, or to demand a full week's output from them.

In time of recession, with a deteriorating labour market, changes in working hours are likely to be detrimental to workers, *unless* there is a strong campaign within the labour movement to maintain existing provisions, extend their coverage to more sections of the workforce and to ensure that innovations build on rather than replace these entitlements.

Employers on the other hand are likely to seek to reduce their labour costs. Employing part-timers is one way, another is to increase outwork – work done for an employer at piece rates in the worker's own home. Outwork includes sewing, packaging, light assembly work and repetitive tasks such as folding leaflets. Because existing laws regulating outwork are rarely enforced, little is known about the extent of outwork and the conditions under which outworkers are employed. However, one study by Denise Cusack and John Dodd for CURA estimated that there may be 8000 outworkers in the clothing industry in Melbourne, and it is likely that the numbers are increasing.[8] Most outworkers are women whose child-care responsibilities inhibit them from working outside the home. They are marginal to the labour force and are especially vulnerable to exploitation – they are isolated, usually non-unionised, paid at piece rates and, because of their dubious terms of employment, have no recourse if they are underpaid. The situation of outworkers is discussed further below.

One aspect of the current recession is capital-intensive investment, that is, investment in equipment, particularly new technology that reduces the size of the labourforce. This potentially could lead to the elimination of dreary work and the reduction of everyone's working hours. However, under present political and economic circumstances it is more likely to displace workers without passing on the benefits to them of increased production. The demand for the shorter working week, the thirty-five-hour week, has been suggested by some unions as a more equitable solution.

Since employers have invested so heavily in equipment it is in their interests to operate it twenty-four hours a day. So although technological change is reducing the size of the workforce it is also resulting in proportionally more shiftwork. The impact of increased shiftwork will be felt not only in terms of working hours but also in the social lives and employment conditions of workers.

Working and living in a society that operates around the clock may provide flexibility but the question is – for whom? Is it flexibility of employers to deploy their workforce around the clock, or is it flexibility for workers to choose working hours that suit them? And if working night shift is the only option because there are no other jobs, or no adequate child-care services available, how meaningful will it be to speak of choice for women workers? If shiftwork increases as employment decreases, then it is likely that more and more people will be forced to take shiftwork because they have no alternative.

The social impact of shiftwork is already immense. Increased shiftwork will bring a social cost as the health, family and personal lives of workers will suffer. It is unlikely that all of society would operate twenty-four hours a day, so shiftworkers, while increasing the convenience of the service they provide to others, would not themselves benefit. The social costs of shiftwork are now partially compensated by shift allowances and similar higher payments. However, as shiftwork increases, employers can be expected to argue that it is not abnormal and should not carry penalty loadings. At present, the main inducements for workers to do shiftwork are extra money for men, and fitting in with child care and family needs for women. However, with higher unemployment and fewer day-shift jobs available, no further inducement or compensation may be needed. Clearly, in that situation, the bargaining power of workers would be lower, and the important safeguards for workers such as control over rostering, length of breaks between shifts, provision of canteen facilities and health services, would be harder to achieve.

Possible changes in working hours and arrangements, whether they involve part-time work, casual work, outwork, shiftwork or other non-traditional arrangements, all contain some potential for giving workers greater flexibility and choice of suitable working hours. However, at present they also have disadvantages which could grow worse unless workers have the industrial bargaining power to make sure that working conditions are not eroded and that the social impact of work is recognized.

The following section looks in more detail at developments in non-traditional working hours.

Part-time work

Throughout the 1960s and 1970s part-time work increased much more rapidly than full-time work, so that by 1979 over 15 per cent of the workforce was employed part time. Four-fifths of these part-time workers were women, the majority of whom were married. Part-time work has become part of the career pattern of an increasing number of women, especially married women rearing children.[9] Part-time workers made up over a third of women workers, and over four-fifths of married women workers compared to only 5 per cent of men. While most male part-time workers were in the younger and older age groups (probably students and men approaching retirement) the majority of women were in the 25-44 age-group. Young women (i.e., those aged between 15 and 19) were students and, increasingly, school-leavers affected by a deteriorating labour market.

The largest occupational group for both full-time and part-time women workers is clerical. However, part-time workers include a higher proportion of service, sport and recreation workers and a higher proportion of sales workers than full-time workers, probably because of the peak-hour and 'after hours' requirements of those occupations.

There is some evidence that part-time work gives women the opportunity to re-enter the paid workforce or to keep up their job skills and confidence while bringing up children. Sample surveys in areas of both Melbourne[10], New South Wales and Sydney have shown that at least a third (36 per cent, 33 per cent and 43 per cent respectively) of women not currently employed wanted part-time work. And the majority of part-timers said they were not looking for longer hours or full-time work. However, it is not true to say that part-time work is desired by women workers in general. From all available research there is evidence that a significant proportion are looking for longer hours.

In a depressed labour market, workers have less control and less effective choice over their jobs and working hours. It is clear, however, that some people want part-time work and are starting to demand better terms of employment and recognition of the needs of part-timers. Others have little choice because their domestic responsibilities, together with lack of good quality, cheap, accessible child-care services, prevent them from working longer hours. And a third group – still a minority but likely to grow rapidly – work part time because full-time work is not available to them. This is particularly true of young people, older men and married women. As one women has put it '$60 a week is better than no job'.

Women who discussed part-time work with me made a range of comments all of which related to the deterioration of the labour market and of conditions associated with part-time work.[11] Comments were that women do not always choose their working hours; in some cases part-time work entails being under great pressure to do more work for less pay, but if jobs are hard to find it is better than nothing. It was also suggested that part-time work could in the long term downgrade women's position in the workforce and detract from gains the women's movement has fought for or achieved.

Several industrial disputes in which the Working Women's Charter Campaign has been involved have centred around reductions or adverse changes in working hours, for example the Newcastle cleaners strike and the Redfern Central Mail Exchange dispute of 1977.

One women, also a Newcastle cleaner, but with a different firm, had been working full time but was cut down to three hours a day when new contracts were negotiated. As she said to me, she had not wanted shorter hours:

Oh, not really, because we get less money this way. When we worked longer hours, of course we had more money. But we can't do nothing about it much can we? The offices everywhere, they are trying to cut down as much as they can. It's not fair really, because they just about want us to do everything for nothing! They still want a good job to be done, but they want it in short hours. I stood up to them. I said, 'I don't want no one to push me about', because they start doing that. They stand there and watch us and all this. And I said 'No, I don't want the supervisor here behind my back because I'm not going to do a better job even if she's standing there'.

And I even do a better job now when there's no one around, because I'm more relaxed. I like the job there. It's not that ... I've been working there for three years. It's just the hours. If there were longer hours it would be better, because of the pay.

Pressure of work on part-timers was also said to be a problem in white-collar employment. As one union official commented:

With part-time and casual there are so many loopholes. They all talk about government, fair enough, in government you can regulate it, but you get out to an employer in the private market, how do you regulate it? I know women who work three and four days a week. Three days a week and do the five days' work in actual fact and get three days' pay. And I am not talking about isolated cases when I say that because it comes from different areas, so it must go on if I can meet them. They must be pretty widespread.

Another woman had changed her job from general cleaning to cleaning the glassware in a science laboratory because 'the hours were better': 'Instead of a 6 o'clock start you start at 8 o'clock, a more civilized time ... I had to get up at half past four in the morning every morning and you start to get a bit tired after a while.'

She then found that her working hours were cut down:

[I work[from eight to one, actually. I am only on part time. The university is cutting down on their staff rather than putting them on and I haven't been able to get anything in a full-time job at uni at all. I would very much prefer to but a half-time job is better than none. [It is particularly hard to get a job] when, as I am, you are unskilled. There's very, very few jobs and ones that are usually very, very hard are ones they tend to put younger women to. You see, I'm only a couple of years off retiring age and it's pretty hard to get a couple of years off retiring age and it's pretty hard to get a job of any sort under those conditions. They much prefer younger women. Even on jobs like cleaning jobs. As a matter of fact when I went to the university I put my age back, because I'd been knocked back so often, and I was forty-seven at that time, and about three years later they asked for my birth certificate. It wouldn't have made any difference as far as they were concerned but on most jobs it does make a difference. It does now at uni. They wouldn't give you a job out there at my age when there is a younger person available in cleaning.

One women expressed the hostility that is common within the union movement towards part-time employment:

One issue we have to be careful of is part-time work. I am not against part-time work but I do see a lot of dangers in part-time work and I do believe there is the necessity for hanging onto the main issue of full-time employment. And I think that women have got to realise that they don't have jobs for hobbies. Jobs are for working and until they do this they are not going to get the promotional opportunity, better rates and all the rest of it that women wanted to get and that we think they should get. And I am frightened of the fact that I feel with people pushing for part-time work that all the work for equal pay will go down the drain, because they will still be on a second rate and they will still be included as second-rate citizens which I for one have always tried to get rid of, and I feel all the work we have done could be lost.

However, this view represents only one thread of the argument. Others, to be taken up below, are that part-time work already exists and effort is needed to improve part-timers' conditions and to ensure that promotion, opportunities in all jobs and so on are available to people working part time; and further, to ensure that other issues such as job creation, a shorter full-time working week, extended child-care facilities and family provisions for workers, are also pursued.

There is no simple explanation of the role of part-time work in the labour market. It varies according to the industry and occupations involved, the ages and sex of the workforce and the changing economic environment.

Gallagher has outlined the impact of part-time employment in several industries.[12] According to him, in clerical work that part-time workforce complements the full-time workforce. The changes likely to occur in that area of employment are introduction of increasingly sophisticated technology, reducing employment but also increasing part-time professional and data-processing work, most of which will be done by women with educational qualifications. However, for many women, increased technology in the clerical area will entail replacement of skills by routine mechanical processes.

Sales and service occupations are represented more highly in part-time employment than in full-time, probably because they operate outside 'normal' hours (e.g., nights and weekends) and have peak hours. The part-time workforce is young, with many casuals being employed. Although this situation will probably continue, there is pressure from government and employers to reduce penalty rates and keep conditions and entitlements to a minimum.

One example of this has been the dispute between the Liquor and Allied Trades Union and McDonalds, the fast-food chain. The Labour Resource Centre, in co-operation with the Victorian Branch of the Liquor Trades Union, has produced a booklet called 'Rip Off Ronald: How McDonald's exploits kids'. It outlines complaints the union has received against McDonalds, some of which include dismissing workers when nearing twenty years of age in order to avoid payment of adult wages, failing to pay annual leave entitlements to casual employees, and attempting to employ juniors under 'work experience' schemes for as little as $3 for an eight-hour day. The booklet states that the majority of McDonald's employees do adult work for about half of adult wages, and that the extremely low wages force both casual and permanent workers to work excessively long hours. Other complaints were that some casual workers were 'on call', sometimes being rostered on but not paid if business was slack, or sent home without being paid. It was alleged that the company was 'very slack' about payment of overtime and penalty rates. In order to continue these practices, the company maintained a notoriously anti-union stand.

This type of operation could be setting a pattern for retailing in future for the large numbers of unemployed young women are prime targets for employment under similar conditions. However, as the booklet says, 'it should not be a choice between a rip-off job and no job at all'.[13]

More and more retail outlets, especially those selling food, household goods and products related to cars, are following the pattern of staying open all or most of the night, staffed by one or two young people operating computerized cash registers. This style of business relies heavily on low wages, which explains the employers' preference for young people, and increases the likelihood of failure to pay penalty rates for night time or shiftwork. Retailing and service industries are likely to draw an increasing number of young people into shiftwork.

In manufacturing industry there is relatively less part-time employment, although it is possible that as employment in manufacturing declines and capital-intensive investment continues, there will be more part-time work and continuous shiftwork. This is consistent with employers attempting to reduce labour costs, provide flexibility in production runs, and make maximum use of equipment. The workers most affected will be migrant men and women. Migrant women will further be affected by labour-cost cutting, for instance through increase in outwork in the clothing and other manufacturing industries.

A final feature that Gallagher mentions is that part-time women workers are more strongly represented in the higher status occupations such as administration, executive, managerial, professional and technical ones than their full-time counterparts. This may be, as Gallagher suggests, that part-time work provides women with some access to these jobs, but it could also mean that professional and administrative staff are in a better position to demand part-time work and, being relatively higher paid, are able to earn enough by working part time. Although these women, for instance part-time teachers and public servants, have been used as a model in the argument in favour of more part-time work for women, they remain a relatively privileged minority compared to the women in clerical, sales, service and manufacturing industries.

Gallagher concluded that:

Part-time work may function to re-inforce the segmentation of the labourforce by sex, age, ethnicity, occupation and industry ... The point is that part-time employment will not have a uniform effect on the structure of the labour market and accessibility to employment. Rather, increasing part-time employment may entrench inequalities.

Gallagher, while not denying that part-time employment with adequate terms and conditions, suits some people, links the trend towards part-time work and other 'flexible' arrangements with a deteriorating labour market, and therefore worsening conditions for workers.

This analysis is partly acknowledged in a booklet published by the Women's Bureau of the Department of Labour (now Employment and Youth Affairs) which states that the high demand for labour in 1945 to 1970 'may have held back the acceptance and spread of flexible work arrangements'. Part-time employment grew over that period in order to draw up otherwise 'unused' labour of married women, whereas now it may grow in order to *reduce* the workforce.[14]

The demand for part-time work has come largely from people whose health, lifestyle or other commitments make them reject full-time employment. It is clearly progressive to demand shorter working hours and more flexible arrangements that do allow greater and more flexible arrangements that do allow greater opportunities for personal or community activities. It is important for both part-time workers and full-time workers that the labour movement give priority to increasing the pay and fringe benefits of part-time workers, and links this to campaigns for reduced full-time hours.

For many women, however, entering the paid workforce is only possible 'if adequate child care facilities [are] provided and fi working hours [are] arranged to meet family responsibilities'.[15]

Women's organisations (such as WEL) have, therefore, argued for more 'permanent' part-time work (i.e., carrying pro rat terms and conditions).

Unionist Jozefa Sobski has questioned the effects of 'permanent part-time work' on the advancing status of women in the workforce in the long term.

She has listed several possible ways in which part-time work could 'backfire' on women; it could institutionalise the inequality between men and women by continuing to channel women into jobs with lower status, less responsibility, fewer prospects for promotion, and by widening the income gap between men and women; it could contribute to the perpetuation of sex roles by restricting men's involvement with their children and retaining prime responsibility for children with women; it could also, by allowing women to combine paid employment with child raising, reduce government responsibility for providing child-care facilities; it could also divide workers into groups with different levels of 'needs' for employment, and play on women's 'self sacrificing' role in times of high employment; it could lead to decreased interest by women in unions; it could reinforce the myth that married women do not have a proper place in the workforce; and finally, it might seriously disadvantage the working-class women who do not command the same salaries as teachers and public servants.

While these dangers do exist, they are more likely to become a reality if unions regard part-time work as a threat rather than as a basis for a progressive demand for better paid, more humane working hours. Sobski ends by asking a series of questions which fail to discuss how the issue should in fact be dealt with:

Whose interests in the long term, will permanent part-time work serve? Will it alter significantly the status of women in the workforce and importantly, in the home? Will it redistribute power to income in the workforce or in the home? Should the struggle be centred on shorter working hours for all rather than the institutionalization of conditions suitable for a few and forced on the many?[16]

Some unions continue to be hostile to 'job-sharing', part-time work and other flexible working arrangements. The Australian Post and Telecommunications Union (Victoria Branch) has stated:

Job sharing schemes, while suiting some individuals, decrease the number of full-time positions in the community, without creating any additional work. At this time, it does not seem to make much sense. In addition, job sharing could leave a detrimental effect on working conditions, from meal breaks through to penalty shifts.

This union is currently fighting a battle with Australia Post . . . to prevent jobs disappearing through the conversion of full-time positions to part-time positions (not job sharing), against the wishes of the holders of these positions, and without the creation of new positions.

Although the union recognizes the advantages to some members of the community of part-time work, which may include job sharing, the major employers in the communications industry are attempting to use it to cut staffing costs.

A shorter working week and additional leave entitlements would create more jobs, but would not disadvantage those members of the community holding and wishing to retain full-time positions.[17]

The ACTU has accepted part-time work for women in the adoption of the Charter for Working Women, which advocates the 'Introduction of broadly defined flexible working hours where appropriate. The concept must be interpreted to include part-time work, tandem employment, etc., and must attract appropriate loadings.'[18]

The ACTU, however, is yet to adopt a policy on part-time work for male workers. It has produced draft guidelines for unions to use in the course of negotiations and puts forward four principles:

1. Part-time work should not be created at the expense of full-time jobs.

2. Part-time work is not a panacea for overcoming unemployment and its introduction should not be viewed as a substitute for effective economic policies. In the current economic climate it must be made absolutely clear that changes in working hours do not detract from full-time employment.

3. Part-time work should be *voluntary* and based on the demands of workers for a more flexible working life.

4. Any change in work hours or mode should be introduced only after consultation and agreement with unions. In this regard, unions negotiating part-time provisions should consult with other unions who have member which may be affected.[19]

These are followed by a longer list of specific guidelines concerned primarily with ensuring part-time workers have equivalent terms and conditions to full-time workers.

Penny Giles, an employee of the Victorian Teachers' Union, presented a paper to an Australian Teachers' Federation seminar in October, 1979, which dealt with many of the issues contained in the debate for and against part-time work.[20]

In it she pointed out that while many unionists were against the introduction of part-time work, it already exists. In fact in some industries – entertainment, recreation, hotels and personal services – over one-third of the jobs are part time. Despite this fact, 'the structure of jobs – and thus people's lives – is an issue which the trade union movement has never really taken up in a co-ordinated manner'. In fact, she argues, part-time workers have been largely ignored or excluded by unions, as have women, so it is not surprising that they are now regarded as hard to organise'. As a result, there are now over a million part-time workers whose conditions need to be improved and protected. This being the case, it is clear that many of the objections to part-time work are to poor conditions associated with casual employment rather than part-time work as such. The other major objections – that part-time work encourages the perpetuation of sex-role divisions and inadequate child-care facilities – are, according to Giles, misplaced. She argues that other measures, including broader community action, are needed to bring about change in these areas.

Whereas according to Giles the government and organizations such as 'Future Lobby'[21] campaigned in 1978 to ally arguments for permanent part-time work with those to abolish penalty and overtime rates, 'allowing maximum flexibility for employers in deploying the labourforce', she puts forward a set of preconditions around which the labour movement could argue for part-time employment. These include the demand for job creation, consideration by unions of job security, banning of shiftwork in all but essential industries, a shorter full-time working week, expansion by unions into providing child care and extension of family and parental leave provisions. These are important demands which have come from the charter campaign's ability to introduce radically new ideas to the labour movement.

She concludes that 'relationships between employers and employees have meant that the control of working hours has not been in the hands of employees. Thus people have been forced to structure their lives around the needs of industry and their employers.'

Women in particular feel the pressure that these demands have created. As the Working Women's Centre in Melbourne has pointed out:

The consequences of attempting to fulfill work obligations, raise a family, run a household and participate in union activities are very often marital and family problems, mental stress, physical fatigue, industrial accidents, etc.[22]

The answer is not as simple as reducing the number of hours women spend at their paid job. For instance, Jan Harper and Lyn

Richards found in their research into families that mothers working part time showed more confusion and guilt than mothers with full-time jobs.[23]

In order to provide workers with more flexibility and to maintain employment standards, it is important that unions continue to accept, organize and work on behalf of part-time members, as well as pursuing provisions such as child-care services and family leave which will give all workers, men and women, a better chance to determine the balance between work and the rest of their lives.

Shiftwork

'In terms of damage to physical, mental and social well-being, shiftwork is probably the worst of all.'[24]

Despite the heavy human cost of shiftwork, and despite the fact that a quarter of the Australian workforce work at night, it has received very little attention. Unions have recognized the need for shiftwork in some essential services, but in most industries, for example, in steel manufacturing which operates twenty-four hours a day with three eight-hour rotating shifts, they have settled for shift allowances. Men have taken shiftwork principally because of the extra money while absorbing such long-term costs as poor health, disruptions to family and social life and higher rates of industrial accidents.

Linda Rubinstein in her study of women shiftworkers found that women have been drawn into shiftwork for different lessons – it allows them to look after their children during the day or while their husband is at work, and go to work at night.[25] Paid work and unpaid work are combined but only at the expense of opportunities to sleep, rest and spend time with family and friends. The chronic fatigue and stress that is part of life for many women workers must be at its worst for full-time shiftworkers. It is a clear illustration of the pressures women undergo bringing up children in a society that does not recognize their need for child-care services and paid employment. Most women have jobs in which their personal and family commitments are ignored.

The ILO estimates that 20 per cent of workers in Western industrial countries do shiftwork.[26] In Australia only one survey has been done. It was carried out by the ABS in November 1976, and included all people who had worked after 7 p.m. at night in the previous month.[27] They included shiftworkers people doing paid overtime, people doing unpaid work and people 'on call'. Shiftworkers made up three-fifths of all those who had worked at night. It was interesting to note that while women made up one-third of all those who had worked at night, they made up a higher proportion (40 per cent) of actual shiftworkers. Most of the women worked between 7 p.m. and midnight, with 20 per cent working between midnight and 5.30 a.m. Three-fifths of the women shiftworkers were married, which corresponds closely to the female workforce as a whole. However, the occupation composition of women working at night was very different from that of women generally.

One-third of female night workers were in professional and technical occupations, most probably nursing and related jobs. Over a quarter were in service, sport and recreation, traditional areas both of shiftwork and female employment. Clerical occupations also figured prominently, accounting for 16 per cent of night workers. As technological change transforms white-collar work, shiftwork in this area will become characteristic.

The ABS survery also attempted to guage people's attitudes to shiftwork through their assessments of advantages and disadvantages. However, the results should not be taken too seriously, since a necessarily superficial survey cannot probe the complexities of people's attitudes to subjects like work and family life, especially when people's choice is limited by constraints in the work situation and pressures of domestic life.

Women reported fewer disadvantages of shiftwork than men. As the Women's Bureau has pointed out, 'the reason for the different attitudes of men and women towards shiftwork probably hinges on child-care responsibilities. For many women with family responsibilities who were unable to make satisfactory child-care arrangements, employment may only have been possible in the evening or at night.'[28]

Thus three-quarters of the married women working at night said that the hours suited their personal or family routine. However 45 per cent of the married women also felt there were disadvantages in relation to the families, social life and health.

As Linda Rubinstein has said, 'for women with children, their paid job is in a very real sense their second job'.[29] If you already have a full-time unpaid job during the day, it is not surprising that you will see advantages in your 'second' (paid) job being at night. Nor is it surprising that, given the necessity of work, the consequences in terms of health and stress are played down.

In a study of women shiftworkers in the western suburbs of Melbourne, Linda Rubinstein interviewed seventy-two women. She found that 'generally they had only begun shiftwork after the birth of the first child or when for some reason, they were no longer able to make child-care arrangements'. There was some evidence that shiftworkers tended to have younger children than other women workers.

The majority of the women were dissatisfied with their present working hours, 57 per cent saying that they would prefer to work day shift. Most of those on rotating shifts wanted permanent shifts, as one women explained:

Just when I get used to one shift I have to change, so I don't sleep regularly. You don't get enough sleep at home because of the housework and the children need a lot of attention. When I work night shift I hardly have two hours sleep during the day.

The need to care for children was the main reason given for wanting shiftwork: 'I do not like the idea of leaving them at any child-care place because I am afraid they would not be looked after properly'.

Some women spoke of the inadequacy of existing child-care facilities and service: 'It's very expensive to have the children minded. I would leave them in a good centre, but there are not enough, especially in the West.'

Others mentioned lack of choice, higher pay and time to do housework during the day as reasons for doing shiftwork. The majority (69 per cent) mentioned adverse effects such as lack of time to spend with their husband and children, not being able to see friends and relatives and not being able to go out. Many comments revealed emotional strain and problems with their relationships with their husbands: 'Sometimes we argue all the time because we both get tense and tired and we take it out on each other. Some weeks pass and we only see each other on the weekend if I'm not working then.'

Many had problems with insomnia, lack of sleep and tiredness – 72 per cent said they felt tired a lot, and 64 per cent said they felt tense or nervous. As Linda Rubinstein comments, this is partly due to shiftwork and partly due other general pressures on women with domestic responsibilities. The extent of this pressure is illustrated by the fact that some women said they would prefer part-time work – not so they could get more rest, but so they could do more housework.

Many of the women interviewed were migrants from non-English-speaking countries which made their social problems worse:

Many women seemed to have very little social life. Although working hours did have something to do with this, problems of migrating to a strange country, the isolation of women in the home and lack of time due to working both at home and outside were major factors.

Despite the need for extra entitlements to protect shiftworkers, unions generally have less contact with them than with day workers. The women interviewed in this study were union members, but had little knowledge of or contact with their union. Night shiftworkers were most isolated from union activity.

Rubinstein concludes that the issues raised go further than just shiftwork. The difficulties revealed are experienced by women with children who combine two jobs. However, she argues strongly that there are good reasons, both financial and social, for women to be in the paid workforce, and rejects the idea that they should be paid to stay at home. Instead, she puts forward two main areas of reform to overcome the problems of working women, and shiftworkers in particular.

The first if the provision of child-care services, developed in such a way as to overcome the fear and mistrust of high-cost, poor-quality private minders, and the guilt which many women still feel at leaving their children. The second is to improve shiftwork itself by limiting it to essential services, introducing greater choice and flexibility of hours for the worker, improving leave entitlements and breaks between shift changes, and making more part-time work available.

The cost of shiftwork in health and social disruption is high. This much is clear, despite the need for more research of depth and sensitivity to be done. As the incidence of shift work increases, wit technological change and pressure to operate equipment twenty-four hours a day, workers will be pushed to further adapt their lives to the demands of the job. Unions adapt their lives to the demands of the job. Union and social scientists should be ensuring that the impact of night and rotating shiftwork in understood, so that adverse changes can be recognized and rejected.

Outwork

In 1895, the Chief Inspector of Factories in Victoria reported that outwork in the clothing industry was leading to widespread exploitation of women workers. He described the outwork system in this way:

A contractor or middleman approaches a factory owner offering to get work done for him both quickly and cheaply. The factory owner, under pressure to meet his own contracts, agrees to the middle man carrying out work on his behalf. A rate is agreed for each garment to be thus manufactured, a rate which is often less than the rate which the owner is paying workers in his factory to make the same garment. The workers employed by the middleman are paid even less than the agreed rate – the middle man pocketing the differences. The factory owners can shrug their shoulders in all innocence because the home workers are not employed by them, but by the middleman, yet the middleman is ruining the trade while sweating the women.[30]

The government's response to the problem was to attempt to control the growth of outwork by registering outworkers and restricting the circumstances under which they were allowed to work. That legislation is still in force. As of mid-1978, only seventy-nine permits for outworkers were on issue from the Industrial Registrar of the Arbitration Commission, and fewer than twenty-five were on issue from the Victorian Department of Labour and Industry.

Various union and employer representatives have put the number of outworkers in Melbourne at somewhere between 2000 and 8000. This generally refers to the clothing industry. Numbers in Sydney would probably be similar. Although outwork is typically associated with the clothing industry, it exists in several other forms, such as packaging and light assembly work. No one knows how many outwork jobs have been created with the advent of a multitude of plastic products and with the increase in packaging in recent years.

The legislation governing outwork had the dual aim of protecting the industry as a whole and protecting the workers. In practice, employers now just ignore the law, so it does neither. Applicants for an outwork permit must demonstrate that they are in 'necessitous circumstances' and 'cannot reasonably be expected to seek employment in a factory'. Permits are issued for a fixed term of six or twelve months, implying that the outworker's circumstances are temporary and that outwork is a stop-gap form of employment.

The little research that has been done on outworkers suggests that his is not so. In the small pilot study by Denise Cusack and John Dodd, twenty women outworkers were interviewed. They had on average three-and-three-quarter years' experience as outworkers. Some were due for long service leave. Their reasons for doing outwork arose from long-term circumstances, such as a husband's low wage, lack of child care that they could afford or trust, or inability to cope with the pace of work in a factory.

Since outwork is associated with the clothing industry, the distinctive features of that industry should be explained. The clothing industry in Australia is labour intensive. Many of the manufacturers operate on a small scale. Despite import duty of 40 to 45 per cent and import quotas to protect them, they have trouble keeping afloat. Competition is strong between small manufacturers who make up garments for wholesalers and distributors. Using outworkers, small manufacturers cut their costs and are able to undercut competitors. Although there are some large firms in which all stages of production, distribution and retailing are carried out within the one company, it is more common for the various stages of the process to be contracted out. Thus a garment may be sewn by a woman working at home for a piece rate of , say, $2.50, and sold in the shops for $50 or more, after several 'middle men' have taken their cut.

In Australia, as in the rest of the world, textile and clothing workers are mostly women. The piece rate system of pay prevails and conditions are notoriously bad. It is notable that in Australia migrant women are concentrated in the clothing trade.

Outwork is primarily a way for employers to cut down on their labour costs and overheads. At the very least, they avoid the costs of sick pay, workers' compensation, power, lighting and maintenance that would be incurred in a factory. However, since outworkers are isolated and vulnerable to exploitation, employers can cut costs further by paying underaward wages, not paying for public holidays, annual leave or long service leave, and by a variety of deceits and sharp practices.

It is likely that the number of outworkers is increasing as more and more employers try to cut costs in time of recession by transferring overheads such as purchase and maintenance of machines, rent , power and supervision to the outworker and not paying workers' compensation, holiday or sick pay. However, direct and reliable information simply does not exist to confirm or deny this.

Cusack and Dodd found cost cutting to be typical. The manufacturer or 'maker-up' might have a skeleton staff on small and probably substandard premises, and twenty-five machinists working at home. Clearly the cost of maintaining a staff of thirty on award conditions in larger premises would be considerably higher.

Another reason for employing outworkers could be to accommodate seasonal peaks. No doubt there are other ways of doing this, such as taking on casual or temporary workers, or providing more overtime, as is done in other industries. However, outwork gives the manufacturer flexibility without the costs associated with the other options.

For the workers it means that work is irregular. Periods of little work or no work are followed by periods of too much work. At short notice a woman will be under pressure to finish a large volume of work very quickly. Outworkers are more severely hit by fluctuations in production rates than machinists in factories. The advantages of outwork disappear if the work resembles a cycle of floods and droughts, because periods of no money are followed by periods of no time to spend with the children. Only one woman interviewed knew how much work she would have from one week to the next. Much of the tension and pressure of outwork was due to the irregularity of the work. In some cases, the outworker's husband also had an irregular income. One of the women had changed employers because of the irregularity of the work.

Manufacturers also use outworkers in order to expand production without increasing costs. For instance, if a factory has reached its limit, employment of outworkers can increase the production capacity without requiring new buildings or machines. In these circumstances the outworkers may be former factory employees who have left to have children but still want some of their former income. If so, they are more likely to be paid at the same rate as the factory workers, and are less open to abuses.

Whatever the situation, though, the effect of outwork is to reduce the manufacturer's costs. The greater benefit probably goes to the retailer who is able to make a large profit, especially with fashion wear, because the retail price may bear little relation to the piece rate paid to the machinist.

In theory outwork in the clothing industry is regulated by the Federal Clothing Trades Award of 1964 and, where this does not apply, by the various State Acts. However the regulations are largely disregarded. Most outworkers seem to be unaware of the provisions covering their employment and, in the absence of official complaints, the regulatory authorities have been inactive. Unions too find it difficult to do anything about the situation of outworkers who are not union members, and this would be most outworkers, because they are almost impossible to locate. One organizer in Sydney told me that the only way they could think of was to drive around following the employer's delivery van and noting the addresses of the outworkers. Unions are further hampered by the lack of information collected by the regulatory authorities. For example, in Victoria female outworkers may only be inspected by female inspectors, of whom there were only two in 1977. The Federal award applies only if the outworker has a permit, is a union member and is employed by a respondent to the award. Few outworkers fit these conditions. Those who do have several entitlements: the same rate of pay as indoor workers; weekly employment – that is, entitlement to a week's notice and a guaranteed forty-hour week; paid public holidays; four weeks' annual leave; and long service leave. Employers must provide materials, deliver and collect the work and keep adequate records. They may not employ more than five outworkers.

In Victoria, the State Act has somewhat less stringent provisions. Employers are supposed to submit information to the Department of Labour and Industry, but it is not checked and is certainly not accurate. There have been no prosecutions in the last fifteen years, despite the fact that violation rather than observance is the rule.

Working long hours at piece rates, without any holiday or sick pay, is probably the most typical experience of outwork. As one woman said:

Don't ask me, don't ask me. About twelve hours a day, sometimes six days a week, sometimes seven days a week. Sometimes I have some spare time, you know, I'm not working for two or three weeks. At Christmas I have six weeks off, but I don't get any holiday pay. They don't pay me for the days sick. I just get paid for each piece. If I work, I get paid, if I no work, I don't get paid. For a dress they pay $2, #$1.50 or $1, you know. If they are more difficult, they pay more. If they are easy, they pay less money. I'm working on slacks. I make three slacks in an hour and pays me $1.35 for those slacks. But sometimes they are difficult and I only make $2 for an hour. So on average I would get less than $3 for an hour. And that's with no holidays, no sick pay, no nothing.

Of the twenty women who were doing outwork on the clothing industry interviewed by Cusack and Dodd, all but one were migrants from non-English-speaking countries, including Turkey, Greece, Italy and Spain.

Comparing actual practice with the award requirements for outworkers, Cusack and Dodd found that of the twenty only one person was being paid the award rate, one had been paid long service leave, three had been employed on a proper weekly basis, three had paid public holidays, four had paid annual leave, four had their work collected and delivered by the employer and all were provided with the necessary materials by the employer. In no cases were correct records of work and payment kept.

Only three of the women interviewed were union members. Fifteen were non-members, and two were independent sub-contractors. Most of the women seemed reluctant to discuss the matter of unionism.

Some were critical of the union's inattentiveness. One women saw little relevance in the union to her situation. Of course, the isolation and vulnerability of outworkers make feelings of intimidation more likely. As one women said: 'If you complain or want to join the union, the boss will sack you'.

Another said: 'We need the work, so we have to stay quiet and take it'.

Similarly, although registered outworkers have some guarantee of somewhat better working conditions, sixteen of the women were unregistered. Clearly employers realize that it is in their interests to employ workers illegally so they are not bound by the regulations and do not have to give the workers their entitlements. Neither the regulatory agencies, the unions nor the women themselves have as yet practice. 'I contacted many factories and wanted to do the right thing, but if I ask about registration, then I am told there is no work for me.'

Knowing that other employers may be more unscrupulous, an outworker may simply put up with an abusive employer. One woman whom I interviewed said:

Oh well, like all the bosses. Sometimes when he needs you, he's very good to you. He talks to you and asks you about your problems and everything. But when he doesn't need you, when he's not busy, he's very angry and he looks at your work and if he finds something is no good, it's no good. He says, 'I don't give you any more work'. But when he's busy he comes again, because he knows I work very hard. And when he's busy I have his work ready. But when he's busy he comes again, because he knows I work very hard. And when he's busy I have his work ready. But everybody's the same. I change three or four factories, but everyone's the same. They don't care about you. He's alright. This boss is alright. He pays you. But somebody else, they don't care. They pay you when they like, and sometimes they don't pay you. They say, 'I'll pay you $2 for one dress', and then they pay you $1.50. You can't do anything because we don't pay tax, and we can't do anything. This boss is a bit better than someone else.

Many aspects of outwork – the way it is organized, the rates of pay, the hours of work, the regularity of the work, the power of the maker-up the isolation of the outworker – contribute to exploitation of outworkers.

Compared with machinists in factories, outworkers usually have several extra tasks. For instance, bundles of work have to be unpacked and the number of garments checked. Finished articles have to be tied into bundles and stored. All this takes time but the outworker is paid by piece rate, not by the hour. In a factory these related tasks would be done by another employee. Other small jobs are done by the outworkers. Collars, cuffs and belts have to be turned, threads between garments have to be snipped, and so on. Sometimes these related tasks are done by members of the women's family, often her children.

Outwork, of course, also requires space. Four of the twenty women interviewed by Cusack and Dodd had a spare room in which to work. The others worked in the kitchen or in a corner of the livingroom. Some had bundles of work in storage up in the ceiling or all over the floor the outworkers then had the additional task of cleaning up, which in a factory would also be done by another employee.

All outworkers paid their own electricity bills, and fifteen of twenty paid for the maintenance costs on their sewing machines. Three machines had been provided by the employer. Three women had bought their machines from their employers, and were paying them off by weekly instalments. None of the women took their machine costs into account when calculating earnings.

Lastly, outworkers incurred transport costs for picking up and delivering work. According to the regulations, this is the responsibility of the employer.

Cusack and Dodd found that the information they were able to collect on rates of pay was 'incomplete and confusing'. Although outworkers in theory are entitled to the award rates for machinists, in practice they had little opportunity to find out whether their pay was correct, and often seemed to accept it on trust.

All of the women were paid by piece rates, but the rates varied considerably. Fifteen of the women said the rate varied according to the garment. The other five received a set rate, sometimes irrespective of the complexity of the garment and how long it took. One garment might take two hours, another as much as four hours. Most of the women did not know if the rates they were being given were correct, and often asked the interviewers what other outworkers were paid.

The amount of money earned per week was variable. Furthermore, it was impossible to calculate accurately the hours a woman spent on her work each week. Only one women had kept a record of the hours she worked each week. The others did not seem to think of their work in terms of hours worked for pay received. Thus, because of the extra little tasks and because of the tendency to do another hour of sewing whenever possible, the total time spent on outwork can be far greater than it seems.

One women was doing outwork because she did not like the long hours of factory work. But when she was asked to describe her working week, she realized that she had worked for sixty-eight hours. Her starting times in the morning were irregular. Some mornings she started as early as half past six, some evenings she did not finish until ten. She also worked on Saturdays and Sundays. Like many others, she had never sat down and calculated how many hours she worked, and did not realize that she was working much longer hours than she would have in a factory.

She was amongst the better paid outworkers in the study, being paid at the same rate as factory workers. Unlike others, she received work regularly.

The most extreme example of exploitation was the case of a woman who had worked for six months and earned $700 which she had never received. She knew another outworker who had lost $75 in wages from the same employer.

Another problem reported by several outworkers was that disputes arose about the rate that had been agreed upon or the number of pieces completed. For example, one women had agreed to a rate of 50 cents for each pair of trousers that she machined. She completed thirty-one pairs in a week, and expected to be paid $15.50. The employer told her that he had offered 40 cents and that she had given him fewer than thirty pairs.

Eleven of the women interviewed said they knew nothing about tax and presumably did not pay any. Five had tax deducted regularly by the employer, and two were registered as independent sub-contractors. Irregularities had occurred in the remaining two cases. In the first, the employer claimed to have paid tax, but did not provide a proper statement of earnings. In the second, the employer had agreed to pay tax, but did not produce any group certificates.

The pattern of payment for five of the women was suspicious. They were paid less and less per week as the pay period lengthened. Only one of the women interviewed was paid correctly. The fact that her husband was a foreman at the factory supplying her work probably accounted for this.

Outwork makes the close relationship between women's paid work and their domestic role very clear. Granted, there are some advantages of outwork that may lead a woman to choose it in preference to factory work, for instance, when she cannot maintain the pace demanded by supervisors but can reach a steady pace in her own time. However, from the women's point of view outwork is another way of resolving the competing demands for work on the one hand and time to look after children and home on the other. Caught between these two factors, most outworkers are vulnerable to exploitation but unwilling to protest.

With the shift away from the family component in the minimum wage, there is now often a need for two incomes to support a family. At the same time there has been a greater social acceptance of the role of women in the paid workforce. However there has not been a corresponding growth in community support services, the most important of which is community-controlled child care within the means of working people. One of the options that is sometimes suggested to make this resulting strain a little more bearable is to have more part-time work with flexible working hours.

One outworker I spoke to in Sydney said:

No, no it's not fair. It's not. But the problem is the children. I have no one to leave the children with. I better stay at home and work by myself and keep my children in my hands with me. I don't have to run next door to leave the children, and pay, and I don't know if they looked after. This is the worst problem, I am waiting till my children grow up and go away. They go to school, but in the morning I have to prepare them, and 3 o'clock I have to be there. If I go to work from 9 to 3 o'clock I get about $60, no more than that, a week. And I have to get a bus to go to the city and come back.

She explained that as long as outworkers were isolated, as a result of language difficulties and being at home looking after their children, they would be unable to change their working conditions.

Yeah. Thousands and thousands of women is working like me. Worse than me. I know quite a lot of friends, they're working like me. Just about all members of the family have got work. My sister-in-law, here sisters, they do the same thing. Because they are all married and got kids and they can't leave them. And they can't speak the language to be able to do something like an office job where they can get out for a few hours. I know a lot, but there are thousands who I don't know. Yes, I am thinking about it, but I can't find, you know, what to do. One, two, five, six, seven, ten, eleven, we can't do anything. We must be all together to do something. If I stop working I do nothing because someone will take my position. We must be all together. Now we have no unions, nothing. I tell you, the problem is the children. The other ladies will tell you. I have nowhere to leave my children, that's why they are here. Nobody is happy to work at home, nobody.

Again, while some of the women interviewed by Cusack and Dodd were doing outwork for health reasons, most of them said they had worked as machinists in factories but had taken up outwork in order to care for their children, as these comments indicate:

I have two young children and cannot afford child minding I would rather care for them at home.

My mother was never there, was always out working; it left a scar on my life.

It's good for the kids to have mum at home.

The factory hours are too long. Then I have to travel and the children are on their own.

Now my mother is getting older and is sick. She is not able to look after the children.

The women saw child care as their responsibility and did not expect any help from their husbands. They considered flexibility of working hours to be a relative advantage of outwork over the oppressive routines of factory work, rather than any preferable or ideal situation. It is also apparent that in fact the daily routine of outworkers offers very little freedom, despite the comments that some women made:

You are your own boss. You can stop work for a while and talk if you want to.

If you don't feel like working at home you can sit down for ten minutes. You can't do that in a factory. If you don't feel well, you still have to keep going.

At home I am free. In the factory workers have no dignity and are always pressured by the boss.

The overall impression gained from the interviews is that despite the flexibility, outworkers work hard, for long hours and under as much pressure as factory workers if not more because the work is always there, claiming every moment between household tasks:

You feel trapped by the work. It is always there.

The effects are worse when working at home. When you work in a factory, you can come home and relax; but with work at home, the job is never finished. You get no rest. You still have to do all the household chores, knowing that more outwork remains to be done.

Women whose outwork was irregular had to give it priority until the work was finished. This meant working in bursts of very long hours. One Turkish women said she hated the work: 'But when it's here it takes priority'.

In between the work, I am confronted with so many jobs that I do not know where to start.

I clean the house between 7 p.m. and 12 p.m., when the children are in bed.

It will be better when she goes to school. I will have more time during the day to get things done, and won't have to work so much at night.

The typical daily routine was for a woman to get up and do housework between 6 and 7 o'clock in the morning, prepare breakfast, send or take the children to school, do housework followed by a stretch of outwork, with only a short break for lunch, until it was time to get the children from school; do a little more outwork, perhaps with the children helping, prepare the evening meal, and resume outwork until about 10 o'clock at night. Only two women said that they had very little to occupy them when they had finished their housework. Outwork kept them busy for most of the day and some evenings as well.

One women said her husband was always pushing her to get the work done. There was a lot to get through and she was under pressure to finish it on time. She sewed evening dresses. When work was available she would start at 6 o'clock in the morning and work until 6 at night, with short breaks to prepare breakfast, take the children to school, have lunch, collect the children, and prepare the evening meal. She had worked until 2 o'clock in the morning about three times a week and usually at weekends too. She said that once when she could not keep up the pace, she told the boss that her child was sick, but it did not make any difference. 'He came and took whatever I had', she said, '. . . pushing the life out of you'.

Another woman whom I spoke to found the pressure of work and financial need greater with outwork than with factory work:

I am very tired, I am. But I got to make do. My husband, he get only $120 or $130 a week, and we are four or five persons. That money is not enough to eat very well. And you have to pay rates: $400 a year. You have to pay water for the house. You have to pay for the car. A lot, a lot, a lot of things. We are still paying for the house. Anyway, clothes are very expensive for the children, shoes, everything. So I have to work. I don't like to work. I like to stay here to keep my house clean, to keep my children clean and nice, and to talk to them. Because if I work I get tired, and sometimes I fight with them and I smack them and they scream with my sister, sometimes. That's true. But I have to work a bit more, one or two years and then my children grow up a bit. Then I'll go out to work. Only eight hours, you know, is better. Go out, come home, cook and stay with my family.

Outworkers are far more isolated than other workers. It means that the individual outworker can be kept in ignorance of the prevailing standards of employment, rates of pay, legal rights and conditions of employment. Quite often, women being interviewed would ask about the pay and conditions of other workers, or ask what they had right to expect.

The following case study by Cusack and Dodd shows the degree of pressure that an employer can put on an outworker, especially if she is very isolated:

A Greek woman, aged forty-seven, lived alone in two small rooms at the back of a house. She had been in Australia for fifteen years, and had worked in various factories as a machinist. In Greece she had been a dressmaker. She had begun working at home because her health was bad. Because of the problems she had encountered doing outwork, cause of the problems she had encountered doing outwork, she had tried to go back to factory work. Three times she had taken a job in a factory, and each time she had been unable to keep up the pace.

She had done outwork for three different employers. The previous one had been just as bad as this one. At the time of the interview, she was sewing skirts for $1.80 each and shirts for $1.40 each. The employer had told her that the price of shirts had to be lowered because he could only sell them for $13.00 but he got $20.00 for skirts.

'I asked for skirts', she said, 'and he said he would bring them, but he never did anything'.

This women was not paid regularly. She had to ask for her money and was then paid in a lump sum. For a while she had been paid weekly.

'Then I got $75.00', she said. 'Then, on the second pay, I was paid $120.00 for a fortnight's work. Then I was paid $200.00 for a month's work.' She asked Cusack and Dodd what they thought a reasonable wage would be. She did not know anything about permits or registration and had never been a member of the union.

She found the job by answering an advertisement in the paper. She had rung up, and the boss had arrived with work within two hours. He came around about every two days with more work, and was putting pressure on her to do more work. He wanted her to sew one hundred articles a week, and told her that one of his other workers could do fifty a day. She was able to do eight or nine a day if she put in long hours. She said she worked from 8 a.m. until 10 o'clock at night, with a break of an hour and a half in the middle of the day to rest. She worked nearly all day on Saturday.

Isolation is also a social problem. As noted earlier, some outworkers felt relatively free but many outworkers feel lonely working at home:

At home by myself, you have no one to talk to. You have to work harder.

I liked working in the biscuit factory. There were other Turkish women to talk to. You could stand up and walk around and do different jobs.

A factory? Oh, yeah, much better. You go to work only, you haven't to anything else in your mind. You work eight hours. You stay for lunch. And then you finish. You go home and cook and everything.

And stay and watch TV. But here, you can't. You can't because you're very, very busy, and you have to have the work ready. The boss is coming in and screaming, he said I don't do my work. That's why I don't like it here. If you go out you talk and see somebody else. It's different. But here, I have nobody. I don't see anybody.

One women said she had worked in a factory where talking was not allowed. She said that even that was preferable to the isolation and loneliness of outwork. Another woman had tried to work in factories because she was lonely, living alone and doing outwork at home. She had lost her job three times because she was not well enough to keep up with the pace of work. Other women said that there was an opportunity to make friends and to learn English if they worked outside the home.

However, on the whole outworkers have little freedom from the pressure of work, and their isolation simply makes it impossible for them to safeguard their rights as workers.

In summary, women who do outwork have little or no choice. Usually they desperately need money for without their income from outwork they would either have nothing, or they would be dependent on poverty-line wages of their husbands or social security benefits. Most outworkers are migrant women whose isolation and lack of knowledge about rights and entitlements is made worse by their language and cultural difficulties. However, the foremost motivating force for outworkers is their desire to be at home with their children. Usually, this does *not* mean that they have rejected using good-quality, community-based child-care service. On the contrary, it usually means that they have quite understandably rejected the poor-quality, commercial child-minding businesses which proliferate in Australian cities. Lack of government funding of good child-care services for working parents has allowed commercial establishments to flourish, to the detriment of many children. It has also meant that thousands of women are trapped at home with no alternative to exploitative working conditions, in isolation from the mainstream of the workforce.

Government attempts to regulate and limit outwork have been outstanding failures. As manufacturing industry, notably clothing, declines, more employers will use outworkers. And as unemployment leads to more widespread poverty, there will be more women who will accept the employers' terms.

Unless working women, and in particular migrants from non-English-speaking countries, have more child-care services, regular jobs with adequate wages, and higher social security benefits, outwork in its worst form will increase over the 1980s to the point where there is another public outcry against 'sweated labour' a hundred years after the first one.

Conclusion

The lives of many women doing part-time work, shiftwork and outwork show that substantial inequalities exist within the workforce.

In the context of the development of capital-intensive technology, declining manufacturing industry and unemployment, the proportion of the workforce employed in these under-privileged and less unionized forms of work is likely to increase. Overall, it will mean a reduction in the share of national wealth received by employees, not directly because of wage cuts but rather because of changes in the terms and hours of employment. At the same time, cutbacks in government spending have reduced the social benefits that people receive as members of the community. Services that are particularly needed if women are to overcome some of the barriers against equality, for example job training and retraining, child care and English lessons for migrants, will remain inadequate, thus contributing to the persistence of oppressive working lives.

There has been much debate over whether changes in working hours are beneficial or detrimental to workers. The short answer is that it all depends . . . In particular, it depends how much control people can gain over the organisation of their work lives. To ensure that changes in the hours and arrangements of the working week are not detrimental, people need effective control or enough bargaining power to demand equitable payments for all 'alternative' modes of employment; work systems that take the health and personal needs of workers into account; and social services within the community as a whole that recognize the need for both employment and family or social needs, amongst men and women.

Achieving the bargaining power necessary for this will require a broader approach by unions. They will need to be more attuned to the needs of their women and migrant members, as well as paying greater attention to organizing the marginal and underprivileged sections of the workforce. They will also have to take up in a more systematic way the social issues related to the experience of work. A greater linking between work-based and community-based activity concerned with child care, health and welfare will be needed.

If such a massive program of social action came about – at the moment, only a few seeds are apparent – then the continuing recession of the 1980s could be the arena for historic changes rivalling the eight-hour day, the minimum wage and equal pay. Such changes, while starting with the goal of providing child-care services, tailoring working hours to people's needs, limiting shiftwork and extending the benefits of regular full-time work to part-time and casual work, could profoundly change the role of women in society and the place of employment in people's lives.

CHAPTER 7

'What are the needs of a woman?'

Health and Safety

In 1928 the Commonwealth Department of Health conducted a major survey of women in industry in Victoria. Many of the problems it uncovered still exist, along with new hazards resulting from increased exposure to toxic chemical and from changes in production processes. The 1928 report found that:

There is no legislation at the present time providing for the needs of the large number of females engaged in office work nor has any investigation dealing with their health been made.[1]

This statement, made in 1928, is still true more than fifty years later. The findings of the 1928 survey of women in Victorian factories make interesting reading. A total of eighty-four workplaces employing over 4000 women were investigated. Physical working conditions, such as ventilation, temperature, lighting, dust, fumes and noise, were studied in detail. Work operations, seating, posture, weight-lifting, job rotation and work systems such as piecework and bonus rate were also studied, along with amenities including toilets, eating areas, first-aid facilities and drinking water. Personal interviews were conducted with women workers, covering not only the work they did but also fatigue, headaches, menstrual problems, coughs and cold, eating habits, exercise, time spent doing housework and general health problems.

Many of the investigators' observations about working conditions indicate that little has changed. The 'repetitive and monotonous character' of the work was noted. Job rotation was thought to be very important, but in practice little attention was paid to it. Pieceworkers and women paid according to a bonus system were seen working at a high speed using 'rhythmical swaying and jerking movements of the body'. In some factories, extremes of heat and cold were felt, natural lighting was inadequate ventilation allowed dust and fumes to remain in the air, and considerable noise was reported. Complaints of fatigue were made by women over twenty-one years of age, and were largely attributed to piecework and bonus systems. Women were asked how much of their time was spent doing housework, and, incredibly, three-quarters said they spent less than three hours a week. This was true even of the adult women, one quarter of whom were married. I suspect that housework was not defined broadly enough to include the vast number of tasks that most women do in the home.

The motivation for the 1928 survey was not simply to protect the health of workers. The author of the report did not see a healthy and safe working environment as the right of all workers. Women workers were regarded as 'the actual or potential mothers of the next generation' and the government was therefore concerned to 'protect and safeguard their unique contribution to the State'.

This approach to occupational health and safety contains assumptions which are still central to the debate today. The principles could be summarized as follows.

Women should have the right as workers to a healthy working environment for their own sakes as well as the sake of their reproductive capacity or an actual foetus they might be carrying. If this is so, men too should be equally concerned about occupational health and safety, firstly because men, as workers, should have the same right to a safe and healthy working environment simply for their own sakes as individuals and secondly, because men also have a reproductive system. Increasingly evidence is showing that hazards affecting women's reproductive capacity also affect that of men.

Past concentration on the impact of working conditions on women's reproductive health has led to a distortion of the issue: a neglect of the health of women as workers, and an even greater neglect of the health of men. This is not to say that there are no differences in the occupational health needs of men and women, simply that those differences have been overstated.

The effects of a double working life on women's health and safety

A study of women's occupational health cannot ignore the interaction between conditions in the paid workplace and the work that women do at home. 'Housework' is an inadequate term to convey what is involved in the emotional and physical care and maintenance of a whole household of people, especially when young children are involved.

The work that women do at home affects their health and safety at paid work in a number of ways.

Most commonly, the strain of having, in effect, two jobs leads to tiredness and emotional stress. These are made worse by child-care problems which can cause worry and even lead to accidents at work. Child-care problems are the major reason for women doing work in otherwise inconvenient and anti-social hours such as shiftwork which contributes further to health problems because of disrupted eating and sleeping patterns. Chronic fatigue and stress when combined with boring and repetitive work requiring unnatural movements and posture result in further symptoms such as headaches, backaches and general muscular aches and pains which are commonly treated with analgesics, tranquillisers and sedatives. Consumption of these drugs is staggeringly high in Australia.

In many occupations at home there is also exposure to heat and cold, dust, fumes, noise and toxic substances.

Housework, the most common form of work for women, is not usually recognized as 'work' by the medical profession and has rarely been considered in literature on occupational health and safety. The Liverpool Women's Health Centre has pointed out that there are five times as many accidents in the home as in the 'real' workplace. However:

No one thinks of home as a place of work, or of housewives as workers, with the same needs as other workers for safe equipment, adequate training and working conditions that make for a safety-conscious attitude towards work.[2]

They also state that it is not enough to consider work in the home and outside the home as if each were being done by separate people – when both jobs are done by one person the effects are multiplied.

Because of the accumulated stressed, women's health may break down and flu, ulcers, migraines and high blood pressure follow. However, many women keep working, or go back to work very quickly, because they feel they must continue to look after their families and conserve their sick pay for the days they take off to look after sick children.

Dr Hazel Halse of the Australian Department of Health found in her study of blue- and white-collar women workers that tiredness was by far the greatest complaint. Next came anxiety and depressions, followed by domestic tension. Over half the women surveyed said they were tired, and 7-8 per cent said they were exhausted. Tiredness, according to Dr Halse, resulted from many factors: women were doing two jobs out of a sense of obligation which itself caused tiredness, especially if the work was unsatisfying and achieved no definite goal. Long hours of activity at home and at work left 'little or no time for relaxation'. Equipment and work areas were designed for comfortable operation, especially for women who were often too short to use standardized equipment with ease. Lack of time for shopping and cooking encouraged use of 'convenience food' and faulty nutrition. Dependence on analgesics, tranquillisers and antidepressants became a problem. The social and psychological factors causing tiredness included the vicious working outside the home, lack of involvement in any social or community life outside work and home and 'the dreadful rush'.[3]

I have also been told of many instances of family pressures contributing to tiredness at work. For example:

You should talk to a few women I knew when I was on night shift here. One in particular lives somewhere out at Gosford or the Blue Mountains. She had about five or six kids. Two under school age and her husband was an alcoholic. He was beyond that. She was virtually the whole supervision in the house and when those two under-age kids slept she would grab a few winks. She got on the average three hours sleep a day. Really good, you know. The department gives you five minutes break every hours! A health break it is called. A health break and the buzzer goes and you relax and the buzzer goes and you work. That five minutes she would clunk and she's out to it. It's really tragic.

The extent of occupational deaths and injuries

Frequently claims are made that hazards have been eliminated from the workplace.[4] However, this does not stand up to scrutiny. One newspaper article pointed out that in 1974, 187 workers were killed in New South Wales and that there was a 'world-wide trend' in increased workers injuries.[5] Records of injuries at work are inadequate, and research into long-term effects of the work environment on workers' health is almost non-existent. However, those figures that are available show a rate of working days lost through 'accidents' or injuries: thirty-five days were lost for every million hours worked in 1975.[6] In 1976 the NSW government was investigating ways of toughening industrial safety regulations.

There are 300-400 deaths a year in Australian industry, and some 3000-4000 injuries officially recorded.[7] However, these figures represent only the most obvious occupational casualties. They do not include the over-tiredness and worry that become part of the daily routine for many women. They do not include the tenosynovitis, a painful inflammation of the tendons in arms, wrists and hands, that is attributed to housework or 'old age', or described as rheumatism or arthritis, or simply put up with by working women until they are sacked because they can no longer move their hands fast enough. And they do not include the results of exposure to toxic chemicals such as cancer, miscarriages, infertility and birth abnormalities that may not develop until the person has left her job, and are in any case difficult to link directly to their cause.

Are women different?

The ILO has published a massive encyclopaedia of occupational health and safety which has a short discussion on women in employment.[8]

It discussed some of the ways in which women's jobs and therefore women's occupational health problems are different from men's and gives a careful account of the debate about 'protection for women' versus 'no discrimination'.

According to the ILO, protective legislation has had the aim of protecting women's 'special function of reproduction', and secondarily 'to protect women, as a weak and unorganized group in the workforce, from exploitation and abuse'. Some of the special protective laws have related to maternity provisions, hours of work, night work, working underground, heavy work and dangerous or unhealthy work.

The argument in favour of removing protective laws usually states that both women and men should be 'free to choose' their hours of work, occupations and so on, and that no protection is needed unless a situation involves unique hazards for women, or is more dangerous women than for men. This ignores two important points. One is that freedom of choice may simply mean that the employer is free to require both women and men to work under undesirable conditions, to work unlimited overtime or to do shiftwork, while the employee does not have the power to determine what the conditions should be. The second point is that there are few hazards that are unique to women. It is more important to remove hazards that are general to both women and men. Removing protective legislation may simply expose women to hazards that men currently accept.

As the ILO puts it:

With certain clearly defined exceptions, the answer to health hazards is not to prevent women from working in certain industries and occupations but to ensure that the conditions obtaining in these industries and occupations are such that women as well as men can work in them safely.

The ILO view is that protective legislation should be used sparingly, and that to protect maternity does not necessarily 'compromise equality of the sexes in regard to employment'.

There is also some discussion of the ways in which women's health is adversely affected compared to men's because of the greater family responsibilities of women that lead to over-tiredness. The ILO suggests that fatigue should be reduced by providing shorter working hours for all, longer weekends and holidays, and improved household services and technology. A resolution adopted in 1965 urges that women with family responsibilities be enabled to work outside their homes without being subject to discrimination, and urges changes in hours of work and better child-care services to achieve this.

Types of occupational health hazards

Speaking at a seminar on workers' health, organized by the Melbourne Workers' Health Action Group and held at the Victorian Trades Hall, Lyn McKenzie, a doctor with a particular interest in women's occupational health, discussed three main types of health hazards: those affecting both men and women, those characteristically found in 'women's work', and problems associated with reproduction.[9]

She stressed that it was important to recognize the hazards that affect both men and women. Often in the past the effect of various hazards on women, or specifically on the foetus, has been recognized and used as an excuse to exclude women from areas of employment. However, she argued that fertile men were just as susceptible because of changes in their chromosomes or their sperm motility and structure. Furthermore, hazards which have in the past been associated only with harm to the foetus could also affect adults, for example by causing blood disorders, liver diseases and cancer.

The problems that are characteristically 'women's occupational health problems' are the result not of the differences between women and men, but differences in the work that they do. For as stated earlier, the majority of women work in sex-stereotyped jobs, such as clerical and secretarial work, process and assembly line work, especially involving fine details and rapidly repeated movements, and service work such as preparing and serving food, cleaning, laundry work, health-care work and looking after people.

Lyn McKenzie states that the emphasis should be on making the work environment safe for the foetus and both male and female reproductive systems. However, she adds that there are other problems related specifically to birth control. Women who want to stay in the paid workforce in the long term usually have the responsibility for contraception and suffer the consequences of any side effects.

Fear of pregnancy is particularly strong in women whose families depend on their financial support. This is a subject which has been almost totally ignored in Australian history. *Bobbin Up*[10] which is a novel, *A Hundred a Day*[11] which is a short fil, and *Zelda*[12] which is an autobiography, deal with working women resorting to 'backyard' abortions because they could not afford to leave their jobs. But this is not a topic normally covered under the subject of occupational health.

The Working Women's Centre has called for family planning services to be widely available, particularly at the workspace.[13] Some of the reasons are that since child bearing is used to discriminate against women, knowledge of family planning is needed; many women are unaware or have limited knowledge of the means available to limit their family size, even when they want to do so in order to stay in the paid workforce; and all women in any case have the right to determine whether or not they will become pregnant.

The centre cites studies which indicate inadequate knowledge of contraception amongst large numbers of people, and restricted access to information and services, especially amongst migrants. Unions can play a vital role in education in dissemination of such information, not simply from the point of view of individual family-planning problems, but also in relation to working conditions affecting fertility.

The Working Women's Charter Campaign has specifically included the need for 'comprehensive sex education and birth control advice; free and freely available contraception; free, safe legal abortion on demand, but not forced sterilization or abortion'.[14] The ACTU initially left out this controversial issue. In 1979, at the ACTU congress following the adoption of the charter, the Victorian Trades Hall Council put on notice a motion to amend the charter to include the right to abortion, sex education and family planning. However, because of the extended debate on uranium, the motion did not come up for discussion, but was accepted by the ACTU executive after congress.

It is not feasible here to attempt to state all the possible hazards to which women might be exposed in the workplace. The list would be enormous and in any case would soon be out of date as, for instance, new chemicals continue to be introduced into the workplace.

Technological change is also accompanied by new substances, processes, procedures and ways of organising work, which constitute possible hazards, some known and some unknown.

The hazards discussed here are those most often mentioned as arising from the work that women usually do. Perhaps 'hazard' is too specific a term, since I am looking at overall health, not just 'accidents', injuries or specific diseases whose cause has been pinpointed. The most common health problems of women in the workforce are true of all occupations. Bearing the similarities in mind, we will now look at some of the problems that are mentioned in relations to factory, shop, office, health and service industry occupations.

Factory work

The greatest volume of information available is about factory work indicating in part the lack of attention that has been given to other occupations. A woman interviewed at the Liverpool Women's Health Centre said:

I work night shift a factory making cans. Mainly women work there. It is extremely noise; most women use powders constantly. They supply ear muffs but we remove them as they are uncomfortable and hot. Safety shoes are compulsory, but we have to pay for them ourselves out of our wages. There is a fast pace on the line, 250 lids on cans a minute and all the work is tamped with the worker's number so they can trace mistakes. We get covered in oil. There are two five-minute breaks to go to the toilet, besides a twenty-minute meal break and ten-minute tea break.[15]

An article in *Link*, a metal-workers' newsletter, highlighted nine hazards that are typical of the sort of work women do in factories like this one.[16] They were high noise levels, analgesic consumption, oil on the skin, having to wait to go to the toilet, fast pace of work, night shiftwork, tenosynovitis, fumes and tiredness. Dr Margaret Raphael mentioned some of these at a seminar held by the Health Commission of New South Wales and added two other hazards: deterioration in eyesight as a result of doing fine-detail work, and strains due to uniform machine design which does not take into account the stature of most women.

Dr Raphael, however, is of the opinion that 'outright health hazards such as noxious fumes, unsafe machinery, etc., have largely been eliminated from workplaces, and are, in any case, no different for women that they are for men'.[17]

Her assertion that hazards have been eliminated I open to challenge by the numerous examples given below. Furthermore, with her final point she falls into the same trap that many other writers have previously – concentrating on hazards that are unique or special for women, rather than the majority of hazards that are harmful to both sexes, or the hazards that women face as a result of their work rather than their sex.

Chicken-processing factories have become notorious for the conditions under which their employees – nearly all migrant women – work.[18]

One factory in which conditions were videotaped for a submission to the Jackson Committee inquiry into manufacturing industry, displayed a sign saying 'Work Safely: Safety depends on the operator'. When asked about the machines they worked on, migrant women said: 'Of course they're dangerous. Women have lost fingers. Only a little mistake and your finger is gone. If you think of anything else, your finger is gone.' Their supervisor remarked later: 'They all get their aches and pains'.

Conditions inside the typical chicken factory are very cold, as this article from *Women at Work* shows:

Ice covered the floor in Ayse's section, and although the women wore protective boots, the cold went right through their bodies. Since leaving that section five months ago, Ayse hasn't had a menstrual period. She feels this is directly related to the work conditions at the factory.

Exposure to fumes and caustic chemicals used to process the chickens affected the workers' skin and eyes:

As the chickens passed through a moving drum of chemicals which washed them and whitened their skins, Ayse pegged them onto a moving line. After a month, her eyes were red and painfully swollen from the chemical fumes. They dripped continually.

A local doctor gave her a medical certificate for five days off work, but the company paid her for only four. Although her eye was still inflamed, she returned to work.

The company moved her to a different section at her request, but the work was just as bad. Her eye trouble continued and after two months she resigned.

Ayse's eyes are no longer swollen, but they still occasionally drip. She has not yet claimed workers' compensations – the factory did not give her forms to fill our and at the time she did not know she was entitled to it.[19]

The Liverpool Women's Health Centre saw many women who worked in a chicken-processing factory.[20] They mentioned dermatitis, tenosynovitis, cuts, traumatic injuries and exposure to fumes:

One woman had dermatitis really bad. They paid her light duties for a while and she was on compo – her hands and arms were a mess. They insisted that she went back to her old job or they would sack her. Their compo doctor backed them up. She went to her own doctor then and he insisted she stay off the line where she gets wet, but they'll get her now for fighting them.

A lot of the women's hands 'go' near the wrist. I think it has something to do with the nerves and tendons. Even when they sack them, their hands never recover – they can't use them properly.

Your hands have to go into the birds to get all the guts out – a machine does it but it doesn't come all away. Of course they are full of small bones and your gloves tear. You can't get a new pair unless they are badly torn. Your fingers get little cuts and get infected. It attacks the nails, they swell up and the nails fall off.

The safety factor there is practically nil – women are continually being injured. One had her hair caught in a machine and ripped out. Another had her fingers caught in a machine – cuts from the blades. The safety shields are inadequate. It's the pace they are supposed to work at.

If you've ever smelt ammonia, you would know what I mean. You just can't breathe. It attacks everything wet – hence it gets into the mouth, throat, nose and eyes . . . I've seen women get affected and panic . . . They just drag them out, some vinegar and water – outside in the air for a while – then back to work. It leaves you with a dreadful headache that no powder or pill will cure.

Frequently poor ventilation was mentioned to me by women working in various jobs. The problems ranged from overheating, temperature controlled for the sake of equipment rather than people, inadequate protection against dust and other irritating substances in the air, and a high incidence of respiratory and bronchial ailments.

One group of packers and sorters working with a lot of paper and dust discussed the problem. As one put it:

Another thing too I dislike is the airconditioning system. Actually there is no airconditioning system at all. What it is a constant level of heat or coolness or whatever, just to keep the machines cool. It has got nothing to do with the employees. It doesn't matter about them. It is just to keep the machinery at a constant temperature.

Another woman added: 'Keeps the dust circulating.'

And a third:

Oh doesn't it. It is really good. Everybody that works in that place has bronchitis. Everybody, just about. In one appliance factory women refused to work unless conditions were improved:

The first thing we went for was fans. I brought a thermometer to work, put it on the workbench and you could see the mercury rising.

It starts rising up 98⁰, 100⁰, 105⁰. Ingrid down the front starts to get sick, cramps. Someone else has to go out to the toilet. It was loss of salt and it was getting hotter and hotter and the word is going up – fans are needed. The foreman comes round and murmured and I said, 'We need fans'. I said, 'The girls are going to have to turn their solder pots off. We can't work.' I said to Ingrid 'Turn your solder pot off.' He resented me saying it. I said, 'I'm turning mine off and when I turned mine off all the others did too. He got very upset. I said, 'Well, we have asked and asked again for adequate ventilation and fans. People cannot work.' The result of that was that we got fans and things were a little bit better.

In another factory, manufacturing furniture, the Department of Labour and Industry (DLI) had been called out to inspect the problem of sawdust in the air.

You'll hear the noise when they're working. It's pretty high. I don't think any of the saws have got silencers on them. Since they've moved the woodwork down the sawdust is the main problem. They use a lot of saws without a bag or anything on them or dust collectors. We rang the DLI, asked him to come out, and instead of coming to see us who rang him, he went to the manager, or the industrial officer or whatever, and he brought him out and when he brought him out of the office, everything was turned off. So the DLI inspector had a look, and he said, 'Oh that's all right'. Soon as he went again it was all switched back on again, and sawdust flying everywhere.

Noise can cause headaches and temporary hearing loss which after a time can result in permanent hearing loss. It also tends to produce nervous stress. Workplaces – usually offices and shops – that have 'white noise', or piped background music to obscure noise, are thought to induce increased tiredness and stress and even metabolic disturbances. As I was told:

In my section, we have to put the plastic moulds into cast-iron clamps and throw them down a metal chute. There is a constant crash of metal on metal. You can feel yourself tense up waiting for it to hit. You have to shout to be heard even by the person next to you. It doesn't take long to get a headache. They put nearly all Greek women in here.

There is a lot of noise which gives us headaches. Most of the women take Vincents.

We have got to do something about dust and sound. The noise in there is incredible. I can't complain on our floor but other floors. Like the third floor especially and the fourth. They are incredible, the noise. People shouldn't have to work with that noise. As Cheryl said, you are just like zombie, which they are. Especially when they are treated just like another piece of machinery. It is quite unreal.

In 1977 the National Health and Medical Research Council recommended that industrial noise regulations be introduced, that workers should not be exposed to more than 90 decibels (dBA) for an eight-hour day, and that this level should be gradually reduced to 85dBA. Journalist Ian Davis reported that a multi-million-dollar noise-control industry had developed and was lobbying for more stringent controls, whereas employers generally wanted higher noise levels to be allowed.[21] The Workers' Health Centre maintains that 80dBA should be the recommended level for eight hours' exposure. They recommended that anyone exposed to over 75dBA should have regular hearing tests, and bargain with their employer for noise-reduction measures.

Finally, comments were made by various women about dangerous or toxic substances in the work environment. One of the problems, apart from exposure itself, is the general lack of information available to workers about the substances with which they work. As a shop-steward in a whitegoods factory pointed out:

Well there again the union has got no facilities or no control on the job to know what the substances are that are used. They use all kinds of oils, kerosene, waxes, spray painting, spray enamel, glass enamel, caustics in washing the oil off the metal for painting and spraying and enameling and so on. Who knows what effect those things have on people?

And fiberglass is another one which would interest me. Fibreglass is a terrible irritant and I don't know whether it does anything more than just irritate. But I mean anything that irritates your skin is bad because the skin is a really sensitive area. What workers tolerate just to earn a living – it is just incredible. I remember when I was working over in Alexandria we started to do some jobs cutting out things in fiberglass. WE had a lot of problems with it because it is not the only things you know are irritating you, it's the things you work with and you don't know what effect they have. I've been a press operator all the time and you are using oil all the time and then they started to use something else instead of a lot of other more expensive metals they used to use. It has white coating on it and it powders. And anybody that does spray painting for any time, or enamel spraying, you can see that it has an effect on them. They are all a bit chesty, a bit sinusy. Bronchitis is a very common problem among industrial workers. In assembling fridges you're using some kind of powder put in plastic. You don't know what effect that has, do you? And making that insulation – plastic insulation, slab plastic.

The International Chemical Workers' Federation (ICF) has warned the fiberglass and other inorganic fibre substances are carcinogenic – minute particles lodge in the lungs and induce cancer.[22]

The chemical, plastics and pharmaceutical are probably the most rapidly growing industries in the industrial countries in recent years. They expose workers to unnatural substances, whose effects, in most cases, have not been thoroughly tested. Many are suspected of causing cancer, mutation and birth abnormalities. In the pharmaceutical and cosmetic industries, 95 per cent of all production work is carried out by women, according to union official Brian O'Neill.[23] The usual health problems arise, but are supplemented by less visible chemical hazards which may have long-term effects. Talc, for example, has effects similar to those of asbestos on the lungs.

Respiratory and bronchial disorders and allergic diseases are especially common among women in the textile and clothing industry where dust, fibres and other airborne particles act as irritants. Ventilation and systems for screening out particles are usually either non-existent or inadequate. However, these traditional diseases of the textile industry are now overshadowed by the more recent problem of exposure to numerous chemicals used to dying, shrinking, waterproofing, oiling, permanent pressing and cleaning of fabrics. According to Anne George, a Canadian researcher:

Because of the enormous range of substances, nearly every part of the body could be affected adversely in some way or another through exposure to the work situation in the textile industry, if proper precautions were not adhered to.[24]

Tenosynovitis

I worked in a factory making mowers. I was putting screws on, twisting my thumbs all day at a very rapid pace. I started to get pains and numbness in my thumbs. My doctor put me on compensation. I eventually had to have an operation. When I went back to work they put me back on the same job. Now my hands are bad gain. I'm not working at all now.

The woman who made these comments has tenosynovitis, a painful inflammation of the tendons and tendon sheaths of the wrist and hand. Sufferers usually also have 'severe muscle strain in the forearm, upper arm, shoulder, neck and back on the affected side'. The pain and swelling make it had or impossible for the person to do simple things such as opening doors, writing or peeling vegetables, let alone working on an assembly line.

Tenosynovitis is caused by rapid, repetitive movements of the hands of the sort that are typical of factory process work, especially in the metal, electrical and other assembly and packaging industries, and increasingly typical of clerical work consisting of unremitting rapid keyboard operation.

There are three astonishing features of tenosynovitis: it is found in epidemic proportions amongst women workers; until recently it has been largely unrecognized by the medical profession, even amongst those concerned with occupational health; and it is entirely preventable.

The bind that grips women workers is that the only cure for tenosynovitis is to stop doing the work that causes it. While some do just that, many cannot; they are working because of economic necessity.

Technically it is correct to say that tenosynovitis is caused by movements of the hands; but what makes these unnatural movements necessary? Primarily, it is the organization of the production process. In the name of efficiency, tasks are broken down into minute components, each one repeated hundreds, even thousands of times a day by one worker. Coupled with this is a system of strict supervision, production quotas, bonus rates for a certain volume of work, and a fast pace of work that is not set by workers but by management. This is how one assembly-line worker in a vehicle factory described it:

Everybody had fucked-up hands and wrists and arms. I mean, I had awful trouble with my wrist, and they x-rayed it and carried on and kept assuring me that it was all right. Other people had the same thing, tenosynovitis, tendon trouble. They had operations and months off because they were doing things, continually heavy things, with one hand, and tendons just weren't built to cop it and they broke down. Every second person you see has got it or had it, because it is that kind of work.

They can go along and the doctors can scream at them now and again to rest, but how can they? If they had a wage, it wouldn't be nearly as bad, but as it is, you know, people are on like the basic wage plus production bonus and it doesn't go very far. So that if people can see that if they work a whole lot harder than they would otherwise they can get more money, well they do. What happens then is that in a very short time, quite often only in a few months, they've got tenosynovitis or some other thing and some of them complain about pains up in here, and muscles trouble, so they get sent to a doctor, and they do x-rays, and the x-rays show up nothing, so they get told to go back to work. And quite often people just can't stand the pain any longer, so they just go.

One shop steward from factory manufacturing household appliances pointed out the role of management in creating the conditions for the tenosynovitis epidemic:

Over half the compensation cases on my job are strain and tenosynovitis, and that is bad supervision and bad engineering because the engineering is done on the cheap to cut costs and produce more or less, and the speed up on the job carried out by the agents of the company, the supervisors. Any attitude they have of being humane usually turns out to be just a front in the final analysis.

Attitudes of management were described as being to get rid of a worker as quickly as possible when she developed tenosynovitis, and if possible to avoid having to pay workers' compensation:

All the time there are problems with women going off on compo with it, not being able to have very long off, coming back being put on to the same job again, not being able to do the job, and then being sacked.

One woman told me that when she went back to work, she was harassed and given particular hard work to do, so that she eventually broke down.

Stories abound about the appalling way tenosynovitis is treated. Firstly, it is frequently not recognized as an occupational disease, and diagnosed as arthritis. This is not surprising, given the neglect of occupational medicine in medical courses. According to Dr Jim Walker of the Lidcombe Workers' Health Centre, medical courses contain only a brief mention of a rare form of tenosynovitis.[25]

Secondly, if it is diagnosed as being caused by work the prescribed 'cure' is rest. In practice, this means the worker is given some time off work on workers' compensation, and then sent back to work, usually to the same job, whereupon the disease returns. Many women, faced with the choice between having no job and working on in pain with their hands getting worse, choose to keep working. Deborah Vallence, a medical student who spent a year doing a case study of 'repetition diseases' in a Melbourne metal-work factory, has described women sitting at their work benches in tears from the pain, consuming analgesics and forcing themselves to go on working. Some find that they simply cannot maintain the pace required of them and are sacked.[26]

Thirdly, when tenosynovitis and related diseases persist, operations are performed on the wrists. Most reports from women who have had these operations indicate that either there was no improvement, or the problem became worse. For example:

We had one case on our job. The company brought a doctor in. God knows where they found him. And we had a lass – she'd only been on the job three months and she ran into a wrist problem. Nobody had spent time to get through to her, although some people had tried, but the company hadn't accepted the responsibility to assist somebody like that to work properly. Anyway she ran into trouble and this doctor sent her to hospital, operated on her wrist, gave her no information about anything. Sent her back to work and she was just in agony. Eventually we had to send her to the union solicitor who sent her to another surgeon. It was a botched job but she had to have another operation on it and he eventually sent her back to work fit to work. In the meantime the company had sacked her and we tried to get the company to put her back on again but they didn't.

The study by Dr Walker showed that of nineteen people who had been operated on for tenosynovitis, only one said she was cured. This woman, in fact did not have tenosynovitis but carpal tunnel syndrome which has similar symptoms. Of the others, thirteen said the operation had made them worse and eleven said they felt the operation had permanently crippled them. Walker maintains that the operation, a carpal tunnel release operation, is entirely inappropriate for tenosynovitis, and that a misdiagnosis occurs because patients' occupational history is not taken.

Walker describes tenosynovitis as a 'crippling new epidemic in industry'. Crippling and epidemic certainly, but it is not new. It is an intrinsic part of the production process as it is now organized. Its recognition is new, and is largely the result of work by groups such as the Lidcombe Workers' Health Centre, the Liverpool Women's Health Centre, the Melbourne Workers' Health Action Group and the Working Women's Centre.

Given the devastating effect of tenosynovitis on countless number of women workers, it is amazing that employers and even occupational health professionals can go on saying, as they do, that women are suited to work involving rapid, dexterous small movements on the production line.

The fact that a preventable disease is so widespread is an indictment of the way Australian industry is organized. It reflects two main features: firstly, that workers themselves have no control over the organization of work processes; and secondly, that the priorities of management are to maintain the highest possible production and therefore profit levels that they can, even at the cost of disabling workers. Tenosynovitis could be prevented if these two features were changed. There is general agreement that job rotation, slackening the pace of work, removing the bonus system and allowing each worker to perform a longer, more complex and varied task which is repeated less often throughout the day are all ways of reorganizing production to avoid tenosynovitis.

However, there is great resistance to this by most employers. One shop steward put it this way:

There is very little attention given to rotation and no education of the workers on the question of rotation so workers become wedded to their little job and that suits the boss at certain times because that person becomes quite fast and expert on that job. But then the job often does them a lot of harm. You have got people with distorted hands, fingers, ripped arms, shoulders and elbows just from constant repetition. You see, you could do one job till morning tea time, another job till lunch time, another job till afternoon tea time and another job until knock-off time. It's just not necessary that people are doing the same thing over and over. It's just easier for the boss to organise it that way.

Reorganisation of production will not take place unless workers themselves have more control over their jobs. This means, in the first place, getting more information about hazards and how to avoid them, forming health and safety organisations on the shop floor, and putting forward demands about aspects of the way work is organized.

Shops

The hazards discussed so far have been primarily associated with work in factories. However, the majority of women work in clerical, sales and services occupations which are usually regarded as safer, cleaner and less hazardous overall. While some of the more obvious hazards of factory work are absent from other occupations, there are nevertheless many that present problems which have been largely ignored. While industrial inspectorates cover factories, albeit not very thoroughly, women in other occupations have no such protection. The Victorian Labour and Industry Act 'does not really apply to offices, schools, shops or hospitals, the areas where most women work'.[27]

Shop assistants have to contend with long hours of standing, and the emotional strain of having to keep up the appearance of being friendly, polite, charming or attractive. They also, in some cases, suffer stress because of sales quotas and job insecurity. Their physical working conditions 'backstage' – for example, lunch rooms – are often a contrast to the shop itself. One shop assistant told me: 'We sat on wooden packing cases on bare concrete out the back of the shop. We had to apply for a key to the only toilet, which was across the arcade and shared with other shops.'

Technological change is affecting the nature of work in retail sales. Sales workers now are likely to be check-out operators rather than counter staff. They sit all day (which can be as bad as standing all day), often in cramped cubicle, having to make tiring and unnatural movements, twisting sideways from the waist to face customers, and rapidly punching keys. Hand, wrist, arm, neck, shoulder and back strains can result in much the same way as they do from process work.

Another hazard that affects supermarket workers is 'meat wrappers' asthma'. The *Women at Work* newspaper published a report on it:

You probably haven't heard of 'meat wrappers' asthma', but the Australasian Meat Industry Employees' Union is currently conducting a campaign to eliminate this disease from the industry.

Meat wrappers' asthma is caused by the hot wire method used in the meat rooms of most supermarkets to cut plastic (PVC) film.

When the hot wire cuts through the plastic, it gives off fumes. Sometimes bits of plastic stick to the wire and continue to smoke.

The smell and the effect on the eyes can be bad enough. But after a time, the person using the machine can develop asthma.

Doctors don't know everything about asthma, but it is known that once some people get it, they may have it for the rest of their lives.

Here are some examples of members of the AMIEU who have used the hot wire cutters and developed health problems.

Anne had never had asthma in her life. She worked for five months in the meat room of a supermarket and had to give the job away because of shortness of breath and asthma attacks. A specialist said it was probably due to the fumes from the machine.

She received $6500 after the union took up a compensation claim. But she is still ill. The asthma spray she uses makes her feel sick and the money is no substitute for her health.

Flo worked as a meat wrapper for three and a half years. During the last year she suffered breathing problems. She had an operation on her nose and sinus and has now lost her sense of smell. She suffers from headaches, dizziness and nervous tension. A compensation claim is under way but nothing can replace her health.

Mary worked in a supermarket meat room for five years. She developed asthma recently. A specialist from a big hospital took his equipment to the supermarket and tested her breathing while she worked on the hot wire cutter. Her asthma got worse. The union has pointed out the dangers of these cutters and asked the Retail Traders Association to look at alternative methods.[28]

Offices

Office and clerical work too have hazards that go largely unrecognized. They include exposure to noise, solvents, fumes, photosensitive paper, high-intensity light, ultraviolet and infra-red radiation and electrical hazards. Duplicators and photocopying machines are often housed in small, badly lit, inadequately ventilated areas. Operators may be exposed to liquid chemicals and treated paper capable of causing dermatitis and unknown longer term hazards. Even short periods of operating photocopying machines can cause headaches.[29]

Keyboard and key-punch operators, like factory workers, are subject to tenosynovitis and backaches caused by rapid hand movements while sitting rigidly in a (usually non-adjustable) chair. Technological change has added to, not eliminated, hazards of this kind, which are typical of stereotyped 'women's jobs'.

Linda Rubinstein interviewed Sylvia Hall, General Secretary of the Australian Telephone and Phonogram Officers' Association:

Ms Hall says the union is very concerned about the health of its members: 'The automatic exchanges look much better than the old ones, with beautiful décor, new furniture and rest room facilities.

'However, they are windowless building and people suffer from sensory deprivation. In Adelaide, the girls go up to the canteen, where there are windows and stand there watching the pigeons. If a pigeon craps they go berserk; something has happened.

'The temperatures are bad because the computors have to be at a certain temperature and the operators have to suffer that.

'During the ATEA dispute last year the airconditioning broke down and management opened all the doors. My member were sitting there freezing, with their coats on, so I closed them again. I was accused of industrial sabotage.

'We have a lot of people suffering from sore eyes. A friend of mind has had to change her glasses three times in the fifteen months since she has worked with the computer. Her specialist says staring at the screen all the time has accelerated the deterioration in her eyesight over that time.

'You can see that people coming off work with the video display units have sore eyes. They come off exhausted because they sit looking at the screen for three hours without stopping. You can't look the wrong way, or you're in strife. You can't even turn around like you used to be able to do.

'The operators are given typists' chairs, but they are not doing typists' work. They punch only a few keys and they don't use all their fingers. We made a film of them recently showing that they use the left hand more than the right and that they were sitting at peculiar angles. Telecom still hasn't solved the problem of where the screen should be in relation to the keyboard.

'Recently we had three cases of tenosynovitis and those members are receiving workers' compensation. I think this is because they didn't have enough room to put their hands down between calls.'[30]

A Telephonists' Action Group has been formed in Sydney in response to health hazards in the new exchanges. They quote examples of women who had been convinced by doctors that they were suffering nervous breakdowns, or even had a brain tumour because of headaches, dizzy spells and memory blackouts. It turned out they had contracted middle-ear infections from the airconditioning.

One typist described her working conditions in this way:

It does not take many typewriters to be clustered in an area to create a volume of noise. Even if the noise volume is only about 70 decibels, it could be a health hazard if you are subject to it over a number of years, because typing also calls for a measure of intellect.

It is time some standards were set for working in these conditions. A penalty rate for the exposure would be one way, thus encouraging employers to install noise-breaking partitions or padded mobile screens. The majority of typists in typing pools are quite young – average age under twenty – but because increments usually cut out a twenty-three and promotions are hard to come by, many older women are finding themselves in the 'pool' for a long time.

These 'typing ghettos' are also increasing with the number of highrise office buildings. So much for 'progress'![31]

Health and service occupations

Just over half the women working in the health-care industry are service workers such as nurses aides, cooks, cleaners and food handlers. About 20 per cent are nurses, while only a tiny minority are doctors, scientists or administrators. They are subject to a wide range of chemical hazards, anaesthetic gas which is suspected of causing miscarriages and birth abnormalities, and ionizing radiation from x-ray equipment, Laundry and drycleaning workers are exposed to high temperatures, soaps, detergents and solvents that can cause skin irritation and dermatitis, and their work may be heavy and require long hours of standing. House, office and industrial cleaners are exposed to similar hazards. One industrial cleaner commented:

I suppose I've got used to it, but the machinery is pretty heavy, especially if you have got too much to do; it gets dirty and all. You need two people to lift it – industrial machine, polishing machine, you can't lift it by yourself. You have to carry it up and down. When we worked for [company A] we had to carry the machine because they got upstairs in the building and I used to carry that upstairs and downstairs. Many times by the time I got up, I thought I was going to have a heart attack! My heart was just beating like mad!. It's a big machine, it's a big monster, you know, real heavy. At [company B] you don't have to carry it upstairs, because they got upstairs machines and downstairs; it's very good. In my building where I work it's no upstairs, so I don't have to carry up and down anyway.

Nursing staff also suffer injury from lifting patients. Some hospitals have mechanical lifting devices, but in others understaffing puts pressure on nurses to lift more than they can cope with. A nursing aide in a State psychiatric hospital said:

Well officially you're not allowed to lift anybody on your own, there should always be two of you, that's why night staff are not supposed to do any day duties because it involves lifting people and helping people in and out of the baths. I mean you do do it sometimes but it's up to you; you're not expected to do it, let's put it that way. There are a lot of cases where girls have gone off with bad backs from doing things that they're not supposed to do. Some of those patients can be very very heavy, although in the geriatric wards now they have lifting things that lift and sit them in the chair and you put the thing on and it lifts them into the bath and the bed and brings them out again. And we have chairs for them and hand-held showers which we didn't have before and which makes it easier.

Alcoholism

Tiredness and emotional stress as a result of both home and paid work have been discussed, and the alarming use of painkillers and 'nerve' tablets has been pointed out by many writers.[32] Alcoholism amongst women, especially women in the paid workforce, is a far less aired topic.

Speaking to women in some factories and service industries, I was struck by the extent of alcoholism and heavy drinking amongst workers. In one pharmaceutical packaging plant, a woman estimated that about three-quarters of her fellow-workers had a 'drinking problem'. One was fired shortly afterwards, and another was starting to be unable to turn up on time, skipping days, and not returning from the pub after lunch. Some would go to the 'early openers' before work, consume a few cans during morning tea, pattern for Australian-born women rather than migrant women. Some women had extremely distressing situations waiting for them at home and would stay at the pub after work until closing time. They would drink because they didn't want to go home, and because they didn't want women to work. Although drinking is part of a social pattern that goes beyond the workplace, it is an aspect of occupation health, firstly because the tensions of work contribute to the abuse of alcohol and secondly because drinking adds to the possibility of an accident at work.

One woman described the problem at her job:

To work in a place like that I think you should be able to bear it. I mean you are actually there nine hours a day if you do a day shift because you have an hour break for lunch. Everybody races to the pub madly to get out of the place. If you are going to be there for eight hours working in that building I think you should be able to put up with it – I think you should have a choice of what job you do. Something that would suit you. I mean I'm no person to talk because I work my own shift more or less. I'm never there and I can say the same for other people, not mentioning names of course.

What do you mean you are never there?

Well I go into work. Get there on time everyday. Get there on time just about. But I go to lunch at 1 o'clock and go to the pub and that is it. I just can't go back. I detest the place. Everybody detests it. Most people think about the money and they go back.

I went to [the welfare officer] about the alcoholics in the building. Quite tragic, oh God. This place turns people to alcohol. You've got people coming in in the morning with half a dozen cans, everyday. They go into the locker room for half an hour, an hour at a time and the supervisors go in there after them; they see the problem but they ignore it. They don't care.

In one large workplace, shift arrangements were going to be changed, with far-reaching consequences:

What are these people going to do if they cut down all the weekend work? Because so many people work seven days a week and a lot of these are alcoholics. If these people aren't going to be able to work, the department should open centres to give them something to do. They are alcoholics and keeping them at work is actually keeping them away from the alcohol.

There is so many alcoholics, especially the older people in the place because they have been there for so long and they need it to tolerate the place, and I can understand that.

There is so many alcoholics, especially the older people in the place because they have been there for so long and they need it to tolerate the place, and I can understand that.

A lot of these alcoholics, they have got no real home life. Some people even sleep at work because they have got nothing to go home to. They spend twenty-four hours a day in the place. They will sleep in the locker rooms just waiting for the next day to come so they can get back on the job because there are people there. They are so lonely it is incredible, and in such a big place like that it is really bad. They are really out of it but they will keep going because they don't want to lose the job because it is the only thing they have got.

Health and safety problems of migrant women

The health and safety problems discussed so far all affect migrant women. Particular problems of migrant women are due to their concentration in particular jobs – those industrial process jobs where are found poor physical conditions, bonus and piecework systems and tenosynovitis. Tiredness and emotional strain are probably worse for migrant women than for Australian-born women for several reasons: their financial situation is likely to be more desperate, their access to acceptable child-care service may be more limited, and the responsibility they are expected to take for work in the home may be greater. Added to this is the strain that results from having to cope with a strange culture, and not having work procedures and safety measures adequately explained. Probably the greatest disadvantages faced by migrant workers in relation to occupational health is the lack of bilingual health service personnel, and lack of access to information about workers' compensation and the procedures it entails.

A survey by the Brunswick Community Health Centre found that in one industry, the clothing industry, two-thirds of the workers were migrants but less than one-third of the union's compensation claims were for migrants. Similarly, men were twice as likely to claim for compensation as women were. Claims made by women resulted in less compensation being received, and took longer to finish.[33]

The Working Women's Centre has found that:

Those who are aware that they do have rights frequently encounter problems, owing to language and culture, in explaining their problems to doctors, lawyers and unions, not to mention the Workers' Compensation Board when their case comes before it.[34]

What can be done?

Like the women who 'turned off their solder pots', some women have been able to have changes made by refusing to work under unsafe or unhealthy conditions.

At a Rosella Foods factory in Richmond, Victoria, a small group of migrant women, many of whom did not speak English, walked off the job.[35] Their action followed demands by the Food Preservers' Union that the company slow down the line, and provide bigger boxes. The women were expected to pack 20 000 packets of soup a day. They had to cram twenty-four packets into a box that was too small. The speed of the line and the repeated banging of boxes to fit the packets in was causing bruising and injuries to the women's arms, hands, wrists and shoulders. Some had severe cases of tenosynovitis.

For three days the women worked for an hour and then sat in the canteen for an hour. Then they went on strike for ten days. Their action resulted in a complete victory. They won payment for three days of the strike, two extra twenty-minute breaks, a slow-down of the line from a hundred packets a minute to ninety packets a minute on some lines and ninety to eighty packets on others; and the company agreed to introduce bigger boxes.

According to union organizer, Gail Cotton, it was the first time there had been a dispute in the industry over tenosynovitis:

The women used to sit at the machines with their hands bandaged, saying nothing because they were scared they would get sacked. Then they decided they had had enough; they could not stand it any longer.

In the meat industry increased organization of workers also led to better health conditions:

They used to make us work with stitches in our hands. People cut themselves a lot in this job; we've got three off this week. We had a lot of stoppages about that. We went to arbitration and we won.

I've got tenosynovitis in my arm. They put me on light duties at the same rate of pay. That wouldn't have happened before.[36]

However, in other workplaces where rank-and-file organization is lacking or where the union is more concerned with traditional issues, hazards go unchallenged. A process worker in a power transformer company stated:

Nothing could happen in a place like this unless the union did take a really strong line and a really major organising role, and there's very little likelihood of that happening. Conditions, too, were really bad that people complained about all the time but nothing was done; like the noise and the dirt and the oil which was really bad, machine oil. I went in to find the union rep and just talked with him a bit about it and his approach was, 'Oh well, you might get cancer, but you never get . . .' – I forgot what it was, something absurd like 'bronchitis, working with oil'. It was sort of like, well, we might get that but working with oil prevents this other thing from happening, so just forget about it.

All too often occupational health professionals dismiss problems by advising workers to take care, avoid hazards, rest, rotate their jobs or work at a slower pace. They do not realise that although these simple solutions might be effective, they are beyond the worker's control. Taking care and meeting production quotas are mutually exclusive; hazards may be unrecognized. And in any case are usually part of the work environment and could only be avoided by reorganizing processes; rest periods, job rotation and speed of work are all issues over which workers and unions have to fight hard, even for minor changes.

No matter what the specific problem, it arises from the fundamental facts that workers do not have control over their working environment and that employers, who do have that control, organise work with the primary aim of maximizing production, not safeguarding health.

Increasingly occupational health and safety is being seen in the context of 'industrial democracy', 'workers' control' and similar movements aiming to increase the effective power that workers have over their employment, conditions and working arrangements. The Liverpool Women's Health Centre takes this further by saying that it is a question of women controlling their own lives:

Seen in this light, free twenty-four-hour-a-day child care, communalisation of housework, health care in work hours, information on conditions and access to research and records, and training on the job are as much industrial health demands as the demand that certain substances be eliminated.[37]

They discuss the powerlessness of women and their lack of involvement in union organization and state that it is essential for women workers themselves to be involved in forming demands, setting priorities and determining the pace of work and the style of its organization.

Ben Bartlett, formerly of the Lidcombe Workers' Health Centre, has commented on the recent emergence of health centres and workers' health action groups in Sydney, Newcastle, Wollongong, Melbourne and Perth. He makes the point that health professionals can redirect their research and other work towards the health problems of workers, and play a useful part in providing information about various hazards, their effects and how to deal with them. However, he says:

... the main way changes in occupational health are likely to occur is through the action of workers themselves. For this, some form of worker organization is essential. The value of work by professionals can be gauged, to a large extent, by the degree to which they assist this process.

He lists a number of short-term goals, including increased epidemiological research, more enforcement agencies with adequate legislation, more workers' health centres, accurate labelling of industrial substances, more emphasis on occupational health in the training of doctors and nurses, making occupational health staff answerable to workers, and establishment of a national research organization to provide information on request.

One shop steward summed up the situation in this way:

These health centre initiatives that have been taken by health workers will play a part. As workers start to go to them for a few times they will probably build up some statistics and start putting a bit of pressure. But it's only when the workers have control themselves that these sorts of things will be done.[38]

CHAPTER 8

'Not paid and never done'

Child Care

I t is obvious from previous chapters that the issue of child care touches on all aspects of women's situation in and out of the paid workforce and therefore it has high priority in the ACTU charter and in the Working Women's Charter Campaign. Child care, and how it is provided, is central to many issues raised by the women's movement such as the value of unpaid work in the home, the definition of 'work' in Australia's society, and the 'caring role' undertaken by women without adequate resources to back them up. Child care has been linked to women's right to work, and lack of suitable facilities identified as a major barrier to women's equality in the workforce. Child-care problems are known to be especially of concern to migrant women, many of whom speak of bad experiences with commercial and unregistered child minding. Lack of satisfactory child-care services, along with the pressure of taking prime responsibility for work in the home, are central to women's health problems. Many women structure their working hours around their child-care arrangements and, in the longer term, participate in the paid workforce according to a pattern set by their child-rearing activities. Thus, the role of women in relation to child care, and the extent and accessibility of child-care services, constitute a powerful force in shaping the labour market, and in turn are influenced by labour market conditions. The emergence of women workers demanding greater responsiveness from their unions, along with the gradual broadening of trade union concerns to more 'social' issues, have combined to produce a movement urging unions to add their weight to the lobby for better child-care services for men and women workers. As unemployment and technological change break down old certainties about the nature of work, the child-care debate, focusing as it does on paid and unpaid labour, will continue to raise central issue about work and society.

Historical background

Historically in Australia child care has been seen primarily as if the responsibility of individual mothers. Services and facilities have been limited to benevolent or charitable day care, kindergarten or pre-school education for children whose mothers were not in the paid workforce, and commercial child minding. In all cases, only a minority of children have been catered for.

During the 1960s there was a resurgence of interest in child care, prompted especially by the number of married women entering the paid workforce and people realizing how many children under school age had both parents in the paid workforce. Furthermore, at this stage, the government and employers were keen to attract and retain married women workers, and some sort of provision for child care was needed. In the 1960s unions too began to take an interest in child care as part of their activities to raise living standards. However, the result has been described by Winsome McCaughey of Community

Child Care as 'a patchwork of single purpose services' controlled by bureaucracies and philanthropic agencies.[1]

In 1970 a number of organisations began to act on the issue of child care, mostly focusing on 'working wives' or 'working mothers'. The Employers' Federation held a seminar on day care and absenteeism while unions, spearheaded by the Amalgamated Engineering Union, launched an organization called Action for Adequate Child Care. Public meetings were held and a Child Care Charter was put forward. This campaign was one of the forerunners of the Community Child Care movement which developed in the 1970s.[2]

That movement was concerned to establish that:

. . . children's services are a right, that there should be parent participation and community control of services, that services should be for the convenience of the users, that integration of services is part of the process in creating community and that future problems can only be met if there is flexibility in planning.[3]

From about 1975 there was particular concern about the possibility of unions being involved in the campaign for child care. Winsome McCaughey has stated that:

Traditionally the unions have used their skills on campaigns around wages and work conditions. Today there is a whole range of social issues beyond the workplace which affect the lives of the working people, and that, 'Trade unions and community organisations need to jointly campaign for services which genuinely improve the quality of life'.[4]

One important focus for child care in the late 1970s which is continuing into the 1980s is union involvement in community child-care services. The principles and actions of this campaign are discussed in this chapter.

Another focus is the struggle to maintain government funding of non-profit child-care services.

The Community Child care organization and those associated with the broader child-care movement have been at pains to point out the child care should be linked solely with women in the paid workforce; strategically because there would be a risk of losing child-care services when women's paid labour was not in demand; and in principle because all children are seen as having the right to a range of services and all women, whether in the paid workforce or not, need access to child care at times in order to do business, shop, participate in community activities, take courses or simply have a break.

However, the Child Care Act (1972) was introduced by the government because it thought that, as women were making a major contribution to the GNP, it should be doing something for their children, and, as labour was short, women's labour was needed, so more child-care centres would help release that labour supply.

Now that the labour market is quite different, the government's concern is with cutting back public expenditure, including child-care services, and encouraging women to leave the paid workforce to look after their children full time.

Figures on child care

The Women's Bureau's 1970 report on child-care centres[6] estimated that there were 13 725 children in child-care centres throughout Australia – 2171 in 40 government-subsidised centres and 11 554 children in 515 unsubsidised and commercial centres, two-thirds of which were in Melbourne and Sydney. Only two centres, both in Melbourne, were operated by employers for the children of their employees. While only 1 per cent of children under six years of age were in those centres, 30 per cent of married women between twenty and thirty-four were in the paid labourforce, along with 58 per cent separated, widowed and divorced women in the same age group. The report did not say how many children there were and what sort of care they received .However, the figures pointed to grossly inadequate child-care services, and minimal government support.

In 1977 the Australian Bureau of Statistics did a survey of child care.[7] The number of child-care centres had increased markedly, and there were an estimated 20 000 subsidised 'places' and 45 000 commercial 'places'. Although it is limited by the assumptions it makes about women being responsible for children, except in the case of sole fathers, the survey does give an overall view of the labourforce participation of people responsible for children, their hours of work, afterschool and school holiday arrangements, existing and preferred child-care arrangements for children of and below school age, and whether people looking after children were seeking paid work.

The survey showed that 40 per cent of people 'responsible' (in the bureau's definition) for children under the age of twelve were in the paid workforce. Only 2.3 per cent of these were men. Just over half (52.1 per cent) of these people worked part time. When asked about their child-care arrangements for after school, half the people said that either they only worked during school hours (26.9 per cent), or their spouse (usually the husband) was home at that time. Other people said that their children were cared for at home by older children (12.7 per cent) or by someone else who came to their home (9.5 per cent). A further 15.2 per cent said that their children were sent to another person's home where they were looked after. Only 3.2 per cent had some alternative arrangement while 9 per cent had no arrangement. The striking feature of these figures is the lack of use of organized child-care facilities such as community after-school care programs. When asked what they did during school holidays, a similar picture merged. One-third of the people said that they continued to work as usual. Half as many said that they either resigned or altered their working hours to cope with school holidays. The proportion saying that their children were looked after in their own homes either by older children or by another person was similar to the proportion making those arrangements for after-school care. A slightly higher proportion (17.9 per cent) said that their children were looked after in another person's home. The proportion with other arrangements was again very small (4.5 per cent) while the proportion making no arrangements was slightly lower (4.3 per cent). Once again the lack of organized child-care facilities or programs stands out. This at least partly reflects the way child-care programs in Australia have not been designed to meet the needs of parents in the paid workforce. In particular, it has often been assumed that child care for children of school age is not needed.

Child-care arrangements for children not attending school reveal a somewhat different picture. While over two-fifths of workers said that their children were cared for at home, either by a spouse (28.7 per cent) or by some other person in the home (13.2 per cent), a larger proportion (34.2 per cent) were cared for in someone else's home. There was a higher reported usage of organized child-care centres (16.3 per cent) although this figure, representing the only one in six families, is still very low.

Although the Bureau of Statistics produces valuable data on the population from which the need for children's services can be inferred, it does not really tell us much about the range of existing child-care services because it fails to distinguish between kindergarten, co-operative day care, commercial day care, family day care, private paid minding and private unpaid minding.

Nor does it indicate how adequate those services area, or what specific needs exist. According to Community Child Care, some of the people whose children are cared for by the other parent at home would be shiftworkers. Their difficulties have already been discussed. Children cared for in other people's home would include some of the unsupervised private minders who may be unreliable or unable to meet adequate standards, and themselves receiving no support and meagre financial reward. 'In short, there remains a drastic shortfall between supply and demand for full- and part-time care. And indications are that the demand will continue to rise.'[8]

The survey certainly revealed this strong demand for organized child-care centre either at work (16.5 per cent) or elsewhere (25.8 per cent) for children under school age, but a much slighter demand for such care for children of school age (5.1 per cent and 5.7 per cent respectively). Parents of children under school age also favoured having their children cared for by someone in their own home (25.4 per cent) or in another private home (20.6 per cent). Once again the figures do not distinguish between commercial and non-commercial care. Almost one-third (31.0 per cent) of people with school-age children said that their preference would be to work only in school hours. As has been seen, there is an increasing number of women, especially married women, seeking part-time work for this reason. It is also clear that if more part-time work opportunities existed, more women would enter the paid workforce. The child-care survey states that 30.2 per cent of those with school-age children were looking for work, while the rest said that child-care problems prevented them from looking for work. Likewise, of those not in the paid workforce who had children under school age, 20.6 per cent said that they were looking for work while the rest were not because of their child-care responsibilities.

The context of child-care needs

The growth of a community child-care movement in the 1970s was probably a response to changes in population and behavior as well as changing attitudes to some of the major myths about families, work and children.

Myths about the 'normal family'

Historically, of course, we have had the persistent myth of the male breadwinner and the dependent female engaged in full-time child rearing. The division between economic support and caring has left its mark on most Australian men and women. Against this myth is the reality that there has always been a high proportion of lone women with dependent children in Australian society, of whom a steady minority have been in the paid workforce despite low wages, limited opportunities and social disapproval. Furthermore, large families, those on low wages, and migrant families facing the prospect of establishing themselves from scratch, have not found it possible to live on one 'breadwinner's' wage.

Nowadays, departures from the 'normal' family are more frequent: one in four mothers of children under school age are in the paid workforce, and about one in ten families are single-parent families.[9]

As stated earlier, the life cycle of women today is different from that of a generation ago. To summarise, they spend longer in education, marry later, have fewer children in a shorter time and return to the workforce more rapidly and for a longer time, having greater past experience of employment and of some period of independent adult life. Furthermore, they can be less confident of having supportive social networks of family or friends to provide child care.

However, it is not simply the increased number of women in the paid workforce that has led to a call for extended child-care services. Three-quarters of children under school age are cared for by their mothers at home .For many, this is a lonely isolating experience.

Furthermore, the children have limited access to variety and social contact unless a wide range of community services are available.

Thus the myth that the 'normal' family of mother and children, supported by a male breadwinner, can get by in isolation is challenged by the evidence of women both in and out of the paid workforce.

Actual situations of child care

Although systematic and thorough research has yet to be done on child-care arrangements, several surveys including the by the ABS have built up a fairly consistent picture that the movement of women into the workforce has not been accompanied by an adequate development of community services. Women have continued to take primary responsibility for children, and in doing so have sometimes been stretched to the limit. Some arrangements have been makeshift or inadequate, and have caused much stress. Women have bent their working hours in accordance with child care to the extent of undertaking shiftwork. Some children have been left with relatives, older children, or even alone. Many parents have turned to informal arrangements, usually paid, with private minders. This system, along with the organized commercial sector of child minding, has grown unchecked despite its cost to the parent and the doubts frequently expressed about standards of care.

It is notable that only a minority of parents use organized child-care facilities such as creches, day nurseries and centres. This is partly because of the inconvenience of their hours or of their location, and misgivings of the parents about the quality of care provided.

However, most mother in the paid workforce have made some sort of arrangement for their children, even though they might be unhappy about it. Many are probably so affected by feelings of guilt at leaving their children that they find it hard to think about the quality or standard of care available. However, the problem that the majority of women in this situation face is that their regular arrangements do not usually cater for times when the children are sick, or for school holidays. Many women have said that if a child is sick they take sick leave, or simply take time off work to stay home. Others take annual leave, or resign during school holidays. Apart from the disruption to their employment that this causes, it is a massive source of insecurity.

Child care and organised recreation programs before and after school and during school holidays have been put forward as an answer to the problems of working parents with children and it is astonishing that so little use is made of school facilities for this purpose.

Care of sick children (and indeed of other people) requires a rather different solution since it is unpredictable and almost invariably parents do not want to take a sick child away from home, preferring to stay home themselves rather than have an 'outsider' come in. The most appropriate solution put forward has been for the introduction of special leave similar to sick leave, which would allow both male and female workers to take time off to deal with emergencies, illness of dependants and so on. This is clearly an idea which cannot be implemented without union support – in fact it is one reform that unions are uniquely placed to achieve.

The Women's Trade Union Commission in Sydney has been particularly involved in promoting child care related to the workplace and enlisting the support of unions. As well as establishing a model child-care centre on a new industrial estate at Eden Park, the WTUC has produced a film which documents the story of four families with typical child-care co-ordinator, says, 'Migrant women, single parents and unskilled workers all have little choice in care for their children, mainly because they are low-wage earners and on the job full time, all the time'. She sees the prospect of organized labour demanding quality, low-cost child-care service' helping to overcome the problem.[10]

Child-care problems of migrant women

The FILEF (Federation of Italian Workers and their Families) Women's Group has encountered similar problems in the Melbourne suburb of Coburg, where they have sought to have a child-care centre built in the grounds of the Commonwealth Clothing Factory for the use of workers and people living in the surrounding area.[11]

They have had meetings with clothing workers and with several unions in the process of their campaign. The CURA study of migrant women showed that they felt strongly about child care and were keen for their unions to be more involved in trying to get more facilities made available.[12] A survey of working mothers and their children published by the Electrical Trades Union in 1974 also showed that migrant women were anxious about child care.[13]

For migrant women, the problem is not just the lack of child-care centres with suitable hours and reasonable fees. Centres, like schools, have usually been set up and staged by English-speakers who have automatically dealt with food, activities, relationships and so on according to Anglo-Saxon Australian cultural values which have been confusing for the children and threatening for the parents. Barbara Gayler, a Melbourne social worker, has pointed out that ordinary day care employs few bilingual staff members, and migrant children attending such centres live in two different worlds.[14] Many parents, therefore, prefer to put their children in the care of a private minder from their own culture. However, this reduces their choice, renders them vulnerable to the abuses of the more unscrupulous minders, and denies them access to a share in subsidies and funded facilities. She suggests that one solution would be the development of small neighbourhood centres with multilingual or bilingual staff catering for migrant parents and sensitive to cultural differences in child rearing. Municipalities such as Fitzroy, which have a high migrant and refugee population and a huge diversity of ethnic groups, have found that one of their needs is for the teaching of English as a second language in child-care centres.[15]

A woman who worked in a factory with many Spanish speakers told me:

And then the worry is often the language thing. I remember a South American women, who eventually got a child into this preschool centre, and just for the first month or so, until she knew it was going to be all right, was really worried just because there was no one there who spoke Spanish, and no Spanish-speaking child, and he had no English and how was he going to tell them that he had to go to the toilet and that he was thirsty?

Commercial centres

One alarming development is the increasingly strong lobby of the commercial child-minding industry. Community Child Care points out that there is a conflict of interest between the commercial or profit motive and the public interest, where the first priority is to ensure that the child receives the best possible level of care. They fear that a franchise system of day care may take hold in Australia, as it has done in the United States. Under this system, chains of day-care centres are set up as business ventures. They have been criticized for their poor standards of care and their lack of accountability or parent involvement.

Ruth Crow, an advocate of community-based child care, has shown how 'private child-minding businesses have become a growth industry for investers'[16], and lucrative child-minding freeholds have been advertised in Melbourne. Senator Guilfoyle has responded sympathetically to the commercial child-minding lobby, suggesting that the government could contract out to private day-care firms.

Some common views on child care

The women I interviewed agreed that child care was one of their major concerns, and had experience most of the problems already mentioned.

It was clear that many women feel bad about leaving their children, even if satisfactory arrangements are available. They also feel vulnerable to criticism and to getting into trouble if their arrangements are inadequate. This must surely cast doubt on the validity of some surveys on child-care arrangements for, as one woman pointed out, women will not always speak frankly about their child-care problems:

Whenever you start asking the women about their kids, and who looks after them, they're always really wary and watchful that you aren't going to be making value judgments about them being bad mothers, because they aren't looking after their kids. And so long as you made it quite clear that you aren't, and what you think about the whole situation, then they talk about the experiences and the troubles and the worries they have about it. Otherwise on the whole they try and paint a pretty rosy picture.

It was clear that many women did not have any organized child care, and took recourse in shiftwork:

Apart from those sort of alternate shifts, opposite shifts, there don't seem to be any other arrangements anywhere.

Well I didn't get much sleep, but I managed. I think when a woman has to go out and you can't get a job that works in with you family you will put up with anything.

Some women said that they had been unable to find suitable child care, so they had simply stayed out of the paid workforce until their children were old enough to be at home by themselves after school.

My kids are big now, so I got no problems about that. I can leave them alone, one is thirteen and one is eleven, so don't need a baby-sitter or anything. And my husband is home. Only one week when he goes on afternoon shift, and the kids are by themselves, otherwise he's home and can look after them.

I have never worked before, like since I came to Australia; it's only about three years ago I start, because the children, I didn't want to leave them when they are little.

However, others cannot afford to spend years out of the paid workforce:

They look for baby-sitter, of course, and many leave the children home by themselves, even the little ones. They tie their little baby like into those high chairs. They went out in the morning and left that baby all by itself, you know all day, eight hours. It's a bit dangerous. I wouldn't do that. Couldn't.

These informal and unregistered arrangements are invariably a source of worry:

Yeah, most of the women here have kids, and their child-minding arrangements almost always, that I know of, are relatives minding a child, or a lady, usually of their own nationality, who they pay, and they worry all the time, not being sure of how the kid is being looked after. You know, you say, 'Well, how did you find the woman', and they say 'Oh, I put an ad in the newspaper', or someone told them about someone. And then they always say, 'Well, she seems all right, you know, but you never know, do you?' And some of them tell of really and incidences of things, of how they hadn't been feeding the kid, or leaving them in dirt nappies, and they have arrived half an hour early one afternoon and discovered it and taking them away. There are a couple of them who have them in pre-school-type things.

Alternatives, in the form of high-quality, subsidized child-care facilities are often inaccessible: 'The council has got two quite nice places, beautiful they are, but there is a five-year waiting list. The kindergartens are the same, there's a big waiting list around this area.'

The hours that some existing centres are open, their location and the travelling time required to reach them and then go on to work or home constitute a further problem:

A lot of factories now are on shift work or you are on different hours and again where does that leave you with child care?

I travel three hours a day. June is travelling three and a half hours a day. That's taking a great big slice out of your day for a start and then this business of child care. In some suburbs they've got really terrific facilities but in other you've got nothing. You haven't even got a bus service that you can get anywhere within half the places. I've got a private baby-sitter for my little four-year-old now. Only because I know her personally or have known her for a long while that I leave here there. I'm lucky. But then what do you do when you are on shiftwork? You see, most of the child-care centres are from 7 a.m. to 5 p.m. – this is why we do the early shift.

There was a widespread feeling that government funding should be provided to reduce the costs of child care:

Trying to get into a kindergarten that's reasonable price that's subsidised is very hard, unless you put over a story that you are desperate or pay $25 a week to have them minded in those hours with no meals or anything. But this is something I think should be provided by the government. They forced this situation on us. Why aren't they providing us with more cribs? They do it in other countries.

For women working part time, the high cost and inflexibility of child-care centres made working hardly worthwhile:

A few, they pay around $20, $25 for a baby-sitter. Like, they take the children to the baby-sitter's home, and then that person feeds them, the baby and all, like a little child, from Monday till Friday. And they have to pay for it. But it depends, like, if I was working I couldn't afford to pay $25, $30 for the baby-sitter because I only get $65 a week so. I'd rather sit home and do nothing, stay with the children.

Employer involvement in child care

Opinions vary about the role of employers in child care. Although many women feel that employers should take more responsibility, especially through financial contributions, for child care, some are wary of the employer's influence on the quality of child care and concerned that employer control of facilities could be used against women workers.

I think that we have got to have community child care. I suggested a school holiday program and they have just taken the whole thing over and the workers – their kids go along but they have got no say in anything and it is not in the workers' hands to resolve the problems. It is just the same old tight institutionalized thing and just a status symbol for the company and a bit of help to the women who use it for their children. Very little opportunity taken to promote it amongst the male workers to give mum a bit of a break. People only want to talk about child care for the working mothers and that's a very narrow concept and, of course, being such a narrow concept it can be used against the workers.

Some people advocated community-based child care serving the needs of women in a number of workplaces in one area:

Look, child care is an issue I heard from one end of Sydney to the other when I was going around in International Women's Year. It is a big issue when women want to go to work. Now there were no real places for them to put their children at reasonable rates, or at any rates anyway, but at reasonable rates I think we should be able to do this. I don't think they should be attached to tone establishment but have one community-based type of thing. I think the government should be involved in setting them up. And I think that the employers in that area could contribute to them in some way but I am not very keen about single-factory-based child care. I'd take it but I am not very keen. I think it allows a stick to be held over a woman's head.

Whereas others felt that there were advantages in having children minded nearby:

You know we'd advocated that if they had a big meatworks, say, there's not only women, there's men too or single fathers. If they wanted to they could go over at lunch time and see those children. This is what greatly concerns me. Or where there is a lot of factories a centralised place. But I would even like to see a twenty-four-hour service with it because a lot of people, single people and that, they put their child in or else they lock them up in the house all night. Now what if there's a fire? They lose their life while that parent is away. A lot of the employers aren't interested. A lot care. They say well, the union put half of it and we'll put half of it. The union isn't going to put half of it but the people would pay the running costs whereas they couldn't afford to put the building up. I think it would pay the employer to do it – you know the women would be more relaxed and a happier environment at work if they knew their child was close by and safe.

In one case, at a university, child-care facilities existed but were not made available to non-academic staff:

Well since I've gone back to work after having my daughter – I had to give up work then; I didn't work for about seven or eight years until she was old enough to cope on her own and I was able to get a part-time job then. Because at that stage there was just no child-minding facilities available and there's not too many now although at university there is a staff one which is mainly for academic staff. There is also one which students have been fighting to run but neither of them is anywhere nearly sufficient and none of them take in, say, women on the cleaning staff. The in-between group have just got nothing really and unfortunately there's about half a dozen unions involved out there and none of them with a huge membership – other than probably the clerks would be the biggest – and none of them showing much interest in the question of child-care facilities. Particularly, like in the cleaning staff, a lot of them are older. Mainly the younger women would probably be working in research jobs and that type of thing, and lab work, but most of the cleaning staff wouldn't probably need child-care facilities. But they need child-care facilities particularly during school holidays because some of them have young kids going to school. When I was on the cleaning staff we discussed the possibility of the child-care facilities that were set up for the academic staff being made available to the cleaning staff because when the children are on holidays usually the kindergarten is closed down. So it was just lying empty. There was no way in the word – they weren't going to have us or our brats.

'Work-based' versus 'community-based' child care

Since the child-care problems of women in the paid workforce have been receiving attention, the debate about where centres should be located has spilled over to some extent to the more important question of how centres should be run.

So-called work-based child care is usually taken to mean child-care facilities located in or near the workplace. Often ownership or management by the employer is implied, usually with access only to employees of that company. The disadvantages of such a scheme are easy to list: many workplaces present physically unsuitable environments for child care; they may require children to become commuters instead of being cared for close to home; company-controlled centres may not be eligible for public funding nor subject to public regulation; standards may be minimal, and not based on the best interest of the child; the service, which out to be a right, may be used as a lever in bargaining about working conditions; and the ideals of parent or user participation and control may be impossible to achieve given the employer-employee relationship.

There are only a few work-based centres of this type in Australia. Most advocates of work-based care have something rather different in mind, which will be described below.

So-called community-based child care has been taken to mean child care located in residential areas, open to children of parents whether in the paid workforce or not, and managed by a co-operative system involving parents, local organisations or possibly local government. It has been criticized for being, in practice, less responsive to the needs of parents who are in the paid workforce full time, who lack the opportunity or skills to influence participatory planning processes.

Doubtless the pros and cons of each approach could be explained in far greater detail – and have been. However, the debate has been rather misplaced. Fortunately, most people involved in trying to establish child-care services have made sure that the debate has moved on and, broadly speaking, a consensus has been reached on two points: the management and control of child-care services is enormously important, and should be quite firmly in the hands of the used without being influenced by financial interests or other pressures; and secondly, the needs of working parents, especially women, call for urgent attention, not because of the labour market policies of the moment, but as of right. Once these principles are established it becomes clear that location is not, in itself, an important consideration, except in the sense that facilities should be accessible. This could mean establishing them on public transport routes near residential areas, schools, shops or workplaces. In fact, although land-use planners tend rigidly to separate functions, mixed land uses are still found, and women more so than men tend to work relatively close to home.

Union involvement in child care

One good outcome of the debate about work-based child care is that it has focused more attention on the question of what women workers want, and how they might get it. This has led child-care workers to turn to unions, partly because unions control access to the workplace where women can be asked about their child-care needs and preferences, partly because the shop floor or local branch level of union activity may become a forum for women to articulate their child-care needs and jointly take action about them, and partly also because unions are perceived as having power that the community service sector lacks.

For example, in 1976 Merle Brown, former Childhood Services Officer of the Melbourne suburb of Coburg, said:

Unions are in a unique position to create pressure for the formulation of adequate policies by government and employer bodies. However, unless women union members demand a commitment to the issue of child-care services, it is unlikely that the trade union movement will use its power to achieve this essential service for working parents and their children.[17]

In some cases involvement of both unions and employers has been recommended, with no distinction being drawn between the roles of the two. The Royal Commission into Human Relationships concluded:

We consider it important not only to extend the scope of child-care services but also to involve both employers and unions in planning and providing facilities essential to working parents. Work-based child care may have some advantages, provided that physical conditions are suitable and that parents are not tied to the job by the lack of alternatives. There is a clear need here for unions to be involved in planning the arrangements.[18]

However, most community workers have sought co-operation of unions rather than employers because they do not want employers involved in planning or management of services, and because they realise that in order to establish or improve child-care facilities, community organization and political pressure is needed before planning can take place. Unions are seen as part of that process.

At a meeting between representatives from welfare, child care and union peak council in Melbourne in 1979, union involvement in child care was discussed.[19] Community workers expressed a strong view that unions needed to get back to the local grassroots level of organization, and learn from the non-hierarchical approach taken by many community organisations over the past ten years. Participants felt that although progress had been made since 1973, when only two unions had child-care policies, most unions were still uncomfortable about child care. This could be because they fear having to take financial responsibility for it, because their role has not been made clear and they are not accustomed to working with community groups.

The Working Women's Centre in Melbourne has maintained for several years that child care is a union issue.[20] Why this is so will obviously have a big effect on the form union involvement should take. At the joint meeting mentioned above, it was suggested that union involvement 'started off on a bad foot' with the debate over child-care centres located in the workplace. If this type of child care is preferred, then unions have a role in serving claims to employers for the establishment or support of such centres and negotiating about how they are to be managed. However, if child-care services are not to be linked to one workplace or employer, then a different role is indicated for unions. As Ruth Crow has said, the issue in the 1970s was 'who is controlling things?' i.e., who is controlling the planning process, child-care services and other community facilities? However, the issue in the 1980s must take into account technological change and unemployment. Child care should not be exclusively linked to full employment and women in the full-time paid workforce, but to a broader concept of community needs. Union involvement, she suggests, should be built on the broader sense of social responsibility that is developing, and the linking of community needs with the possibility of creating jobs in the service sector.[21]

At a seminar on child care sponsored by the Australian Council of Salaried and Professional Associations (ACSPA) in 1978, Linda Rubinstein, former child-care co-ordinator of the Working Women's Centre, made a similar point when she said there was a need for unions to take up 'alternative economic policies which take consideration of the social needs of our people' in response to unemployment.[22] She saw child care as an important area of union work for several reasons:

It is ludicrous to talk about equality for women in the workforce if this is not linked to taking from them some of the burden of the 'doubleday' – the fact that women in our society have almost total responsibility for the care of children.

She also commented that if unions want to involve their members, they should see child care as a pre-condition. Many women concerned with the under-representation of women in union activities have made this point: until men take equal responsibility at home, women cannot participate equally at work or in union affairs.

Anna Stewart, of the Vehicle Builders Employees' Federation, speaking at the same seminar, said that child care had been denied and ignored by government, employers and unions in Australia. The problem had been 'compounded by the concentration of large numbers of women in the semi and unskilled areas of work, unable to influence their unions or their employers because of their dual home and work commitments'.[23]

Nevertheless, unions have been influenced, perhaps partly due to the long memories of women who become involved in their unions after their children are grown up, and to the priority that women give to the issue of child care.

Child care was one of the five areas of urgent concern of the Working Women's Charter Campaign of 1977. After the ACTU adopted its charter in the same year, child care and maternity leave were selected by a special conference of unions as priority issues for action. Both were related to women's right to work, for even though maternity leave gives a woman a job to come back to after the birth of a child, lack of child care can prevent her from doing so.

The ACTU charter supports child-care facilities that are community based, or controlled by a union committee on the job if located in the workplace, that are low cost, have hours suitable for shiftworkers, and that include a range of services such as before- and after-school care, school holiday care and so on. ACSPA has spelt out principles more clearly in its child-care policy.[24] It calls for government funding of child care, with unions raising the demand that employers take on some financial responsibility. It also spells out that the centres themselves should be low cost to the users, high quality, encourage maximum participation by parents, offer just conditions to employees and be open at suitable hours for working parents.

Several individual unions have developed child-care policies. For example the Australian Clerical Officers' Association supports residential or work-based community child care for the general community as well as calling for centres to be set up for Australian government employees. The Australian Insurance Employees' Union in 1975 recognised the role of unions in pursuing the need for child care. The Vehicle Builders Employees' Federation, the Food Preservers' Union and the Clothing and Allied Trades' Union have all tried, so far without success, to include child care in their logs of claims. The

Clothing Union has also been involved in the establishment of child care related to the Commonwealth Clothing Factory at Coburg. The Hospital Employees' Federation is hoping to establish a centre for its members in the Heidelberg area of Melbourne, and the ABC Staff Association has bought a house in Sydney intended for use as a child-care centre.

Various strategies such as lobbying the government, setting up their own services, making industrial claims and working with community groups have been started by unions. The three Victorian teacher unions have child-care policies that are uniquely important because they touch on the role of schools in the community as well as the needs that teachers, as parents, have for child care. The VSTA's policy supports the establishment of child care in schools, both ports the establishment of child care in schools, both for the children of teachers, younger children of families with students attending the wider community. It specifies that child care should be co-operative, non-profit and run by a committee of parents.

Linda Rubinstein has suggested ways in which unions can be involved in child care, such as discussing the issue at meetings in the workplace, at meetings of shop stewards and officials, conferences, and trade union education courses; distributing information; conducting surveys to provide information about their members' needs and to stimulate debate; making industrial claims; and working on committees with local community groups.

At present, child care is not considered by the Conciliation and Arbitration Commission to be an 'industrial issue' in the sense of coming within the jurisdiction of industrial tribunals. However, some unions are trying to change this. And as Linda Rubinstein has said:

. . . it is however, an industrial issue where it counts most, in the factories, the shops, the offices and in the homes of the many thousands of women who would take paid employment if they could make arrangements for their children.[25]

In Melbourne, two projects have been launched as examples of union involvement in community child care.

The Moorabbin project

The ACTU AND ACSPA (the two peak councils amalgated at the end of 1979) received a grant of $100 000 from the Office of Child Care to set up a child-care centre in Moorabbin, one of Melbourne's southern bayside suburbs. There were good grounds for choosing the area as it has a large industrial region with thousands of parents working, no government-subsidised child-care centres, and there have been reports of unsatisfactory commercial minding centres. The ACTU and ACSPA are working with local community groups, union members and councils to set up the centre, and a survey amongst union members has revealed that there are many parents wanting to use it. It will be a small centre with a 'homey' atmosphere and parent involvement will be encouraged. As well as providing a service, the project will be an educational process for the people and groups involved.

The Footscray project

Footscray, in Melbourne's western suburbs, was selected for similar reasons. It has a lot of industry, many people both live and work in the area and it has inadequate existing services: one council day nursery, one Victorian Association day nursery, two commercial centres and one family day-care scheme. The project was still at the exploratory stage in early 1980. Western Region Children's Services Officer,

Lynne Wannan, has made contact with ten unions and received a varied response. Some have become involved in the discussion of needs in the area. Women in several clothing factories, a hospital and several schools have been surveyed. The problems of what to do when children are sick, during school holidays and before and after school have been mentioned frequently. The project will probably concentrate on improving existing services rather than setting up a new centre.

The experience of these two projects shows that while union attitudes are beginning to change, implementation of policies is an uphill battle, requiring community education and organization as well as pressure on government funding bodies. What is at stake, in this case, is the distribution of resources within the community. Unions can change that distribution in favour of their members in the course of industrial negotiation. However, given the dilemmas that would arise if unions were successful in bargaining directly with employers to provide child care, such as employers' insisting on work-based child-care centres, it is more likely that unions will favour less direct methods such as supporting or joining community organisations seeking government funding for child-care facilities. The danger is that with limited funding available these initiatives will do no more than create one or two models whose examples will not be followed.

CHAPTER 9

'Walking out the door'

Women and Unions

Throughout the discussion of women in the workforce in the past few years, unionism has invariably been seen as problematic.

Firstly it is often said that the union membership rates of women are low. Various reasons are given for this: the type of industries and occupations in which women are concentrated, the number of women who do part-time or temporary work or who see their job as secondary, the competing demands of domestic responsibilities, and the failure of the unions to give a high priority to contacting unorganized sections of the workforce or to regard women as important potential members. The second point in the debate about women and unions is that few women participate at any of the higher levels mentioned in union affairs. The further up the hierarchy, the fewer women there are. Many unions with a large female membership have no women officials and few women organisers.

Thirdly, it is said that unions do not operate in a way that suits women. They do not take up issues that are of relevance to women in variety of ways reflect and perpetuate the sexism of the larger society. For instance, until recently most unions sidestepped the problems encountered specifically by women, such as sexual harassment, discriminatory hiring and firing and the need for child care. It has only been after persistent efforts by the Working Women's Centre, the Women's Trade Union Commission, the charter campaign and the various union women's committees that unions have begun to regard child care as an industrial issue and to recognize that most women have their paid job and their unpaid job in the home.

Union membership alone does not make a great difference to the bargaining power of women workers to command higher pay or better conditions. Unless women are organized as rank-and-file groups or as participating union members, shop stewards, delegates, organisers and officials, these gains are unlikely to be achieved, irrespective of the attitudes of the union leadership.

Union membership

Historically, Australian trade unions have shown a reluctance to include women as members, particularly as participants in the union power structure. Until the 1860s trade unionism was based on skilled tradesmen protecting their interests from employers and other workers. Chinese and women were excluded. In the 1890s the president of the Sydney Tailoresses' Union, Peter Strong, argued in favour of unionizing women on the grounds that if women's wages were equal to men's, employers would prefer men to women.

This background, together with the persistence of the male breadwinner ideal, has resulted in a lower rate of union membership for women compared to men. Throughout the 1960s, women's union membership rate was stable at around 37 per cent. In the 1970s, however, it rose steadily as unionism became more widespread in white-color industries. Meanwhile the proportion of male members has steadily declined.

The Australian Bureau of Statistics has two sources of information on unionism. One is an annual survey of unions concerning their membership. However, since not all unions keep records of the sex of their members, the figures on the proportion of males and females is imprecise. The survey of December 1978 showed that an average of 46 per cent of female employees and 63 per cent of male employees were union members.[1] In Queensland and Tasmania, over half the female employees were union members, whereas in New South Wales and Western Australia the figure was 48 percent, in South Australia is was 44 per cent and in Victoria it was 43 per cent. In Victoria, Queensland and Western Australia, there was a slight decrease in membership rates from the previous year.

The other source of information is a household survey of unionism carried out in conjunction with regular labourforce sample surveys. These surveys probably provide more accurate figures, although they understate unionism slightly by counting only union membership related to the person's main present job. This survey showed that in November 1976, 43 per cent of female employees and 56 per cent of male employees were union members.[2]

Rates of membership vary enormously according to occupation and industry. The general picture, with few exceptions, seems to be that the rate of unionization of women is highest in industries that do not employ many women, and lowest in industries which are the major employers of women. For instance, the wholesale and retail trade, the second-largest employer of women, had the lowest rate of female membership. Only 31 per cent of women in that industry were union members in 1976, despite huge increases following union recruitment drivers amongst shop assistants, and closed-shop agreements with major retailers. By contrast, 75 per cent of women in the communication industry, and 59 per cent in public administration, both employers of relatively few women, were union members. In the community service industries, the largest employers of women, half are union members. Just over half the women employed in manufacturing are union members. Other industries which are significant employers of women – entertainment, recreation, hotels, restaurants and personal services – had 36 per cent of women unionized, and finance, insurance and real estate had 38 per cent of women unionised.

A similar picture is given by comparing the main occupational groupings in which women are found. In the household survey, the highest level of union membership was found amongst tradeswomen, production-process workers and labourers, two-thirds of whom were union members. Yet they represented only 12 per cent of female employees. Union membership was also relatively high amongst professional and technical workers, 54 per cent of whom were union members. Union membership amongst transport and communication workers, and amongst service, sport and recreation workers was about average, while clerical and sales occupations, which together comprised 46 per cent of female employees, had rather low union membership rates of 37 per cent and 30 per cent respectively.

So union membership rates among women vary from about one-third to two-thirds of the female employees in a given occupation, averaging about 43 per cent because of the low unionism rates in the clerical and sales areas. Union membership rates for women overall are about 75 per cent of those for men. This is surprisingly high, given the interrupted participation of most women in the paid workforce.

One of the myths that abound about women workers is that married women are not interested in unions. The ABS figures do not reflect interest, only membership rates, but give no evidence of any differences between married and unmarried women.

The ABS figures give some information about the union membership rates of Australia's increasingly significant overseas-born workforce: 25 per cent of female union members are overseas born, and rates of membership vary according to country of birth. While 43 per cent of women employees were union members, according to the household survey, 55 per cent of women from Yugoslavia, 54 per cent of women from Italy and 44 per cent of women from Greece were union members. Countries such as Turkey, Lebanon and the South American countries were not distinguished in the figures but the general rate of union membership for women from other non-English-speaking countries was 49 per cent, partly because of their concentration in manufacturing and service industries with their high overall rate of unionism. Women workers from English-speaking countries such as the United Kingdom, and Ireland, Canada, United States, New Zealand and South Africa had a lower than average rate of union membership.

Rawson, in his book on unions and unionists in Australia, comments that the changing character of the workforce since 1945 brought with it a decline in the proportion of unionized workers. He claims, perhaps more charitably than most commentators, that 'the later 1950s and 1960s saw Australian unionism responding to the changing workforce but doing so slowly and incompletely, an so falling behind'.[3]

While noting the increase in women union members, he is, however, unsure of the effect his will have on the union movement. He describes women as 'very different from men in their opinions and activities' as union members. In terms of the traditional image of unionists, namely being actively involved, satisfied with their union, supporting the ALP and wanting the union to be affiliated with the ALP, he claims that women are 'not such "good unionists" as men'.

This judgment is a very controversial one and has been opposed by other researchers as well as by women trying to overcome the stereotype of women as 'bad unionists'.

Rawson does make the point that in the past unionists have used their union politically, 'compensating for their socially disadvantaged situation, to bring about extensive social change'. Since disadvantaged groups in the community include migrants, women and Aboriginals, increased political activism within the union movement might be expected from these groups, assuming they can overcome the disadvantages that they suffer within the unions themselves. Yet Rawson agrees with several other writers who have elaborated on the theme that 'trade unionism has so far been slow in endeavouring to accommodate itself to [the] various situations and demands' of these groups.

Ross Martin, in his account of trade unions in Australia, says that:

The typical union member is a white, male manual worker, who is over twenty-four years of age and was born in either Australia or the British Isles, This, of course, is another way of saying that Aborigines, women, white-collar workers, young people and non-British migrants are minority groups in Australian trade unionism. Of all these minority groups, only women are recognized, in the official statistics of union membership.[4]

Participate in unions

A high rate of union membership cannot be assumed to indicate knowledge of unions, support for them or participation in them. When asked what they knew about unions, three-fifths of the women interviewed in the CURA survey had nothing to say.[5] Of those who did comment, three-fifths said they knew nothing about unions and did not understand the English-language information they were given. A quarter made positive comments, saying that unions were good, were necessary or helped to improve conditions.

The lack of knowledge and lack of positive response amongst the women surveyed contrasts with the high rate of union membership found. Over three-quarters said they were union members, although quite a few were not sure or did not answer. This is, nevertheless, a far higher rate than that of the workforce as a whole. The women were asked why they had or had not joined a union. Fewer than half of the members had joined for positives reasons, such as 'to get better wages and conditions'. 'because it is good' or 'because it is important to all', whereas almost one in three had joined because it was compulsory, and the others were not sure why they had joined. Non-union members gave various reasons for not having joined. Almost half said that they either had not been asked or they did not speak English but would be interested if they were approached, especially in their own language. Others felt that union fees were a waste of time and that unions were no help, while a few women said they could not afford the fees.

Many women whom I interviewed about unionism had followed traditional loyalties to the principle of unionism. When I asked them how they had become involved in their union they gave answers such as, 'My father was a strong unionist', or I just believe in it'. Even women who disagreed with what the union was actually doing had a strong commitment to it in principle.

Although union membership may be just a tradition that the worker is upholding, involvement or continued participation depends on what the union does, how it does it and how this fits in with the individual member's circumstances. One woman became interested in her union when meetings were called during a dispute, and continued her involvement after her children had grown up:

School cleaners are pretty well of a union mind – you know, they like to stick with conditions on their jobs. This union has always put out a lot of literature if there is anything going on. Well, in 1966 they tried to put contract cleaners in the school and the union sent us all a letter and we had to go to this meeting. And that was the first meeting I ever went to. Even if you hadn't been union minded, you know, we got so much about this contract cleaning. 'You must be here', sort of thing. It stirs you up a bit. It was the first time I had anything to do with them at all. I was always a bit union minded – my husband [was] – although he is not as much union minded as he was years ago. His father was a real militant, too, because I lived with them when I first came up here and I think a bit of that brushed off on me. I have always gone to union meetings since then, always been interested. But when my son was younger, I couldn't do much. I go to Sydney [from Newcastle] whenever we have problems now, but I wouldn't have like to have gone overnight and stayed when he was younger.

Sometimes joining a union means being involved in a large and important campaign:

So the first thing you do when you go to work at the post office – I was on a counter – you join the union. Just at that time, by late 1966, our union was well into the five-day week struggle. Postal offices worked Saturday mornings in those days. The Postal Clerks' Union and the Postal Workers' Union – that's the union I've always been in – were engaged in this five-day week struggle. In 1967, the counter officers in the post office engaged in their first strike. It had never been known before. The five-day week campaign really hotted up. We had a big Town Hall rally and busloads of people came from Wollongong and Newcastle and marched in a body – 'Newcastle greets the five-day week' – and there were great claps and cheers. It was marvelous. Real consciousness-raising. Wollongong arrives. Western District arrives. We're clapping and cheering and the campaign for the five-day week is on and the government reacted by going for us under Section 55 of the Public Service Act.

Some women were able to draw their fellow workers into a union by demonstrating tangible benefits:

The union was making a drive to get people into the union and the union secretary came out and saw me and I [told him] I had been talking with them about it and trying to convince them and then we started to get the moves toward equal pay and I really drove it home to them. I explained to the girls how the union had never let up, and that this was the result of this struggle from 1950 onwards, when equal pay had been taken away from us, and we were now going to get it gradually. This had an effect on them because when they started to get more money that really made a difference in their attitude to the union. I got one in and then I got another one. Then I asked the union officers to come out and we had a meeting in the lunch room and the ones that were hanging back finally joined. We got all but one man in. And I said to him, 'A lot of your criticisms of the union, some of those things are true. There are trade union bureaucracies. There are good trade union leaders. There are trade union leaders who are just seat warmers.' I said I am aware of all that but a union is the only thing a worker has and a union is as good as its members make it.

By contrast, some employers have compulsory unionism agreements with the unions, and employees' union fees are automatically deducted from their pay. This often causes resentment and reduces the changes of any effective rank-and-file organization. A retail clerk in a large department store put it this way:

I think the firm itself is really more interested than its staff because they at least come in on the deal with five big retailers to have the staff join the union and there was a tremendous lot of kick-up on the staff with the ones that didn't want to join. Some people even left rather than join. There's a bit of a let-out clause where if you're doing confidential work for the boss – well, a lot of people who really shouldn't do so take advantage of that. And there's lots of people who don't really want to be in it, and 87 cents a week gets taken out of your pay, but they never go near the union and they are not interested in it. But out firm won't allow union reps, probably they could break through. I think the union should really do something, but the union has a bit of a cop-out I think because they always say, 'We're very democratic, we'll only do something if you want it.' Well, if you've got a lot of non-unionists who don't want anything, nothing is ever going to happen. But I've always been interested in it, but the other girls, they think that everything comes from the boss.

In some cases, where closed shop agreements between the union and management existed, the management rather than workers supported unionism:

I find, and I don't know whether this is a valid reason, a lot of girls come from the country and they seem to be more anti-union than people who are brought up in the city. Well, I suppose out of our staff, there's three now in the pay office that are originally from the country, and they all pay their money but they are not interested. One time, the union decide to have half-day stop-work meeting, or the whole day it turned out, to discuss an award because the shop assistants were doing it and they decided to back them. Everybody was horrified and in the end it was the boss who made them go! They didn't want the conflict between the ones who went out and the ones who didn't go out. But, anyway, they all went out but they didn't like it at all because they were horrified to think that they would have to do anything like that.   Another woman, a cleaner, was strongly opposed to compulsory unionism because she felt that the union could then neglect members:

One time they used to have compulsory unionism in the State awards here and when that was cut out the unions were really upset. In fact, I got myself very unpopular with them because I said that I thought it was the best thing that ever happened and they were really furious. They said 'All this money we are going to lose'. I said, 'Good, that might force you to get off your bums and bloody well organise the workers on the basis of doing something for them rather than depending on it being done through legal means'. They weren't very impressed. As a matter of fact, I'm very opposed to the idea of the bosses collecting the dues. In fact, I just won't pay my dues through the blooming job. Even now, I go out and pay them at the union office. It is a lot less convenient but I'm opposed to [bosses collecting dues] on principle. For a start-off, it is much harder to develop job organization when you haven't got delegates or when you have got delegates that don't have regular contact with you. At least collecting the dues did force your delegates to go around and see people. It certainly does make for difficulties. Particularly if you've got somebody not very happy about paying dues. But then I think here again you've got to expect that there will always be a few that are going to dodge and duck around it. Certainly you may get those by making it compulsory and taking it out of their pay but, at the same time, I'd much prefer to see the position exist where you convince people about the need for unions and it is a conscious act rather than one that is forced on them. There is a difference between it being forced on them by it being a union job where it is compulsory because the workers say it is and when it is the bosses and the union together.

I'm afraid I resent that very much and I don't care what anyone says, I think that activity at the union – like from the union officials and activity on the job – decreased considerably as soon as ever they got the deduction scheme on the job because people just didn't see any need.

Many women join a union believing that their rights and conditions are thus protected, only to discover later that they are not, as one delegate's comments illustrated. She was speaking about meatworks in Queensland, where the amount of work a women has to do is determined by the ratio of follow-on labour to tally labour:

You know some of those women are working flat out. There are times when the women are so used to doing it, it just comes automatic and they don't have time to do their work properly. And then you get inspector come in and find one bone and they are in trouble. We had one particular place, I went out there for a trip and I was amazed at this meatworks because the union officials out there didn't know a lot about the union and they didn't know a lot about the women's situations. The women had gone home just after 12 o'clock and the boss found a couple of chips of bone in the packing cases. He went to the delegate's home and brought those women back and made them unpack all those cases, undo and rewrap them and they worked until a quarter to four. They never got pain any more. Now, when I found out about it, I reported it and the chap said 'That's not right'. When I went to the organizer, I said 'Well, it is right, I've got the women'. So anyhow, they investigated and I went to the general manager, or the chief industrial officer. He said, 'Well, I didn't realise these things were going on'. Now you see it was just a little shed that nobody knew anything about.

Nor can it be assumed that people working under an award are automatically protected by it. The example below shows that even if a workplace is 'organised' to the extent of having union membership and a delegate, ignorance and intimidation still lead workers to accept conditions which contravene the award. My impression is that violations of awards are quite widespread, and that it takes an exceptionally zealous union member or official to do anything about it. As one women explained:

If you had've seen those women, they were flat out. I would never have believed it possible that people could work like it. I said to the women, 'Why don't you stand up for yourselves and your rights?' One replied, 'Nellie, look we've don't it and we've been told if we cause any trouble, we'll be out the gate'. So I even told the secretary that. Well, he said, 'Nellie, I better get your big boys to understand, otherwise I'll be taking it a little bit further not only with the union. I'll be taking it to the Federal office.' These are things that happen in the works. Those women were not educated enough to know what their ration should have been, what they were really doing and things like that. They just go along their merry way and the boss says you do this and you do that.

The protection afforded by union membership is obvious in some workplaces. But even where union organization exists, its effectiveness is reduced by the recession and the resulting insecurity of employment.

Some women also complained about being undermined by having several unions that do not support each other on the job:

We've got three unions here. We've got ours, we've got the ETU [Electrical Trades Union] and the woodwork. And they won't stand by us, if we fight for anything, like wage increases, although they get it; they won't come out, they won't support us in any way.

Even conditions in the factory – they won't come out for anything at all. I mean we'll go home for a half a day or ban overtime, but there's no such thing as them banning overtime. We've had a ban on overtime for anything up to six months. They create the bad conditions we've got. Like there's sawdust going all over the place, they're right in the middle of it. Anyone with glasses – you can't dam well see, and they're standing there working saws, and they won't move out of it. We'll stop work and the management comes along and says – 'Well, they're working'.

The caution and downright fear about unionism shown by many women when they start a new job underlines again the real weakness of many unions. Although they are often portrayed as powerful, this is belied by the fact that workers in some industries dare not join or even speak about unions, and sometimes have to resort to undercover membership. Not all unions are able to protect the workers' right to union membership without reprisals. One woman, a clothing worker who had recently started a new job, described how circumspect she had to be about union membership or activity:

I've been asking a few questions. I've been very very careful how I ask the questions because nobody knows I'm involved in the union and I don't want to upset anybody. I would like to see everyone be in the union, but I've only been there three weeks. You have to get to know people first. It's no good you walking in and saying, 'Are you in the union? Why aren't you in the union?' and all this because they tell you to jump in the lake. Just got to be patient and it will come natural with the situation. Something would happen and you would say, 'Well, did you ring the union?' And they say "No'. You say, 'Why haven't you rung the union?' Often they want you to, but that will all take time because we have to be very diplomatic. Especially for the factory where management doesn't believe in unions. The boss just doesn't want it and you go and you'll be the first one they are going to get rid of because they can see that you are going to cause trouble.

Even if no one is directly threatened by the sack, intimidation is still effective:

So there is no union. So first of all this union talk. The first thing we go for are extra fans and ventilators. Somehow or other I became the spokeswoman. I was pushed. So I go over to see Lipps, the foreman. The girls called him luscious Lipps. They hated him. He tried to be kind within his rights, but he was also driven by the management up the top and they had a peculiar set-up. Well, the upshot of it was we discussed getting the union out so it was agreed that we should ring the union and I was given that job and some of the old hands said, 'You will never get a union here. No one will ever stick.' Although down in their other factory, the sheet metal workers had got a union.

We had no way, they say, of going to the management. We haven't got a voice. Even the most timid women admitted that then. So I rang the union and I got on to the ETU, the Electrical Trades Union; and yes, they will send someone out. And I said, 'It is in the women's interests as well as the management's, to have a way in which grievances, needs and wants can be expressed.' He informs me that they had had undercover members of the union for seven years in various factories in Sydney and I was appalled. I said 'This is Australia: why do unionists have to be under cover? It shouldn't be so.' He said that was a fact of life, so anti-union were some of these factories. So he did a very foolish thing. He comes to the management and they announce over the inter-communication system that there was an organizer from the ETU outside at the Pittwater Street gate and members may see him in their lunch hour and staff members may interview him if they so wish. When it was announced like this, it was a master stroke from the company's point of view. A lot of the women went to water. Anyway, the whistle goes to 12.30 for the first lunch break and out we go and about three of us joined up.

Myself, this girl who I had told you about who was a rough diamond as they say; and one other woman. Then the big debate goes on. Lots of accusations, counter-accusations about people saying they would join and wouldn't join and so on. I said the best way to look at it is that at least we have got the nucleus. Some of us have joined but we will just have to work at getting the rest in. We keep on this line and we get a few more one by one.

One woman described her involvement in her union in this way:

Well, I was working and the union wasn't getting very far in advancing our conditions and wages so I got myself elected to the council. It's a strange union. You have to live in Sydney to be able to be on the Federal Council. There's no State, there's only divisional committee around Australia who had no real power. All the power is in the Federal Council. They don't fly people even for meetings or anything like that and there hasn't been an election for members of the council for as long as I have been in the union which is something like fifteen years, sixteen years. It is always neatly arranged that only enough nominate every two or three years to get in. I don't like that either, and that is one of the reason I finally got off because I hadn't been elected by the membership and I thought well, until there's an election I won't get back on. But I stayed on for three years and I had dreams of doing all these nice things like child care and things like that, and found that it was so badly run and so badly organized that there were other basic things like conditions and rates of pay that had to be looked at. I found that I was being discriminated against work-wise and so I got off.

Such discrimination against active unionists was often mentioned, as has been discussed in Chapter Four.

Women frequently expressed dissatisfaction with the lack of real organization undertaken by union organisers:

[The union organisers] saw their main job as organizing women into the union rather than actually doing something. We weren't able to get through to them that to really make women conscious of the need to join the trade union you had to do something for them. In fact, I've been told that women that are not members of the union, they refuse to take up their case. That puts you in a pretty bad position no matter what you are trying to take up, if you have got to go and tell a women, 'Well you have got to fork out for dues for a trade union before the union is prepared to do anything'. Then there is no guarantee that they are going to do anything for you!

This can be partly attributed to the financial and practical difficulties of unions, as one official explained, but the story does not end there:

We haven't got big buildings or anything like that and we never have much money in the bank but we have got members and we've driven for members. I can remember being on the executive of the Clerks' Union when we had 19 000 members and we went down to 9000 members after we had the question of compulsory unionism thrown out in New South Wales. From there, we have built up to 31 000 and it's been damned hard work, and we have been broke more often than we have been flush. We've gone to the members a couple of times at election time and we haven't had a penny in the bank. We have been broke and we've had overdrafts and we have been chided by our opposition because we had overdrafts. I don't know how the hell they thought we were going to carry on if we didn't have an overdraft. But that's the politics of the business. But what I'm getting at is that we've made every effort all along the line to always push for membership and I think really and truly at the moment we are doing well. Also, we have tried to give service but in an organisation like ours you cannot give sufficient service to people with you all of the time and this is where you get into difficulty. This is where you lose members too because it's very hard when you've got them in, say, half a dozen different places and there would be hundreds of places that we would have in the commercial area.

The same woman felt that although most workers could see the benefits of union membership, they did not want to incur the costs:

There are other reasons for people not wanting to join a union but in my honest opinion, it is this question of paying for it. And of course it has become expensive. $44 a year now for clerks. You'll only get about 1 per cent of people who are truly anti or truly don't believe in unionism and I would reckon that the rest of them want to trade in on it and they want to get the benefits from it but they won't want to pay for it. I reckon if you gave it to them for nothing they would all be unionized because they can all see the benefits of it and they all come to you when they get into trouble or when there is trouble brewing.

A different view was put by a rank-and-file union member who felt that she and her fellow workers had been 'sold out' by the officials whose salaries are paid out of union fees:

Everybody in the place pays $52 a year union fees, you know. That's a heal of a lot. What annoys me is we are paying this $52 a year and what is happening? [The secretary], for a start, has sold us out. Every year we are paying him and we are paying his wages and what's he doing? We are paying him to kick us in the arse, which he has done and is going to do it again and again and, in fact, it was even said that if the actual union or the union officials didn't lift the bans he would sack the whole lot of the officials and take over himself and he is supposed to be on our side you know. I can't see that at all. And we didn't want to come out to be totally anti-union. They are helping us. We don't want to change the union. We can't sort of oppose the union at this stage because we haven't got any power behind us at all.

We are only just starting out and until such times as we can get more people interested, perhaps then we can oppose the union to a certain extent, and work with them to change them a little bit.

Discussion of the participation – or more specifically the lack of participation – by women in trade unions is often confined to the easily measurable aspects.

In 1977 there were thirty-two unions throughout Australia that could be described as 'women's unions' in that half or more of their members were women.[6] They included unions representing airline hostesses, mannequins and models, nurses and other health workers, clothing workers, teachers, hairdressers, welfare workers, shop assistants, clerks, municipal employees, tobacco and cigarette workers, bootworkers, confectioners, food process workers and laundry workers. Clearly one important characteristic of women in the union movement is that they are concentrated in large numbers in relatively few unions covering areas of traditional female employment.

This could account for the limited impact of women on the labour movement as a whole, but it is not an adequate explanation since in fact women are not represented in the power structures of those unions in which they predominate as members.

It is hard to say how many women hold office in unions. Rhonda Galbally has shown that only ten Victorian unions had a significant number of women in full-time executive or paid positions in 1976.[7] All the officials of the Royal Nurses' Federation, two-thirds of those of the Food Preservers' and Insurance Employees' Unions, half of those of the Airline Hostesses', 4th Division Australian Public Servants' and Victorian Primary Teachers' Unions, one-third of the Shop Assistants' Union and a quarter of the Bank Employees' and Federated Clerks' Union were women. Many of their officials were appointed rather than elected.

Ross Martin, in his account of trade unions in Australia, said:

In recent years, there has been a clear expansion in the number of both full-time and part-time women officials. During 1973, for example, there was a small rash of 'first' appointments which were significantly well-publicised by the unions concerned.[8]

He adds, however, that 'there tends to be an element of tokenism in much of the representation that they do have' because minorities have become 'fashionable' with some union leaders.

Over recent years, fewer than 5 per cent of delegates to the ACTU congress have been women. There are few women delegates to the State councils. Ken Stone, as Secretary of the Victorian Trades Hall Council, commented in 1977 on the 'slow and steady progression of women in trade unions over the past five years'.[9] Fourteen of the 360 delegates were women. In 1978, Gail Cotton received much publicity when she became the first woman to join the executive of the Victorian Trades Hall Council. There were still no women on the federal executive of the ACTU in 1980, although presumably this is only a matter of time. Jan Marsh, the first female ACTU advocate, led the debate on the Working Women's Charter at the 1977 congress. The ACSPA, whose membership included more women than the ACTU's, had only one woman on its federal executive in 1977. The third of the peak councils, CAGEO, had a 'non-participant observer' on its federal executive, along with an active women's committee which was established in 1971.

Despite the increasing activity of women at the rank-and-file level and minor official level, it seems that years will pass before women are regarded as normal rather than novelties within the union movement.

Most unions have both elected and appointed positions. The outcome of elections depends a lot on how they are conducted, how many people vote, how well-informed they are, and so on. Office-holders have an advantage over challengers because of their greater access to members and to the union's communication channels. There have nevertheless been significant victories for women in union elections, especially women aligned with internal reform groups. Change is obviously more tightly controlled for appointed positions, as this comment from a male union official in a service industry shows:

I think that what we should do is say, right-oh, we've got twenty organisers, at least ten of them should be women, because something like that would be accepted. In actual fact, 75 per cent of them should be women, because you've get to reflect your membership outside. I don't know exactly what the female-male ratio is in our union, but it would be high. And none of our organisers are elected anyway: they're all appointed.

Recently we had a woman put in for the job. One of the reasons they didn't appoint her was that she was 'too pushy'. She's very capable; she is 'pushy', the same way that I'm 'pushy'. But she operates in a man's world and she's decided that she's gonna fuckin' operate their way . . . and because she's operating that way, they just wiped her out. She's one of the best delegates we've got in the area, and the main reason for not appointing her was the she just thinks too much like a man. That's what the bastard said.

Most of the women I spoke to were more concerned with participation as rank-and-file members than executive positions. In some cases they felt women who joined the executive or took up some other position within the union lost touch with women workers and became little different from male officials. Mostly their comments showed that Australian unionism lacks a participatory structure and strong rank-and-file organisation. There are many reasons for lack of participation – such as family responsibilities and little encouragement – and few opportunities even for those who are interested. This is especially true with the 1980 recession, because employers have greater power to stop union activities, such as attendance at trade union education courses or the development of shop committees.

Migrant women have additional barriers to overcome. Although the women in the CURA study were critical of their unions, many felt strongly enough about certain issues to be willing to strike, and most felt that the unions ought to be pursuing these issues.[10] in addition to better pay and conditions, the issues of English lessons on the job, flexible working hours, child-care provisions and prevention of abusive treatment by the bosses were mentioned by about a third of the women. Throughout the CURA study women complained of undignified and abusive treatment by managers and supervisors. They felt that unions ought to be concerned about these and other social questions as well as the 'bread and butter' issues. Whereas a third of the women were willing to strike, twice as many believed their unions should be taking some action towards such goals.

When asked generally what else unions should be doing, the women interviewed in the CURA stud said that their union officials should visit and talk to workers more often, tell them more about what is going on, take the side of the women instead of the management, provide multilingual material, centres and interpreters, provide minutes of meetings in translation, involve migrant women as officials, improve conditions and have more consultation with workers, as well as safeguarding existing conditions.

The women I interviewed raised a variety of issues concerned with participation in union activities. They mentioned the difficulties of getting to night-time meetings, especially for women with family responsibilities, the reluctance of employers to give time off for union meetings, the importance of the shop steward in maintaining rank-and-file involvement, the lack of confidence and lack of information that makes women reluctant to act by themselves, and the resistance they meet from male officials when they do so.

The gulf between the rank-and-file membership of Australian unions and the officials in the hierarchy reflects the ambiguous position of unions – bargaining on behalf of workers for better conditions, while accepting the role of employers controlling the economic and work environment. The broad social inequalities based on sex and ethnicity reflect this class structure. It follows that the organisation of women and ethnic minorities is essential if unions are to become working-class organisations. Union officials have been slow to recognize this, as one organizer commented to me:

The issue of women developing, and the question of migrants, are the two main issues facing the trade union movement today. And both of them go together. They are so far out in front, in my opinion, that unless you can resolve those problems, you can't resolve anything. And, you know, the trade union movement doesn't know that.

Encet *et al.* claim that 'of all the voluntary associations, trade unions have been most resistant to women'.[11] however, these authors go on to point out that unions are 'responding to the growth of the female workforce and the impact of radical feminism'. They give a number of examples, including the Electrical Trades Union in New South Wales which set out to recruit women, improved its journal and, through pressure from women, improved safety conditions and amenities at electrical plants; the Hairdressers' Union in Victoria, in which young women took control out of the hands of the elderly men who had been running the union; the various white-collar unions representing bank officers, clerks, insurance employees and shop assistants, in which recruitment of women and appointment of female officials has been on the increase; and growing militancy amongst air hostesses, which led to their association becoming a closed shop.

Whatever the role of unions, and this varies enormously from industry to industry, the fact is that working conditions for many women remain very bad. In an economic system such as Australia's there is drudgery to be done, and there is a constant search for workers who will do it cheaply and uncomplainingly. The reasons why women and migrants from non-English-speaking countries fulfil this function have been explained earlier in this book. While unions cannot be held responsible for this situation, they have been blamed for allowing the poor working conditions of women to continue. Although in many cases they can be criticized for not giving a high priority to improving women's conditions and for failing to develop effective organisation of women workers, most union organisers will point out that it is the employer who sets the conditions and it is very difficult for unions to challenge that prerogative.

For many people who don't have first-hand experience, it is a shock to learn that in Australia, a supposedly rich country with powerful trade unions, many women, especially non-English-speaking migrants, work in squalid and dangerous conditions, where the supervision and the tasks are demeaning, the pay is low and there is little evidence of powerful organized labour at the shop floor, workbench or counter. Despite many labour laws and an intricate system of industrial arbitration in which unions play an important role, the post-war boom in manufacturing industry has left Australians with a large section of the working class enduring persistently poor working conditions.

Not surprisingly, various type of poor conditions tend to be found together. Chris Phillips, in a large survey of working life in Australia, reported that women, migrants, the poorly educated, the unskilled and the aged, were persistently disadvantaged as workers, having low pay, low security and dirty, arduous work with little freedom or opportunity.[12] Migrant women workers seemed to be the worst off, with two-thirds of them feeling they had no opportunities in life. While about a third of the women interviewed looked to management or supervisors to safeguard their interests at work, only 7 per cent looked to the trade unions.

As Phillips found, life for disadvantaged workers can be 'riddled with discouragement, worries, loneliness, and despair – for women much more so than men'. Those who felt most keenly the negative side of work and life were those least able to do anything about it by becoming involved in activities inside or outside the workplace which might provide support, hope or action for improvement. Nor have unions found a way to encourage or support migrants and women to get together for moral and practical support in dealing with problems of the workplace.

Active union members, both workers and officials, often complained to me about women not participating in union activities, and time off during working hours was frequently suggested as an encouragement. But union organisation must be strong enough to put forward the demand. Employers' reluctance to pay for union meetings was mentioned but one woman in the metal industry commented that although paid time for meetings was important, it was only a small step; the first step, perhaps, in making the union's resources available to members. It is interesting that she was talking about workers getting time off work and being paid by the union rather than by the employer.

In some industries, there is little in the way of union activities for rank-and-file members to participate in, even if they are highly motivated:

Rank-and-file people in [our union] just don't have a chance to go to meetings. I used to go to the shop stewards and say 'Look, I want to go to a meeting in Maroubra', and they would say, 'Oh well, we used to have meetings downtown, but they don't have them anymore', and stuff like that. Maree, when she worked there, found out that there was supposed to be a meeting on downtown. She'd waited around out the front of the place, doors were shut. She couldn't get in, and waited and waited. Eventually, this guy comes trotting over and he says, 'What do you want, love?' And she replied, 'Oh, where's the union meeting?' 'Oh look, that's good, but we haven't had to call one since 19--.' I don't know, it was something like six years anyway, since they had had a union meeting, you know, a general branch-type meeting. So he said, 'Oh, it's all right, come again. Next time, you'll have to bring, I don't know whether it's fifteen or twenty people to get a quorum.'

Another comment made quite often was that rank-and-file involvement in a union depended on the grass-roots work done by shop stewards, those workers who are the unionists' representatives.

As Toni, a Maltese woman who had been a shop steward in the Clothing Trades Union explained:

See, you've got to have it in yourself. They can't make you a shop steward. They can make you but a name but the work shop steward you've got to have in you. Not to go by the book, use your own common sense. Like you want to be treated yourself, in a fair way. If you think that way, then you get somewhere. But if you are afraid you're going to get the sack for a start, you say 'Why should I risk my job? Jobs are scarce.' Well then you should not be a shop steward anyway.

She felt that too many shop stewards were just in the position 'for the glory' and preferred to have a dramatic showdown and get the sack rather than slowly build up real strength on the shop floor.

Several women working together in a large service industry in Sydney analysed the reasons for the lack of effective union or rank-and-file activity: 'I have the feeling that management don't care about us – we are just little people in this place and they don't care. As long as the get their work done, they couldn't care less.'

The same women felt that they couldn't look to their union either:

I'm afraid we are not getting much help from the union. We get told about things far too late to be able to do anything about it. I know a lot of people say you should take more interest in what's going on. You try to but then if you're working and your husband is working and you've got a family or it's like June, she's single but she's got still a family and a home to care for. Well, travelling as well is the biggest bugbear. But you haven't got the time to go into these things as fully as you would like to. I feel with union work that you've got a lot of homework to do and I think this is why the structure of the union is falling down because a lot of them aren't right up with the information they should be sifting out and dealing with. I mean, there is a lot of work in being a union rep. I was asked to be one once but I mean, I can't. I've got to say no. I just can't do it, not with five children. How can I when I can't do the homework that is involved in it? To be a good rep, you have got to do this. The ordinary member should be made aware of what is going on and I think if they knew more of what was going on, they would participate more but you feel as though – again you're just a number.

In her article on women factory workers, Helen Hurwitz raises the question of how unions can 'broaden their traditional functions in relation to migrant workers' problems in general and migrant women workers' problems in particular'.[13] she recognizes that some unions with significant representation of women are preparing to try various approaches in dealing with the concerns of women members, 'the major preoccupation being with how to properly inform rank-and-file members about the function of the union and encouraging them to participate more effectively'.

Some of the more active women I spoke to mentioned that the lack of self-confidence and willingness to speak out was a problem with other women at work. One woman, working in the meat industry in Queensland, tried to encourage the other women, and noticed how their confidence developed with experience. Even so, this was done without any support from the more militant male workers:

In union meetings I used to say to them, 'You get up'. 'No, I won't get up'. They had to stand up for themselves. Gradually, after a while, by the time I left there, quite a few women could actually get up without any problems and have a go. That was all right. They would say, 'Have a go'. It was really good. You could see their development. I'm still in touch with some of them. And it was said to me, 'How about we form a women's committee where we have a look at our situation, job situation, our position in unions?' Anyway, we had to go to the union's Southern District Council to see if they would agree to it. The official said 'Yeah, that's all right'. And eventually, it's really quite interesting, they really grabbed onto it. It's not everybody wanted to be in it of course, but those that did, they made number of proposals. Things that worried them were things that they listed down, and I had the job of going to the union and seeing what we were doing about it. I mean, there were such things as, there was no award on the wall. There were many little things at the beginning that were the basis of getting some feelings of militancy. Actually, it was little things that really motivated them – what can be regarded as little things. It means so much to them.

Then we had many stoppages over the general issues that came up, such as the general conditions and wages that concerned everybody.

But there was always the problem that the most militant section was the butchers. They were the key maintenance people. Without them doing the butchering work, you can't do anything. They would at the drop of a hat go off whenever they wanted to, mainly about pay and conditions. But they always expected everybody else to have to go. And there was never any questions of asking or letting anyone else have a say. Again, we weren't regarded as needing to know – we were just women anyway.

One woman, an office worker, said she thought that the women's movement was helping to give women more self-confidence:

That's the problem. They were frightened of expressing themselves and so forth and frightened to put up a case for themselves. But I think this is starting to break down since International Women's Year and the impetus of the women's movement. We find on the jobs that the women do stand up as well as the men do.

The gulf between unionists and organisers makes the former very cynical but also, paradoxically, creates a dependence. Members are reluctant to act without an organizer being present:

Oh yeah, just the attitude of the union coming down! Talk about outside forces coming in; I mean, the worst examples I've seen are, in fact, union organisers who come down from uptown; they're atrocious. I mean on the whole, their attitudes towards people in the shop are just really bad, especially the ones who'd been on a full-time organiser's job for so long that they had forgotten what it's like to be on the other end; and they get so used to hearing their own voice, too, that at meetings they just rave on and on and on and they never give anyone a chance. They have set ideas about how to go about things. Most of them have no conception of helping people's politicization through trying to allow people to work at their own rate, to work out their own strategies, to see where they went wrong, take another tack.

The antagonism is incredible. You know, there's very few places I can remember where people had good words to say about the organisers. It's always put in terms of like, 'They're getting their pockets lined', or 'They drink Scotch with the boss', 'Where's all our union money going to? It just goes down the pockets of the officials' – in fact no true things. I mean, there is a certain amount of corruption, but certainly not of the types that people thought existed.

Yet the contradiction always was, whenever there was a dispute, people always wanted to bring the organizer down, and I was always arguing 'No, let's not bring the organizer down, let's have our own meeting first; let's figure out what's going on, see maybe what we can do about it. If we come up against a brick wall then bring the organizer down, and tell him.' But especially old unionists felt as though they couldn't move without an organizer there, so in fact, the union enough organisers to go around and they can't get the stuff done. On another level, it suits the purpose of union officials and bureaucracies quite well, because it means it's all still in their control.

Only under extreme provocation do cynicism or hostility towards union officials turn into open conflict, such as when officials are perceived to be trying to dampen down a dispute which the rank-and-file wish to pursue.

Marie had been working in a major automobile manufacturing factory in South Australia. She said that the company was pushing workers very hard and stocks of products were piling up. Thinking that this indicated the company's intention to retrench large numbers, workers prepared a strong rank-and-file organization. However, rank-and-file members soon found themselves in conflict with union officials:

We had two weeks day shift and two weeks of night shift, and on this night shift the South Australian branch of the union was meeting and they were discussing one of our shop stewards, and we felt it was important to go to the meeting, so we organized everybody to walk out. It was about [nineteen kilometres] into two and we had discussion about why we should go and what we should put to the meeting and stuff like that. We walked through the plant and got a whole lot of people to come with us. And when we got in there, the bosses had rung the union officials who had closed the doors to the meeting and we weren't able to get in until the last agenda item and the thing about our shop steward had come up. So people were outside chanting 'bosses' union, bosses' union'. And, you know, things like that happened fairly regularly. The union officials would come out to the plant and they were very, very transparent in the way they acted so that feelings against the officials was strong.

Another woman who had been a very active job delegate was opposed in union elections by the ruling union executive. She explained their opposition in these terms:

I think they've lost touch with a lot of the workers and instead of them going out to the workers and asking the workers to join in, they don't. They make the decisions; you've got to abide by them. I think that I was too honest with the rank and file.

A woman who had been retrenched several times said that one important part of the unions' response to unemployment should be the defence of jobs and working conditions if retrenchments are threatened or taking place. Too often, she said, unions treated unemployment as a welfare problem, not an industrial one:

When I just got retrenched this last time, we knew that retrenchments were coming up, although the boss was denying it. People could see it, I mean stores were running down, new orders weren't coming in, orders that had been sent out were coming back because they were no good. People were just really scared, and when the axe fell there was a great deal of concern on the personal level; you know, 'Poor Delia, she and her family have just moved into a new house' and 'Poor so and so, they have just got a new baby' – but there's nothing we can do about it really. The union came out, the management had said that they weren't going to give us management had said that they weren't going to give us loading on our holiday pay – the termination agreement – we weren't going to get that, nor were we going to get paid for any sick days that hadn't been taken. And so the union guy didn't come around and talk to everybody and try to figure out what was going on, he just talked to one or two women who were the union delegates. And they went inside and came out again and said that they had agreed to give us the loading but not the sick pay, so it was quite obvious that the management had been prepared to give us that anyway, and they had just held it back so that it would look like they had given us something as a result of the pressure.

It was a very divisive thing in the workplace, and that has a whole lot to do with the history of that place too. It was a union shop right, but it was a type of union shop where it's union just because it always has been and because they are used to handing over the money. The union was, in fact, controlled by a small group of women, interestingly enough, in about their forties and fifties, who were a very tight clique, and who wouldn't allow anyone else in, but who also weren't prepared to do the work in terms of being a union delegate, except that they were quite good at taking up little things that people were worried about on the shop floor because that was a bit of honour and glory attached to that – like getting real mad and then going to see the boss and coming out and saying 'Yeah, it's all right'. But any of the hard politicization work – this place was a subsidiary of a large company – and any of the sort of hard yakka of shop steward, trying to link up with shop stewards in other areas, none of that was done.

Because of the way in which this group of women controlled the union affairs, people had a fairly bad attitude towards the union. So when the crunch came, there was no sense of a political perspective of what sackings meant or anything else.

As shown in Chapter 1, feminism and activism amongst women in the labour movement was certainly not only a phenomenon of the 1970s. Certainly those years brought a revival, and a challenge to the inertia of the union movement, but some of the participants were simply taking up the threads of an argument current in the nineteenth century, and from the 1930s to the early 1950s.

One of the women to articulate this renewed challenge was Stella Nord. In late 1969 she wrote a paper linking the post-war industrial boom of the 1950s and 1960s with the influx of migrants and women in the workforce. She outlined the implication of these developments, anticipating many of the issue that concern us now, more than ten years later. What seems strange now is that so few people recognised the changes that were taking place so rapidly, and fewer still tried to analyse what they meant. In her paper, Stella Nord asked whether the influx of women into the workforce would strengthen or weaken the trade union movement. Clearly in the face of scepticism from male unionists, she was arguing for the potential of women to strengthen the union movement. She suggested that women in the workforce needed industrial education through involvement in action on the job, and outlined many of the reasons, still valid today, why involvement was limited, including ignorance or scepticism about union activities, fear of victimization and unwillingness to participate in meetings after work.

Her conclusion was that if the union movement failed to take up the rights of women and all the specific issues which follow, such as child care, it would become divorced from the great social and economic problems of our times.[14]

The slow response of unions to the needs of women and migrant workers has increasingly been met by shop-floor action linked to community based ethnic and women's organisations. The demands formulated by women workers' groups have, as Helen Hurwitz put it, reached out into their wider lives, making industrial the issues of child care, maternity leave and English lessons. Despite the remarkable consensus about what the important issues are, agreement on strategies has been less firm, mainly because of different attitudes to the trade union movement, ranging from loyalty to hostility. Sydney feminist Christine Curry focuses on this in an article called 'Union lobby or job action?' in which she comments on the divergence of views at the conference of women trade unionists held in 1976.[15] She summarized the conflict with the question, 'Should working women achieve their demands through a tactic of lobbying union and state bureaucracies or should they do so by the force of the consciousness and power of action of working women on the job?' Those who adopted the first tactic concentrated on getting the ACTU to adopt a version of the working women's charter and advocating that women become active in union politics or enter the union hierarchy to help implement the charter's provisions in their own union. Another view was that the existing union hierarchy should be either opposed, questions or avoided in preference to organizing rank-and-file groups linked through charter campaign meetings independent of any union.

Although the dichotomy between 'job action' and 'union lobby' exists, many women find themselves somewhere in the middle, both sceptical about the performance and loyal towards the principles of the union movement. In fact, much of the activity has taken place within a union framework but at the shop-floor level where union officials are often absent for most of the time.

The conflict reflects a search for identity as well as strategies. Some women identify with the situation of their union 'brothers'. Others identify with their ethnic community and mistrust any English-speaking union or women's organisation. Still others, in reaction to sexism, feel their situation is shared and understood only by women.

Some women have come forward as shop stewards and some have benefited from trade union training courses to overcome their initial lack of confidence. In white-collar unions especially the growing militancy of women has been effective. The Victorian Insurance Employees' Union has changed its character, with a reform group taking power and electing women to the union executive. In Brisbane, the Queensland branch of the Australian Telephone and Phonogram Officers' Association, the union of telephonists, was virtually recreated with women becoming involved and holding eleven out of twelve committee positions. One of the women told me that she felt that lack of an entrenched male union hierarchy had enabled women to become involved and feel as if they had control of their union. By contrast, women who work in industries with strong unions have had to become 'ginger groups' against the ruling executive. Resistance has been most strongly felt in such industries not so much because the men resent the women getting involved, but because the hierarchy is threatened by rank-and-file activism. The problem is the distance between union officials and their members, which has corresponded to a growing gulf between white English-speaking males and the majority of non-English-speaking migrant and women members. It is not simply a matter of how many female union members, delegates and officials there are. It is a deeper-seated structural question of how workers are organized, how the rank and file relate to the leadership and what issues they pursue.

It is a question of great importance for male workers as well. The relative exclusion of women from both management and union structures has led women's organisations to question the traditional confines of union activity, and in doing so they have given a lead to male rank-and-file workers.

As many specific issues such a working hours or health and safety have shown, real gains require workers to control their own work environment. Control of union organization should be seen only as a step in this direction.

One of the major challenges facing unions is whether they can act to improve the social situation of entire disadvantaged groups, such as migrant women. Many of those urging them to do so claim that it is necessary to achieve this aim if the unions are to do their job and represent the general interests of all workers. However it would mean a radical departure from past union activities. It would mean, for example, arranging provisions for multilingualism and for child-care facilities, which are of pressing importance for migrant and women workers, and enabling a greater say for members through, for instance, multi-cultural shop-floor committees.

The distinction between being unionized and being organized has received very little attention in the debate. Many women alck industrial organization and are therefore unprotected and unwilling to take any risks to improve their conditions despite their being fully unionized. For some, this means little more than token membership, little or nor contact with officials or organisers and no shop-floor organization. However, becoming unionized is a hard-won right. Few people realise how much intimidation of employees there can be, especially in times of recession, because there is no law to protect them. The problem becomes circular. If workers can break the circle and organize despite prevailing insecurity, then the right to join a union becomes real, not just token. The important thing is the development of rank-and-file organization. Without it, unions remain remote, irrelevant or, at best, paternalistic.

Sexism in unions

Although many women choose to work within unions around women's issues, they still encounter difficulties with sexism in the form of sexist attitudes, structures that discourage women's involvement and issues that do not reflect the priorities of women in the workforce.

At the 1975 Conference on Women and Politics Robert Goot, an industrial advocate, outlined the attitudes within the union movement that led to less serious effort being put into improving conditions for female union members. Apart from a sexist ideology, one such attitude was that with the 'achievement' of equal pay the end of the road had been reached and women's industrial problems were solved. Another was that women only work to supplement their husband's income, therefore their need for union protection is less than that of men. Goot went on to show that equal pay had not been fully implemented and he was critical of the unions' lack of action on other issues, especially the 'intangible' ones, such as maternity leave and an associated question, the needs of working numbers.

He explained this deficiency largely by the fact that unions reflected the attitude of the broader society:

But I think that it's generally acceptable to describe the trade union vis-à-vis the women as very sexist. Perhaps no more sexist than the community at large, because we've all been through the same environmental conditioning and sociological conditioning. But perhaps it's more disappointing coming from the trade union movement, which one would have hope would have been in the vanguard of change. You look at the peak councils of trade unions, you look at the ACTU, the labour councils and the executives of most unions and look for women – but don't take too long looking because you won't find them.

He also felt that because of the very limited number of women in trade union decision-making structures, 'women's issues don't get pushed'.[16]

When she was working for the Women's Trade Union Commission, Helen Prendergast listed some of the attitudes of trade union men towards women which stand in the way of improving women's conditions.[17] She claimed that there is still suspicion about the breaking of the 'family wage' concept and fear that skilled men would be displaced by job fragmentation and employment of unskilled women. Women were seen by some union men as a form of 'coolie' labour with little bargaining power, more easily banned than unionized. There was also some resentment at women's alleged lack of interest in 'union issues' and greater interest in other issues, such as part-time work, which is strongly opposed by some unions. She also suggested many changes that would be possible within a union structure, for instance, encouraging women to take positions, appointing female staff, including women in trade union training courses, giving special attention to the exploitation of migrant women and the need for English classes in working hours without loss of pay, eliminating discriminatory higher allowances and preferential severance agreements for males and so on. One aspect of this is that it requires unions to go out of their way to encourage women, instead of sitting back and relying on traditional loyalties, or simply claiming that women ought to be more assertive.

Some unions, although recognizing that women workers have unique problems, still fall back on the point that women themselves must do something about their situation. While this is true, it is sometimes used as an excuse for the union not doing anything. In practice, it is very difficult for workers, given the background of the labour movement, to initiate or sustain action without the support of their union leadership and women are increasingly demanding that their union structures should be supportive in backing the claims of their women members. One small example of this was a meeting of shop assistants, mostly women, who roared 'Sisters!' when they were repetatedly addressed as 'Brothers' by their union secretary.

Stella Nord told me of another example:

There were two big dressing rooms, the men's and the women's, and for all the union meetings that were held always the men expected us to go in their place. So we decided one day, let's not go in; let them come into our room. So the women jacked up and decided they weren't going in. And someone called out: 'How about youse sheilas coming in?' And we said: 'No, you come in here'. And eventually it was established that we would take turn about, so that was a bit of a morale-builder.

Although women and men are employed together in many industries, there is often a de factor segregation on the job which help to reinforce the notion that unionism is 'men's business'. Although increasing numbers of women are saying that on-the-job organization is their business too, they resent the assumption that this mean falling into line behind the men. Many women point out that they want to organize on their own terms, giving priority to issues that have in the past been ignored or considered unimportant by male-dominated unions.

Even when support for industrial action is given to women workers, it may still come wrapped in a sexist package. For example, one union journal told of 'girls' who 'manned' a picket line.[18] The events themselves were of great importance, and the women involved deserved to be recognised as adults. The women, who worked in a boutique in Wollongong, New South Wales, were sacked after joining a union and replaced by non-union labour. They were joined by other unionists who felt that the right to organize was under attack. One of the supporters was hit over the head with an iron bar by the manager of the boutique. The South Coast Labour Council called a twenty-four-hour stoppage, and 2000 people marched through Wollongong in support of the right to belong to a trade union, the right to work free of discrimination and the right to receive award conditions. It was an example of how employment conditions of women are so backward that drastic action is needed to gain even the most basic principles of trade union organization.

Overt sexism is more easy to grasp and recognize than the problems of social structure which create the gulf between women, especially migrant women, at the rank-and-file level and union officials. However, it is only one aspect of this overall situation. Severe problems remain for those organisers, for example, who recognize and oppose sexism, and attempt to increase the power of the union membership.

There are, nevertheless, still many challenges left in the form of obvious sexism. For instance, some women find that union men are reluctant to take them seriously:

At the factory I worked in in '75, the power transformer company, when I got there I found out who the union delegate was and I went to him and said that I was going to join the union. It took about three weeks for him to let me in, because he just kept saying for days that it was unnecessary, that women aren't in the union here: process workers definitely aren't in the union. And I mean I could have gone down to the union and just joined myself up, but I wanted him to – I wanted them to – admit that. And so eventually, I did and they said that was okay, and then it was quite fortunate in that a couple of months after I started there, there were these mass meetings about the question of unemployment. So that when we got back to the factory it was really funny, because first of all people were just avoiding catching my eye. Then I thought, 'Oh well, I'll just wait and see what happens', and then a couple of people said something to me about what I had said and how they thought it was good. Only two people actually, about the content of it, and then other people kept on coming up and saying things like, 'I heard you swore' – because I got a bit excited – and that sort of broke the ice in a sense, and the unionists already there realized that I had had some experience, and that I was quite serious about the whole business and so then they were prepared to talk with me about the situation there.

One woman suggested that a code of behaviour was necessary to control the behaviour of the men in the union towards women:

The shop stewards will go up after a meeting to the industrial office and phone through to the big boss to come down and the union organizer will say ' Oh well, he will soon be down with all these beautiful women sitting here'. I looked at him and said 'That doesn't go over here'. But you have to put up with all that. It's pretty disgusting. In fact, I think the first thing a women's collective should do is work out a code of behaviour of male union organisers and shop stewards towards women shop stewards and women members, particularly the way they conduct themselves in from of the boss, as far as the union representatives on the job are concerned.

Women in all situations have to resist being treated as the general servant-cum-secretary of the men they work with. A shop steward's position is no exception:

Until just recently I was the secretary of the shop committee and I was doing full-time union work on the job and I found that it finally became an impossible situation because the male shop stewards were in a way virtually making me ineffective. I think that women have got to have their own organization on the job. It's got to come to that. The women have just got to have women's organization on the job because the men just co-opt all your energies and treat you like the office girl. Because they won't allow you to use any initiative you've got to follow theirs all the time; you just become like a servant to the general union organization on the job. That does nothing for women virtually.

The consequences of built-in sexism within unions can be disastrous, especially where discriminatory retrenchments are encouraged:

Well, I think the women are in conflict with the men if they ever try to do anything. They are already in conflict. They decided to lay off on a job. The previous time workers were laid off it was strict seniority. This time they divided the men and the women into two groups and it was seniority within the groups. Even though we had a women's meeting, the main emphasis of that meeting was job security for our women members. Those decisions of the women's meeting went to the union and were endorsed. From my branch they were again submitted by resolution from the branch I'm in to the union where they were referred on for implementation. Now in May of this year we are having a meeting about it. But on my job the union organizer took no notice of the policy of the union, that our members resist the sack. And so consequently the women were extremely resentful. So as soon as there was any word of retrenchment, the whole grapevine around the place was promoting the man's right to a job and that women should go home. It was forced on us by the men in a shop committee meeting. The women got a tremendous battering and the end result of that was 'Out the gate!' I finished up saying to the boss and the union organizer together, 'Everybody says what the women are prepared to do and not prepared to do but nobody ever asks the women themselves.' And they just both of them pushed that comment aside. So seniority operated for the men and seniority operated for the women and the women just went out in their hundreds.

The resentment becomes evident when union officials treat clerical and office workers with the same lack of esteem or consideration:

This tremendous male dominance. It is absolutely incredible that they downgrade everybody. It's simple things. They refuse to recognize that you exist. They pinch your bloody ideas. You know, you go to someone with a suggestion and they won't say it came from you. They will go and say 'Do you think this is a good idea?' and they will put up your idea and you get no credit. Not that you want the bloody credit but the fact is that you don't even get recognised. I mean, if it wasn't for the staff that work in any office, where would they be? And they go on doing things and discussing things that they wouldn't have a clue about. They don't tell you how long it is going to take you to type out or the technical side. They don't come and ask the technical staff. Oh no, they just go and make their own submission about what they think. Not all of them are like that. I must say there are some of them who aren't too bad. One bloke I work with now isn't too bad.

The women contrasted the union's policy on women with the personal behaviour of the senior male officials:

You tend to make allowances because they are union officials. But I nearly have hysterics when I read in the union minutes – say it's the women's charter and it says 'Brother, we ought to do something about it.' I reckon as far as problems of women workers are concerned, well, they wouldn't have that much knowledge. He wouldn't have a clue in the world and he is a typical mid-Victorian: 'My dear little wife and help-mate will bring my slippers to me', and no doubt she does every night when he goes home and that is his background. What's more, he still has his bloody tea brought to him twice a day by his bloody secretary which is something I put my bloody foot down about when we came in here. I said I'm not serving any bloody cups of tea to any of my bloody blokes and I haven't either.

One group of women shiftworkers were particularly concerned with lack of unionization on the issue of child care: 'Well, it has been brought to their attention several times but nothing has been done about it. To be quite honest, I think this is a typical male chauvinist attitude. They don't really want us here.'

A woman who has been active in her union felt that many women were discouraged by the lack of recognition of their contribution:

There are very few structures whereby if you want to work in the union, you actually have access to do it. At my branch, say, I'm the only woman who's ever come along. At other branches, there a few women who tried to have women's committees; the most that have ever come along have been six. There are obviously female job delegates around, and on shop stewards' councils but, you know, not in positions of responsibility, and the danger of being in a union like that is to have a few token women. And that has a very bad effect. Not only on a union because they just can get by with that tokenism but by the women, when they eventually realise that they have been used, which inevitably, they do. They do a whole lot of the really hard work, the shit work sort of stuff. They get toted out for various conferences to make various speeches, but then when nominations come up for any job which contains any real power or position in the union, time and time again they are overlooked.

In her experience, this made the women either anti-male, in an isolated way without seeing that the men were 'bureaucrats and entrenched in their union position', or encouraged them to try to organize women in that union:

I think it is important that women organize as caucuses in unions around their specific demands, basically supporting the whole idea of unions and principles, etc., and with a clear-cut understanding of why it is that their issues haven't been taken up in the union structure. Otherwise, they are not going to get very far.

Conclusion

Trade unions have a paradoxical role in modern industrial society. They are an accepted, even a necessary part of the system, and yet they contain some potential for challenging and changing that system. Similarly, as far as women are concerned, unions can represent both a confirmation of the sexism that is built into all social institutions, and a means by which women ca learn, gain experience and develop the capacity to change the sexism. It is unlikely that women would have made such gains as having the charter adopted by the ACTU unless there had been a charter campaign based on the women's movement outside unions, as well as the gradual development of women's committees within unions. Both of these groupings have been forums for women workers to articulate their concerns without male leaders speaking on their behalf. However, the implementation of the charter will be feasible only if the resources of the union movement are directed by the leadership in support of emerging rank-and-file structures that are representative of women and migrant workers.

This may happen, partly because union members demand it, and partly because structural changes in the workplace present unions with challenges requiring a decentralized, strategic response that is possible only with a workforce that is confident, well informed and organized enough to act on its own behalf, not only to protect past gains but also to extend them in the direction of workers' control of the work environment.

CHAPTER 10

'And you won't look back'

Prospects for the 1980s

revious chapters have discussed issues of concern to women in the paid workforce in Australia in the 1970s – issues which were formulated in the ACTU Charter for Working Women as a basis from which those concerned might work towards ensuring women's right to work. The 1970s started with an optimism arising from economic security and the possibility of social reform. Groups which had been excluded from many of the benefits of twenty years' post-war industrial development began to articulate demands for greater power to run their own lives and to receive a more equitable share in society's resources. Ethnic organisations, for example, became more active, especially in Melbourne, where two migrant workers' conferences were held. They put forward the now commonplace concept of the multicultural society, and pointed out that migrant had been doing the worst jobs in Australian manufacturing industry, often without political or union representation. Demands for wider job opportunities and equality at work followed. The women's movement, in particular, articulated these demands, as they were specified in the charter, and became a significant influence in changing attitudes. It pointed out that men and women were confined to different social roles that did not allow for individual aptitudes to be followed, and that the female role was undervalued. Women's work was unpaid or underpaid, lower in status, more limited in scope and less recognised for its skills than men's work. Social influences on the upbringing and education of girls were identified as making them less confident and less inclined to gain competence in technical or manual skills. Girls were channelled into school subjects which closed off many employment options. By the time young women entered the labour market they found few occupations open to them. These occupations usually imitated the female role: sewing clothes, serving and preparing food, cleaning, caring for children or the sick and providing support for men. Women had few prospects for advancement within these occupations and fewer still for entering non-traditional ones.

Despite being urgently required in large numbers for such work, women continued to be solely or primarily responsible for their children and their homes. The 'double working life' was seen as a major problem. The women's movement called for two changes: more child-care services and equal sharing of child care and household tasks by men. Unions were urged to support these goals and to work for various other provisions such as maternity leave, family leave and retraining so that women would not be disadvantaged by their career pattern. The women's inequality in the paid workforce and in the community at large would remain entrenched. Paid jobs would continue to be regarded as short term and of secondary importance; poor employment conditions would be tolerated; and women would not have the time or energy to be involved in union activities to improve their working conditions or further education to upgrade their job skills. Attention was focused on the structural barriers preventing women's equal participation in the paid workforce: overt discrimination, lower rates of pay, segregation of the labour market into 'men's jobs' and 'women's jobs', and a union movement controlled by men and allowing little participation by women.

Campaigns to introduce equal pay, establish child-care facilities, to make overt discrimination illegal, to promote non-sexist education, to make unions more responsive to women members and to gain maternity leave were successful up to a point. As we have seen, initial breakthrough were made throughout the 1970s.

However much remained to be done; in particular to implement or extend some of the principles which had become accepted.

Chapter 2 concluded that the implementation of the charter required organisation amongst women workers and a change in the centralized structure that has been typical of unions in the past.

That this is a long-term process can be seen when considering that economic changes in the 1950s and 1960s led to the influx of women into the paid workforce. There is a danger that the labour and women's movements will limit themselves to responding to problems after they become obvious and therefore will fail to come to grips with the fundamental causes. On the other hand, deepening recessing does lead more people to identify underlying economic and social relationships as the problem. If these relationships are to be changed, workers must develop grass-roots organisations which go beyond the traditional union role of responding and bargaining and aim instead for intervention and then control.

The process of shop-floor discussion and development of women workers' groups initiated by the Western Region Centre for Working Women has been successful in building the confidence, interest and determination to act of the women involved. However, there have been problems, the most serious being the devastating impact of economic recession on women's labour organisation, and the second being the unresolved tension between the women's movement and unions.

Implementing the charter requires unions actively and deliberately to organise around issues put forward by their women members. They must encourage women to become shop stewards and delegates, stand for office, attend union education courses and aim to become organisers. To be effective, encouragement must extend to overcoming obstacles such as lack of child care, inconvenient meeting times, limited hours due to domestic responsibilities and hostility from husbands. Organisation should proceed further so that when women do become union delegates, officials or organisers, there are structures and processes through which they can work. These might include a women's committee with decision-making power at policy level, backed up by a network of rank-and-file women's groups in each workplace. A female organizer could work to strengthen such a network, rather than being left out on a limb doing routine work. The initial task of involving women in consciousness-raising and the first steps towards action has been most successfully achieved by the women's movement – either by feminists working within their own union with support from an autonomous women's or charter group outside the union, or by women in those autonomous groups, like the Centre for Working Women, systemically discussing the charter with women in their workplaces. The limitations of these organisations lie not in the type of work they do but in the fact that there are so few of them.

The task of creating processes and structures within unions through which women can pursue work around the charter cannot be achieved by 'outsiders'. However, if women's groups within each workplace begin to link with other similar groups they can work towards creating women's committees with power in their union's decision-making structures, and appointing female organisers to link on-the-job action to the union's women's policy.

These were some of the organizational problems of implementing the charter in the three years following its adoption by the ACTU in late 1977.

However, by 1980 Australian society was entering a new era, one of economic crisis, greater pessimism about the prospect of reform, massive structural change in the economy with drastic effects on work, and widespread uncertainty about the direction in which society was headed.

Undoubtedly, the situation of working women had changed profoundly. The problems facing them in the late 1970s and early '80s had become fear of unemployment (already higher than men's), a dwindling number of jobs, and cutbacks in government spending on child care, education, training or retraining schemes for women and many other services.

Unemployment is certainly the major problem facing the women's movement in the 1980s. Unemployment is increasing for a variety of reasons. Employment in manufacturing industry is declining rapidly as companies close down or relocate overseas because Australian manufactured goods cannot compete with cheaper imports from Asian countries where repressive governments and anti-labour laws keep wages low. Technological change is allowing a drastically reduced workforce not only in manufacturing but also in the tertiary service sectors – banking, insurance, clerical, wholesale and retail, community services and many technical areas. As these sectors became major employers of women in the 1970s in the less skilled and routine jobs as opposed to technical and managerial positions, women will be particularly affected by this trend. There is also renewed investment in development of mineral and energy resources, often by foreign companies taking resources out of the country while providing few jobs. Despite the potential wealth generated by these resources, government spending continues to be restricted, cutting back both services and employment.

All these factors – relocation of manufacturing industry offshore, investment in technology, investment in mining and resource development and processing of raw materials for export, together with government cutbacks – lead to increased unemployment. They are also leading to changes in the types of work available and the quality of working life. International changes in the distribution of labour and capital are presenting immense challenges to the Australian labour movement, and are threatening to have a particularly severe impact on migrant and women workers.

During the 1980s a possible overall loss of 2 million jobs has been predicted, with a disproportionate effect on office, banking, insurance and commerce – all major employers of women.[1] Between 30 per cent and 50 per cent of jobs in these fields could disappear if proposed technological changes go ahead.[2]

These figures – admittedly estimates – sound incredible at first. However, when specific changes in each industry are examined, they appear more realistic. In fact, it is hard to see any areas of new employment, except for some jobs associated with new technology, and these will in no way balance the number of jobs lost. Furthermore, the jobs created in mining and technical areas are likely to be men's jobs.

Sandra Prerost, author of the ACTU and CAGEO submission to the Myers Enquiry on Technological Change, lists five main groups of women who will be affected if current rends in unemployment continue: young women (and married women re-entering the paid workforce) seeking clerical and retail jobs; less skilled women displaced from manufacturing; clerical (mainly fourth division) staff affected by public sector cutbacks; young women now unable to enter the workforce in finance and related industries, as they have done in the past; and finally, women in professions, increasingly affected by technological change and public policy.[3]

Prospects for women's employment in the 1980s are particularly alarming when considering the situation of female school leavers in the late 1970s. Gail Shelston of the NSW Education Department has pointed out in a paper on unemployment and female school leavers that unemployment for girls in the 15-19 age-group is higher than for any other group – in May 1978 it was 17.4 per cent.[4] Furthermore, the majority of them are still only educated to enter a narrow range of jobs. For instance, in 1978, 80 per cent entered clerical, service, nursing, teaching and sales occupations, where there are few vacancies and the impact of technological change is only beginning to be felt. She claims that in February 1979 there were 36 409 unemployed clerks, typists and office machinists with 948 vacancies. She has also pointed out that in 1977 women were being educated in 27 occupations, while men were being educated in 500 occupations.

Girls' job prospects and aspirations remain narrow, according to Shelston, because of low self-esteem, inappropriate subject choices at school, low expectations of their parents, sexual division of labour at home, a narrow view of possibilities, lack of understanding of the real life pattern of most women, expectation of finding a male breadwinner, rejection of tertiary training, perception of jobs as sex-typed, anticipation of conflict between home and a career, a view of child bearing as a permanent occupation and a short-term view of the future. Despite the lack of perception of employment as a long-term part of women's role, it is notable that both female school leavers and older women find unemployment a negative, depressing state. However, even if their perception broadens, changes in the labour market may make unemployment the dominant experience of women in the 1980s.

The decline of manufacturing industry

The reality of unemployment for women can be seen most dramatically in the decline of Australia's manufacturing industry in which female employment fell by twice as much as male employment between 1974-77.[5]

In summary, manufacturing industry, which in 1966 employed 27.6 per cent of Australia's total workforce, employed only 21.8 per cent in 1977, and this figure continues to decrease.[6] This is not due simply to a relative expansion of jobs in other areas, such as white-collar and service industry employment, for ABS figures show that between 1974 and 1977 over 200 000 jobs were lost from manufacturing industry and now fewer people are employed in manufacturing jobs than in the mid-'60s.[7] Hardest hit were workers in those labour-intensive industries which are especially affected by competition from imports from low-wage Asian countries. Between 1974-77, the textile, electrical goods, clothing and footwear industries (in which women are concentrated, making up, for example, over 80 per cent of the workforce in the clothing industry[8]) lost between a quarter and a third of their workforce.

It is too simple to speak of an overall decline in manufacturing industry without looking at output, trade and profits. Manufacturing as a proportion of gross domestic product reached its highest point in the mid-'60s and has since declined. Exports of manufactured goods have decreased while exports of rural and mineral products have increased, indicating a major shift in the economy from manufacturing to mining. Although investment in some manufacturing industries decreased after the mid-'60s, there has recently been renewed capital investment, especially under the Fraser government. The investment tax allowance has encouraged companies to install new machinery to increase productivity but decrease the number of workers involved. Even in the apparently ailing clothing industry, investment increased by 63 per cent between 1977–78 and 1978–79.[9] Investment has been highest in the capital-intensive mining and mineral products industries, which have low employment needs but yield high profits. Overall, the share of profits as compared to wages in the national economy increased between 1974 and 1978.[10]

Peter Robson, who has written extensively on the subject of 'workers control', has pointed out that technological change in manufacturing industry in the 1970s involved mechanization rather than computerization.[11] He predicts that further advanced mechanization and automation will occur, resulting in additional loss of jobs, unless shorter working hours are introduced or unions intervene in decision-making about the use of technology. Specific industries – for example, the whitegoods industry manufacturing washing machines, refrigerators and so on – have been hit by mergers, reductions in the number of factories, specialization and the introduction of new technology. In most cases employers have resisted or avoided redundancy agreements that the stronger unions have called for. Workers have been affected by mass lay-offs in some cases, but there has also been sustained job loss from 'natural wastage', that is, no replacement of workers who retire or leave of their own accord. Other employment practices implemented include early retirement, temporary closure, retrenchment, standing-down of workers for part of the week or compulsory taking of holidays.

The impact on workers of the declining manufacturing industry is not spread uniformly throughout the country. Severe local effects are felt: for example, the problems in the vehicle industry in New South Wales, the whitegoods industry in South Australia and the clothing industry in Victoria had serious consequences for the governments of those States. In the clothing industry the impact has been particularly localized.

Brunswick is an inner municipality of Melbourne with a concentration of clothing factories and a high proportion of migrants, notably those of Italian origin, living in the area and working in the industry. A study in 1979 of the clothing industry in Brunswick and the social impact of its decline found that thirty-six clothing factories in Brunswick had closed down between 1971 and 1979, with seventy-two still operating.[12] Generally speaking, smaller factories had closed while a few of the larger ones had been able to invest in new machinery and some had started to concentrate on the market for higher priced fashion garments. The study also found that 43 per cent of Brunswick's industrial workforce were employed in the clothing industry, and that 66 per cent of women employed in industry were associated with the clothing industry. Most were middle-aged, married migrant women whose prospects for retraining or alternative employment were limited.

The decline in the clothing industry is due mostly to changes in Australia's position within the international division of labour, rather than to technological change. Some new technology has been introduced, however, such as computerised cutting machines capable of replacing sixty workers, and is thought by the Clothing and Allied Trades Union to lead to deskilling and employment of young girls in preference to older women.

The Western Region Centre for Working Women has worked extensively with the Clothing and Allied Trades Union under circumstances which exemplify the dilemmas of the Working Women's Charter Campaign in the 1980s.

The long-term process of creating shop committees and rank-and-file women's groups which are backed by female organisers and women's committees at an executive or policy level is in its infancy in the clothing industry. Progress has been made in a small number of factories; however, lack of job security in a declining industry made the task Herculean.

Several examples will illustrate the problem. In one factory, a group of women had been meeting at lunch times and were about to form a shop committee. The shop steward discovered widespread under-award payments and called in an organizer to rectify the pay and to proceed with electing a shop committee. She was sacked because the boss overheard her telephoning the union. Although back pay was eventually made up, the sacking destroyed the confidence of the potential shop committee before they were strong enough to act. When they later called for improved physical conditions in the factory, the owner agreed to comply with minimal legal requirements but said he could use outworkers or Asian factories if there were further demands.

In another factory, many women were laid off because a normal seasonal lull was worsened by lack of material from suppliers, lack of orders from retailers and orders being given to middlemen using outworkers. About a third of the former workforce was later re-employed.

Another factory, in a provincial city with little alternative employment, took on extra women to fulfil seasonal orders and later sacked a large number – not always those employed earlier – when work was slow. Those sacked were ones with low production records, but no consideration was given to widespread grievances about the arbitrary rates set for each particular job. In that factory, a shop committee that had been formed when work was plentiful disbanded feeling disillusioned and frustrated after the retrenchments.

Another example is a large garment factory where women had been meeting regularly and a multilingual shop committee had been formed. Although work was generally available, a steady trickle of arbitrary or unfair dismissals had continued to take place. The women nevertheless walked off the job one very hot day because of lack of ventilation which, in fact, breached the award. However, they went back to work when threatened with the sack. Inexperience and lack of support caused the shop committee to lose their first industrial action over a disagreement which they clearly should have won. Soon after that, when there were rumours of ten women being sacked, the committee crumbled.

Overall, women in the clothing industry were vulnerable to arbitrary sackings, retrenchment due to lack of orders, temporary and permanent closure of factories, take-overs of small companies by larger ones, and competition from companies using outworkers.

Given the massive loss of jobs from the clothing industry in the 1970s and its uncertain future in the 1980s, there is a clear need for an overall industry-wide policy to secure the jobs of women in the industry or at the very least to protect them from arbitrary fluctuations of employment as the industry declines or adjusts, to compensate them for loss of employment, and to investigate alternative job opportunities. However, these are ambitious goals. The Working Women's Charter Campaign has continually stressed the vulnerability of women in industries with low levels of rank-and-file organization. It is less likely in these industries to be able to stimulate enough strength at the shop-floor level to put job-security policies into action in the face of such adverse conditions.

The conclusion to be drawn from these examples is not that the charter should be put aside as unrealistic but that unions should relate it more specifically to the growing problem of lack of job security. The right to work is basic to the charter, and is therefore at the heart of unions' strategies to respond to new technology, recession and structural change in both manufacturing and tertiary industry.

Changes in the service sector

Despite the growth of the service sector in the 1970s and the decline of manufacturing industry, it is still not generally recognised that the workforce, particularly the female workforce, is predominantly white collar. Unions in the tertiary sector were relatively low key until the 1970s when some realized that technological change and restructuring might lead to massive loss of employment with drastic changes in the nature of work both in the public and private sectors. In the banking industry unions are mobilizing their members around the impact of technological change which, they predict, could result in a loss of between 30 per cent and 40 per cent of jobs.[13] Public service unions are increasingly concerned with staff, ceiling and displacement of junior clerical staff, mainly women, through technology. Employment for clerks, typists and stenographers has already entered a relative decline, while there has been an absolute decline in jobs for telephone and telegraph operators. The loss of jobs can already be seen in the unemployment of young women, and will have a massive social impact over the 1980s, particularly for the less skilled junior clerks and typists. Sandra Prerost predicts the 'permanent decline of office work' in the private sector, and sees the introduction of labour-replacing technology as an integral part of government policy in the case of the clerical, sales and service industries, includes word processors, video display terminals, computerized point-of-sale terminals and more sophisticated and versatile use of computers to store, retrieve and communicate information.

Most of the clerical and general office work done by women in all industries will be affected. The estimate by the large employment agency Westaff, that by 1979 20 000 typists had already been replaced in Sydney alone, has been widely quoted.[15] The price of word processors is steadily dropping – already a word processor which can replace at least ten typists can be bought for roughly the equivalent of one year's salary for one typist.[16]

Linda Rubinstein, in a paper presented to the First Women and Labour Conference, estimates that word processors will allow staff cuts of 50 per cent and make typists, stenographers and secretarial staff redundant.[17] Women will be either trying to compete with men for highly skilled technical work – where they are handicapped by less access to training, less experience and barriers to social acceptance – or they will be limited to jobs in 'data factories', such as key-punching, which is soul-destroying work, entailing higher health risks, and little or no chance of promotion.

The implication of this is that women should refuse to accept these low-status jobs, and must therefore demand access to technical training. In doing so they must challenge the notion that technical skills are the province of a small elite.

Computerisation in the insurance industry has meant a need for fewer staff. The Women's Bureau[18] found that several large insurance companies said their staff numbers had barely risen in ten years despite the increase in the number of policies they handle. Some firms had reduced staff since 1973-74. One company had reduced clerical staff from 100 to 21 and another from 168 to 8 with the introduction of word processors.

The bureau also found that banks had reduced their recruiting by 40 per cent between 1975 and 1977, and were shifting their emphasis from career officers to a short-term, non-career workforce, hiring three times as many women as men. The introduction of automatic tellers and electronic fund transfers between banks and shops, hotels, firms and restaurants was expected to reduce banking employees even further in the 1980s.[19]

In a detailed study of women in the banking industry Anne Game and Rosemary Pringle foresee staff cuts, automation, 'scientific management' techniques, introduction of automatic tellers, increasing EDP work employing women as routine machine operators, electronic cheque-sorting machines staffed by women, almost exclusively married women doing shiftwork and, generally speaking, people employed to do a specific job on one 'tier' rather than as part of their climb up a career ladder. They see also a high turnover rate and a continuing sexual division of labour.[20]

Increasingly, attention is being drawn to the change in nature and organization of women's work caused by new technology. An American study has found high rates of heart disease amongst women office machinists in clerical and sales occupations, especially those who are powerless and in dead-end jobs.[21] Automation is producing clerical jobs that are 'deskilled, downgrading, dead-ended and dissatisfying'. Workers are expected to produce more, and 'there are also reports of a disturbing trend to processing speed-ups and piece-rate pay, and a feeling among clerical workers that their jobs are computer-controlled'. Stress for these women is a major health risk.

A number of unions – including the Australian Journalists' Association, the Bank Employees' Union and the Federated Clerks' Union – are concerned about the health and comfort of workers using video display terminals and units. In particular, eye strain, headaches, tiredness, depression, possible long-term effects of 'electronic smog' (microwaves and x-rays), arm, back and shoulder strains from sitting in an awkward position, and tenosynovitis have all been mentioned.

The Trans National Co-operative, a Sydney-based research group, has also listed the impacts of technology including increased intensity of work (i.e., more shiftwork, faster pace, measured output), and greater centralization of decision-making and control.[22]

The Working Women's Centre (Melbourne), in its submission to the Committee of Inquiry into Technological Change, outlined similar changes including a greater division of labour leading to simpler, more repetitive tasks requiring little training and 'leading nowhere' in terms of career prospects. It said that methods of supervision which have long been typical in manufacturing industry will become more common in white-collar areas: time and motion studies, detailed measurement of work output, 'incentive' or bonus systems, high production quotas (for example for key-punch operators) all resulting in strain on workers and disregard for their health or comfort. The problems of stress, monotony, pressure of work, back pain, tenosynovitis, headaches, eye strain, hearing loss and so on which have been a feature of industrial work will become characteristic of work in 'information factories'. Although it can be argued that technological change requires a general upgrading of the level of skills in the workforce, it has also been argued that the workforce will become polarized into a technical elite and an unskilled majority with the middle ground virtually eliminated, as skills and prospects for advancement are lost.[23]

As machines take over much of the skill involved in many jobs, work becomes more mechanized, more controlled and more monotonous. The same techniques used in factories to increase production and discipline the workers are now being used in offices changing them into paper factories and their staff into process workers.[24]

Apart from changes in the work itself there is more likelihood of casual, part-time and temporary work, not introduced in order to give workers greater leisure time or flexible working hours, but to allow employers to hire the cheapest and most 'disposable' workforce.[25]

A Canberra-based research group, Red Fems, in its discussion of technological change in the public service focuses on the fragmentation of work into specific, specialized tasks, resulting in a loss of skills for employees, an increase in part-time work, with workers having less control over the work process as a whole and a greater gulf between part-time workers and management.[26] They also see the possibility of deskilled clerical work in the public service being 'farmed out' as piecework to women working in their own homes on word processers or other machines linked by telephone to a central computer.

The disadvantages of outwork, as known in the clothing industry, would extend to white-collar workers with women working at home being isolated, and trade union activity virtually impossible. The flexibility that outwork is seen to offer to individuals (often illusory) would be paid for in loss of control over the work situation and, furthermore, the gains made by women in entering the workplace outside their homes would be eroded. Demands for child-care facilities would be undercut and the sexual division of labour in the home would go unchallenged.

The impact of the structural change of work on women is far-reaching: it is felt not just on the job, but in women's role in the labour market and, therefore, since they are so closely linked, in the family and in society in general.

In this context, the women's movement becomes an important force, not only in increasing the involvement of women in white-collar unions but also organizing outside the traditional workplace.

As fewer jobs are likely to be available in the service sector many young women, denied a job, may turn to having children, even though they are socially and financially unable to cope. These women will be even further disadvantaged if they attempt to re-enter the workforce at age thirty or thereabouts. Employers will prefer young women for unskilled routine work in technologically sophisticated jobs, for instance, retailing, banking and administration. Poor working conditions, low pay, lack of prospects for promotion and the large proportion of women reaching child-bearing age will contribute to the high labour turnover of young women. In some cases this exploitable workforce will be supplemented by older, married women working part time. Overall, given the high competition for dead-end jobs and little access to other jobs for either girls entering or women re-entering the labour market, there is likely to be a return of emphasis on women's role in the family and in unpaid community work, and greater devaluation of the importance of education for girls and women.

Several people, including Gail Shelston[27] and Ann Forward[28], President of the ACOA, have further pointed out that women are disadvantaged by technological change because the general social conditioning, education and job training of women is still biased towards non-technical skills .Therefore women, as well as being disadvantaged in an increasingly technologically sophisticated labourforce, are excluded from decisions about the use of technology. Although skilled workers do not make major decisions about the social uses of technology, if they have effective industrial organisation they are in a position to bargain collectively for some intervention in decision-making in their industry. So, as Ann Forward argues, unless women enter technical occupations and are active in unions they cannot be involved in such a process.

A deeper argument put forward is that the sexual division of labour reflects to some extent the separation of technology from social purpose which is part of the Western tradition. Methods of teaching maths and science have been criticized for failing to relate skills to social relationships, problems and context. It has been shown that girls do better in maths and science when they are taught in a social context, and that they are more concerned than boys with the application of skills to human ends.[29] The concern with technological change is not just about the loss of employment that it may entail but also about the uses to which it is put, and its impact on work processes. Therefore, involvement of women in technical education and work could be an added influence in the search for creative, integrated work, serving human needs.

The political and economic context of new technology and structural change

Several commentators have stressed that changes in employment opportunities and in the nature of work are not caused by technology, but are a result of the political and economic framework that determines how the technology is used.

For instance, the Trans National Co-operative sees new technology being introduced for political and economic reasons, as a means of lowering employers wage costs in a recession.[30] Production is maintained and the workforce is displaced. In an international context, labour-replacing technology is a major weapon in international competition. Microprocessors, data processing and communications systems allow further internationalisation to occur as multinationals can operate in several different countries, each country being used for that aspect of the production process which can be done at optimal cost, taking advantage of, for example, a low-wage labour force in one country, a technically skilled elite in another, supplies of raw materials in another, and so on. This process, known as the international division of labour, is becoming more refined as Third World countries become industrialised with new technology and management methods, and Australia becomes more specialized as a supplier of raw materials rather than labour. Large corporations are the major forces transferring technology and production processes around the world, not only increasing their production capacity, but also creating markets for their technologically advanced products and equipment in the developing countries.

The benefits of this process are reaped by national governments to some extent, and particularly multinational corportaions, but they are not generally shared by either the workers who are exploited in low-wage countries or those displaced in high-technology ones. The costs are also felt in communities whose economies are geared towards export, rather than production to meet local needs.

In Australia in the 1960s and 1970s there was a steady increase in production per person employed, due to improved technology and skills. However, the distribution of benefits reflected the entrenched inequalities of Australian society, the power of the various interest group, the multinational corporations, the Australian companies, and wage and salary-earners, amongst others.[31]

Scenarios of the future – the role of the women's movement

In all scenarios of the future, unemployment features to a large but varying degree. Therefore, the role of the Working Women's Charter Campaign will increasingly involve not further establishing women's right to work so much as struggling to maintain the progress toward that goal which has been achieved so far.

Unions presently attempting to gain the thirty-five-hour week, and thinking of other means of shortening working hours, such as the introduction of study leave and family leave, are exercising their power to ensure that technological change leads not only to a greater share by workers in the benefits of increased production, but also to continuing employment. As the TNC points out:

new technology heightens the contradiction between the promise of advanced technology and the reality . . . Automated and computerized equipment could free people at work from routine, soul-destroying, back-breaking tasks and leave them free to engage in more creative work. The reality for countless numbers of workers around the world is an even greater enslavement within the work process or to be discarded by society as useless. Unless the application of the new technologies are brought under greater social control, without a doubt they will contribute substantially to even larger numbers of jobless and to the deskilling and dehumanization of the jobs of those who remain.

They conclude that wage- and salary-earners, through their unions and job organisations, are the only force that can intervene in the political and economic process of technological change and redirect it for the benefit of society as a whole.[32]

Bruce Macfarlane, a political economist at Flinders University, argues that, in unchecked, the 'unbeatable combination' of effective capital and low wages in South-East Asia will wipe out manufacturing industry in countries like Australia, New Zealand and Japan.[33] Intermediate zones of industrial development are being created in parts of Asia with Singapore already encouraging investment in high-technology communications, and industries requiring a smaller but more skilled workforce. Unskilled migrant workers from Malaysia are being repatriated, and labour-intensive industries are being forced to she labour because of changes in government policy. South Korea, notorious for its exploitation of young women in the clothing and textile industries, is developing petro-chemical and heavy industry. Macfarlane's scenario for Australia in the 1980s includes the further decline of local manufacturing, the rising importance of mining, some light and tertiary industry, with the possibility (by no means likely) of some of the wealth thus generated being used to rebuild manufacturing or to sustain public spending.

It is important to realise that many such writers are projecting trends assuming *unchecked* new technology and economic restructuring. However, Macfarlane lists several possible checks on the trends he forecasts, one of which is the international labour movement in which the Australian women's movement will continue to have a major role. Women in Asia are doing the low-paid, labour-intensive work, such as making clothes, that women have always done. When Australia's manufacturing industry was growing in the 1950s and early 1960s, migrant women took on this role. The labour of women in Asia is also making possible the computer-based revolution that will eliminate jobs in Australia's service industry. In Asian countries the labour movement is suppressed, and in Australia it is undermined by unemployment. Only the increasing strength of the labour movement in both developed and developing countries will be able to challenge these trends and propose the creation of employment to provide goods and services available to the majority of people.

Another scenario for the 1980s predicts not high but mass unemployment. It says that if the Australian government did not manage to channel resources back into the development of a restructured local manufacturing industry, and did not build up the publish sector, the trend towards unemployment would be very strong with service sector employment, both skilled and unskilled, being further eroded. The social tensions created by long-term unemployment and falling living standards would be explosive. If the relatively affluent middle class became threatened by downgrading of their skills and erosion of their employment opportunities, they could conceivably form the basis of a radical right-wing political movement. This, combined with international tension about energy resources, could increase the pressure for war as a 'solution' to world economic and political problems. The impact on women would be drastic as sexism and racism increased, and economic and political scapegoats were sought.

The process, described as 'de-development' by Professor Wheelright, Associate professor of Political Economy at Sydney University[34], would entail Australia losing its manufacturing industry and the bulk of its employment, having its natural resources rapidly consumed, and then having either the energy nor the capital to rebuild a manufacturing industry to meet local needs. An increasingly authoritarian government would be needed to control reactions against this trend.

Social tensions created by mass or even moderately high unemployment could on the other hand necessitate some kind of policy of widespread job creation – not the senseless and economically unproductive 'relief' or 'susso' schemes of the 1930s, but the creation of bona fide employment.

Job creation: The private enterprise view

The view of the Australian government, Treasury and business leaders is that if inflation is controlled (largely through lowering wages) the economy will 'recover' and there will be increased investment which will develop internationally competitive industry and create jobs. There are several objections to this view. One is that for Australia to be internationally competitive, wages would have to be lowered to about 10 per cent of their current levels, which would be unacceptable unless, of course, we had repressive labour laws, State emergency powers and intervention of the military in labour disputes comparable to that of countries such as South Korea and the Philippines. Another objection is that investment, according to recent trends, is not increasing jobs but decreasing them, reflecting a fundamental shift in the economy to capital-intensive production.

It seems reasonable to assume that as the international division of labour proceeds, Australia's role will move further away from that of providing an industrial workforce. If private enterprise does create jobs in this context, it will be from its capacity to develop capital-intensive, technologically sophisticated activities which use the skills of a highly educated workforce, and create enough wealth to support a large service sector.

Perhaps part of the concept of creating job through private enterprise is the 'radical' option of developing a large-scale, highly advanced industry supplying automated and computerized components and hardware to the manufacturers in the industrialised Third World. This would require massive development, investment, technological change and long-term planning.

It seems doubtful whether Australian-owned companies have this capacity, and even more doubtful whether an Australian government could claim a high enough proportion of the profits of overseas investors to support such a development.

Job creation through the public sector

An alternative view on job creation relies heavily on the public sector expanding to meet a range of social and community needs: for example, public transport, housing environmental protection, development of low-cost energy sources, health services, education, and care of the aged.

Some of these jobs are not 'profitable' in the narrow sense, and require public funding. However, there are social costs entailed in neglecting them which can develop into problems demanding costly solutions. Furthermore, it is reasonable to expect that social needs of this type should be met at a high standard in a country that boasts of its wealth.

The problem really is the control of that wealth. Various sources of funding for job creation in the public sector have been suggested, such as resources taxes and tax on profits repatriated by foreign investors. This involves both redistribution from the private sector to the public sector and from profits to wages and salaries. Although this may be feasible it depends very much on changes in the balance of power between labour and capital, both industrially and politically.

Those who claim that Australia faces a great future in the 1980s because of its mineral wealth may imagine themselves as ocker uranium shieks, but they show little evidence of having thought about how such wealth could be distributed to maintain living standards and provide employment for the majority of the population, or what will happen when the energy sources are either spent or technologically redundant.

Redistribution of wealth

The distribution of wealth derived either from mineral resources or from high technology industry has two aspects: how much will Australia gain compared with the countries that use the resources or the companies that take profits out of the resources or the companies that take profits out of the country; and secondly, how is the wealth distributed within Australia?

One response to increasing and widespread structural unemployment coupled with exploitation of valuable resources has been to propose shorter working hours, increased time for leisure, education and community involvement, along with a guaranteed income security system. If there are to be few jobs but great wealth produced, why not allow everyone access to a reasonable income, whether it be derived from productive labour or other meaningful activities that become possible? If Australia is rich in natural resources and able to import or produce food, goods and services by means of automation, the distribution of benefits becomes a political rather than a technical problem.

The political problem is one of enormous dimensions. Firstly, such a scenario would require local control of resources, which is limited and decreasing as Australia becomes linked to an international economy in which large multinational corporations are extremely powerful. Secondly, it requires a more equitable distribution of wealth and social benefits within Australia then at present and, thirdly, it requires a drastic change in social attitudes to work.

One such change would be to break the nexus between employment and income. While a small proportion of the population were engaged in economically productive work – or a large proportion of the population were engaged in economically productive work for a small proportion of their time – they all would receive a guaranteed income and would be able to devote their time to personally fulfilling and socially useful activity. However, the institution of employment is so strong to in Australian society – both to distribute income and to structure people's time – that such a change might not be viable.

A comparable scheme would be to employ those who wanted to work in an expanded tertiary sector, designed primarily to meet social needs. Thus, although employment would continue to be central to people's lives, the nature and purpose of work would shift from a primarily economic focus to a social one.

Such a scenario envisages wage- and salary-earners, through their share of benefits by bargaining for large-scale employment in a tertiary sector set up primarily in response to community needs. While this may be a useful principle for both unions and community groups to work towards, it has drawbacks if it takes place within the international context outlined previously in this chapter.

The context, to recapitulate, included Australia's prosperity depending on tis role within the international division of labour as a supplier of natural resources and technologically advanced equipment. It could be profitable in the short term, but another crisis could be precipitated if the energy resources were either depleted or no longer in demand, or if the equipment and technical expertise supplied became redundant. Furthermore, relying on wealth gained from its role in the international division of labour, Australia would be dependent on the exploitation of a massive low-paid Asian working class. Although this might not trouble many consciences, it would entail the possibility of severe international conflict. Some Third World countries are already striving towards a 'new economic order'. If the emerging labour movements and human rights movements of the present low-wage countries are successful, Australia might be forced to take on a different role.

A role that has been suggested by some union officials is for Australia to support the emerging labour and human rights movement in low-wage Asian countries that are seeking higher wages and better working conditions for Asian workers, and a reorientation of Asian industry away from cheap exports towards the development of goods and services to meet urgent local needs. For Australia, they see the possibility of reducing competition from low-wage 'runaway shops', and thus challenging the international division of labour. Such a challenge would have to include serious opposition to the short-term exploitation of energy resources simply to earn foreign exchange, further questioning of the impact of new technology, and a substantial campaign by wage- and salary-earners and their organisations to link employment opportunities to community needs.

The exploitation of young women in factories in Asia, therefore, has a direct link with the decline of Australia's manufacturing industry, the introduction of new technology and the export of its natural resources. The social consequences for Australia are already evident in its high unemployment rate, but if these trends continue the effects will be more profound. The masses of migrants and Australian-born women who entered the paid workforce throughout the 1950s, '60s and '70s, who were essential to both the manufacturing and service sector, will be discarded, along with redundant skills. The social and financial strength of many women will deteriorate as the labour market worsens, although it is likely that the experience of large numbers of women in paid employment since 1945, along with the influential ideas of the women's movement, will create a stronger basis for action than existed in the Depression of the 1930s.

The trend of women entering the paid workforce has meant a broadening of women's role to the extent that women now do both paid and unpaid work. Work as an institution has been criticized in relation to the labour market and social need, the social and environmental effects of production, resource allocation, the priorities towards which human effort is being directed and the distribution of benefits among the population. As we enter the 1980s these issues will continue to be raised.

While paid employment does not liberate women – indeed it creates further stresses and problems as we have seen – it does provide a unique opportunity for them to become less isolated and to overcome the sex-role stereotyping that has for so long confined them to economic and social second place.

However, if Australia continues to specialize in tis role of supplier of mineral and energy resources, the Australian labourforce could virtually be eliminated from the production process, and the power of the labour movement to bargain for job security and expanding employment opportunities fundamentally undercut.

Such an outcome is not inevitable. Indeed, the fact that it is possible and would be so drastic has the effect of destabilizing society, making new forms of organisation likely to emerge and to overcome the inherent limitations of present work and community-based organisations. Over the past decade, the most significant contribution to this process has come from the women's movement.

To sustain the opportunity for paid employment, therefore, will become the essential task of the Working Women's Charter Campaign, acting through participants in unions, the workplace and grass-roots organisations in the community.

Notes

Preface

1   Des Storer, *'But I Wouldn't Want My Wife To Work Here', A Study of Migrant Women in Melbourne Industry*, Centre for Urban Research and Action, Melbourne, 1976

2   Des Storer and Kaye Hargreaves, 'Migrant Women in Industry' in *Social Policy and Problems of the Work Force*, Vol. 1, ACTU Social Welfare Unit, Melbourne, 1977.

Introduction

1   Constance Larmour, 'Women's Wages and the WEB', in *Women at Work*, Ann Curthouys, Susan Eade, Peter Spearitt (eds), Australian Society for Labour History, Canberra, 1975.

1 Working Women – a Historical Perspective

1   Beverley Kingston, *My Wife, My Daughter and Poor Mary Ann*, Nelson, Melbourne, 1977.

2   ibid., p. 31.

3   ibid., p. 51

4   ibid., p. 52

5   ibid., p. 50

6   ibid., p.2

7   Dr A. Smithers, 'Trends in Women's Work', paper presented to the First Interstate Conference of the Council of Action for Equal Pay, Sydney, 1938, p. 1.

8   Janice Brownfoot, and Dianne Scott, *The Unequal Half: Women in Australia since 1788*, Reed Education, Sydney, 1977, p. 42.

9   For a discussion of the history of equal pay, see Edna Ryan and Anne Conlon, *Gentle Invaders: Australian Women at Work 1788-1974*, Nelson, Sydney, 1975.

10 ibid., p. 89.

11 Penny Ryan and Tim Rose, 'Women, Arbitration and the Family', in *Women at Work*, p. 18.

12 ibid., p.20

13 ibid., pp.20-2

14 Muriel Heagney, *Are Women Taking Men's Jobs?*, Hilton and Veitch, Melbourne, 1935.

15 Ryan and Rowse, op. cit., pp. 21-2.

16 ibid., p. 23.

17 ibid.

18 Larmour, op. cit.

19 Daphne Gollan, 'The Duly and Hansford Strike 1943: Find the Strikers', in *Second Women and Labour Conference Papers, 1980*, Vol. 1., Second Women and Labour Conference, Bundoora, 1980.

20 Women's Bureau, *The Role of Women in the Economy*, AGPS, Canberra, 1974, p.4.

21 ibid., p. 12.

22 This has been discussed by many writers. *The Role of Women in the Economy*, gives detailed figures.

23 Katy Richmond, 'Women in the Workforce', La Trobe Sociology Papers, Paper No. 2, Department of Sociology School of Social Science, La Trobe University, 1973.

24 Rosemary Auchmuty, *Australia's Daughters*, Methuen, Sydney, 1978.

25 Preceding figures from *The Role of Women in the Economy*, AGPS, Canberra, 1974, p. 6.

26 Richmond, op. cit.

27 Women's Bureau, *Facts on Women at Work in Australia*, AGPS, Canberra, 1978.

28 Figures in this paragraph are taken from *The Role of Women in the Economy*, AGPS, Canberra, 1974, p. 8.

29 Women's Bureau, *Facts on Women at Work in Australia*, AGPS, Canberra, 1978.

30 ibid.

31 Sandra Prerost, 'Technological Change and Women's Employment in Australia' in *Second Women and Labour Conference Papers, 1980*, Vol. 2, p. 868.

32 ibid., p. 859

33 Australian Bureau of Statistics, *The Labour Force*, May 1980.

34 Prerost, op. cit.

35 Australian Bureau of Statistics, as quoted by Prerost, op. cit., pp. 867-8.

36 J. Selby Smith, 'Implications of Developments in Micro-electronic Technology on Women in the Paid Workforce', September 1979

2 Towards a Working Women's Charter

1 Rhonda Galbally, 'Women, Inequality and Australian Trade Unions: the Development of the Working Women's Charter Campaign and the ACTU Charter for Working Women: two case studies', M.A. Prelim, Thesis, La Trobe University, 1979.

2   Gwen George, 'Why Lobby to the ACTU Congress', *Boilermakers and Blacksmiths' Society Journal,* Sydney, September 1971

3   'Recommendations of the ACTU Executive to the 1971 Congress', ACTU, Melbourne, 1971

4   Report from Syndicate Group G, ACTU School, Canberra, 1972.

5   'The Case For Women's Caucuses', AMU National Women's Conference, Sydney, 1974.

6   Leslie Falkiner, 'Women Join Union Movement', the *Age,* n.d., 1975.

7   The *Australian Financial Review,* Editorial, 7 September 1973

8   Bob Mills, 'ACTU Shirks Equal Pay Issue for "family wage" ', the *Australian Financial Review,* 6 September 1973

9   *Decisions of Congress,* ACTU, Melbourne, 1973.

10   *Women and Politics Conference,* AGPS, Canberra, 1976, p. 90.

11   Women's Bureau, *Comment,* Department of Labour, Melbourne, Summer, 1975.

12   Galbally, op. cit.

13   Catherine Martin, 'Talking About Working', the *West Australian,* 26 March 1975

14   Harold Souter, ACTU Circular, No. 76/1975, Melbourne.

15   'Alternative Union and Working Women's Action', press release, 15 September 1975.

16   'Hawke wants more women on executive', the *Australian,* 18 September 1975.

17   Pat Clancy, *Tribune,* 9 January 1969.

18   *Women and Politics Conference,* AGPS, Canberra, 1976.

19   *Women Unions 1976,* conference booklet, Women's Trade Union Commission, Sydney, 1976.

20   Galbally, op. cit.

21   ACTU Charter for Working Women.

22   Galbally, op. cit.

23 ibid.

24 ibid.

25 ibid.

26 'What Maternity Leave Means to you', Working Women's Centre, Melbourne, 1979.

27 ACTU Charter for Working Women, as amended in VSTA open sub-committee on sexism, minutes of meeting, June 1980.

28 'International Women's Day March 1980', broadsheet by Wollongong International Women's Day Committee.

29 'Jobs for Women!', leaflet, Wollongong Working Women's Charter Committee, 1980.

30 Personal communication.

31 ibid.

32 ibid.

3 The Right to Work

1   Ryan and Conlon, op. cit., p. 175.

2   Australian Bureau of Statistics, *The Labour Force,* March 1980.

3   Australian Conciliation and Arbitration Commission, Decision, Mis. 75/78, MD Print D6553, Sydney, April 1978.

4   ibid., p. 5.

5   ibid.

6   ibid., p.6.

7   ICF Women Workers' Group, *The Right to Work,* ICF, Geneva, 1975.

8   Australian Bureau of Statistics, *The Labour Force,* May 1979.

9   Women's Bureau, *Facts on Women at Work in Australia,* AGPS, Canberra, 1978.

10 Keith Windschuttle, *Unemployment: a social and political analysis of the economic crisis in Australia,* Penguin, Melbourne, 1979, Chapter 7.

11 Australian Bureau of Statistics, *The Labour Force,* May 1979.

12 Windschuttle, op. cit., p. 14.

13 Australian Bureau of Statistics, *The Labour Force,* November 1977.

14 Australian Bureau of Statistics, *The Labour Force,* August 1979.

15 ibid.

16 *Nation Review,* 3-9 March 1977.

17 The *Australian Financial Review,* 21 September 1979.

18 Karen Throssell, 'Part-time work: a middleclass concept?', Labour Resource Centre, Melbourne, September 1979.

19 Australian Bureau of Statistics, *The Labour Force,* May 1979.

20 Women's Bureau, *The Role of Women in the Economy,* AGPS, Canberra, 1974, p. 20 ff.

21 *Female Unemployment in Four Urban Centres,* Labour Market Stuudies, No. 3, Department of Labour and National Service, Melbourne, 1970.

22 ibid., p. 20.

23 Women's Bureau, *The Role of Women in the Economy,* AGPS, Canberra, 1974, pp. 25-7.

24 *Girls, School and Society,* Schools Commission, AGPS, Canberra, 1975.

25 ibid.

26 Kerry Lovering, *Australian Women Workers in a Changing Society,* Women's Bureau, Department of Employment and Youth Affairs, Canberra, October 1978.

27 Women's Bureau, 'Training Available for Women Under NEAT', *Women and Work Newsletter,* Department of Employment and Industrial Relations, Vol. 1, No. 1, Canberra, May 1977.

28 Department of Employment and Youth Affairs, NEAT Scheme guidelines, 1979.

29 Department of Employment and Industrial Relations, NEAT Scheme Operational Statistics, unpublished material.

30 Department of Employment and Youth Affairs, National Employment and Training System, Operational Statistics, September 1979.

31 *Adjusting to Change – the experiences of 60 people retrenched in the clothing trades industry,* ACOSS Report to the study group on structural adjustment, ACOSS, Sydney, September 1978.

32 Eva Cox, Sue Jobson, Jeannie Martin, 'We Cannot Talk Our Rights', *Migrant Women 1975,* NSW Council of Social Service and School of Sociology, University of NSW, Sydney, 1976.

33 *Unemployed Women: A Research Report,* The Council of Social Service of New South Wales, December 1978.

4 Discrimination

1 'Towards Equal Opportunity in Employment', *First Annual Report of the National Committee on Discrimination in Employment and Occupation, 1973-74,* AGPS, Canberra, p.31.

2 ibid., frontispiece.

3 National Committee on Discrimination in Employment and Occupation, *Fourth Annual Report 1976-77,* AGPS, Canberra, 1978.

4 The *Sunday Mail,* 26 February 1978.

5 The *Mercury,* 21 April 1979.

6 The *West Australian,* 1 August 1977

7 ibid.

8 The *Sunday Observer,* 16 October 1977.

9 The *Age,* 26 September 1977.

10 The *Australian Financial Review,* 29 October 1979.

11 Joan Bielski, 'The Case for Legislation Against Discrimination on the Grounds of Sex', unpublished paper.

12 See for example Chris Ronalds, *Anti-Discrimination Legislation in Australia: A Guide*, Butterworths, Sydney, 1979.

13 Personal communication.

14 Ronalds, op. cit.

15 *Report of the Commissioner for Equal Opportunity, year ended 30 June 1978*, South Australian Government Printer.

16 Regina Graycart, 'Federal Awards Get in the Way', in *Legal Service Bulletin*, Vol. 4, No. 5, October 1979.

17 Ronalds, op. cit., p. 5.

18 'Protest "Avalanche" on Bill', the *Sydney Morning Herald*, 2 March 1977.

19 'Discrimination', Editorial, the *Sydney Morning Herald*, 25 March 1977.

20 Ronalds, op. cit.

21 *Report of the Anti-Discrimination board for the year ended 30 June 1978*, NSW Government Printer, 1978.

22 See the *Sydney Morning Herald*, 13 October 1979 and the *Daily Telegraph*, 9 October 1979.

23 The *Daily Telegraph*, Editorial, 9 October 1979.

24 Margaret Thornton, 'Board's First Decision', *Legal Service Bulletin*, Vol. 4, No. 5, October 1979.

25 The *Age*, 9 March 1977.

26 *First Annual Report of the Commissioner for Equal Opportunity, 30 June 1978*, Victorian Government Printer, 1979.

27 *Second Annual Report of the Commissioner for Equal Opportunity, 30 June 1979*, Victorian Government Printer, 1980.

28 Deb Hann, 'Wardley's Long Battle', *Legal Service Bulletin*, Vol. 4, No. 5, October 1979.

29 'High Court Backs Wardley Ruling', the *Age*, 5 March 1980.

30 ACTU Charter for Working Women.

31 Michael Ross, 'Women can drive trains now if only men would let them', the *National Times*, 27 October 1975.

32 'Ban on Women Couriers', the *Daily Mirror*, 17 April 1975.

33 The *Sydney Morning Herald*, 9 October 1975.

34 'Mines Ban on Women to be Lifted', the *Sydney Morning Herald*, 26 November 1975.

35 'Against Discrimination ', *Common Cause*, Miners' Federation of Australia, Sydney, 3 August 1977.

36 'Sacked because she wanted to attend a seminar for women unionists', the *Socialist*, Sydney, 1 September 1976.

37 The *Daily Mirror*, 8 November 1976.

38 'Unionist says sex bias lost her a job', the *Australian*, 8 March 1975.

39 'Sack the Mums!', *Journal*, 2 May 1977.

40 The *Advocate*, 27 April 1977.

41 The *Age*, 4 July 1977.

42 ibid., 9 June 1977.

43 The *Bulletin*, 17 April 1979.

44 *First Annual Report of the Commissioner for Equal Opportunity, 30 June 1978*, Victorian Government Printer, 1979.

45 'Job Bias: Workers Fear the Sack', the *Age*, 15 June 1977.

46 *Women Unions 1976*, Women's Trade Union Commission, Sydney, 1976.

47 Ann Game and Rosemary Pringle, 'Women, the Labour Process and Technological Change in the Banking Industry in Australia', Kuring-Gai C.A.E., May 1979.

48 *Women Unions 1976*, Women's Trade Union Commission, Sydney, 1976.

49 The *Herald,* 17 October 1979.

50 *First Annual Report of the Commissioner for Equal Opportunity, 30 June 1978,* Victorian Government Printer, 1979.

51 L. V. Entrekin, G. E. Popp, C. Jay and L. K. Savery, 'Discrimination in Employment: a look at Australia in the light of current trends', paper to 47th Anzaas Congress, May 1976.

52 Ann Calvert, 'Girls and Apprenticeships', *Female Education and Equal Opportunity,* Doveton Cluster of Schools, Melbourne, 1977.

53 The *West Australian,* 1 August 1977.

54 *Women at Work Kit,* produced by joint TTAV, VSTA and VTU Sexism in Education Project and the Working Women's Centre, Melbourne 1979, and *Pik-a Print* Career Education Project, Education Technology Centre, Education Department of South Australia, 1979.

55 Ronalds, op. cit.

56 The *Courier Mail,* 10 July 1979.

57 Hilary McPhee, 'Women's role in the working force . . . vulnerable in the economic downturn', the *Age* 28 July 1975.

58 The *Mercury,* 13 April 1977.

59 Sara Dowse, the *Age,* 20 January 1979.

5 Migrant Women

1 Storer, op. cit.

2 Australian Bureau of Statistics, *The Labour Force,* February 1980.

3 Women's Bureau, *The Role of Women in the Economy,* AGPS, Canberra, 1974, p. 6.

4 Australian Bureau of Statistics, *The Labour Force,* March 1980.

5 Australian Bureau of Statistics, *Census 30th June 1976,* Table 62 - 'Occupation by birthplace, employed population, females'.

6 Australian Bureau of Statistics, *The Labour Force,* February 1980.

7   ibid.

8   Des Storer, 'Migration, Women and Work', CURA, Melbourne, 1975.

9   The Jackson Committee, *Policies for the Development of Manufacturing Industry,* AGPS, Canberra, Vol. 1, 1975.

10   Helen Hurwitz, 'Factory Women' in Allan Bordow (ed.), *The Worker in Australia,* University of Queensland Press, St Lucia, 1977.

11   National Women's Advisory Committee, 'Migrant Women Speak', AGPS< Canberra, APril 1979.

12   ibid., p. 5.

13   ibid., p. 14.

14   Storer, *'But I wouldn't Want My Wife to Work Here'.*

15   Working Women's Charter Campaign Conference, *Resolutions,* Sydney, August 1977.

16   Working Women's Charter Campaign Conference, FILEF Women's Group paper, Sydney, August 1977.

17   Vivi Koatsounadis, 'Disadvantaged Groups in the Workforce', South Sydney Community Aid, undated.

18   Storer, 'Migration, Women and Work'.

6 Hours and Work Patterns

1   Linda Rubinstein, *Women and Shiftwork,* Western Region Council for Social Development, Melbourne, 1977.

2   Working Women's Charter Campaign Conference, *Resolutions,* Sydney, August 1977.

3   Mike Gallagher, 'A Critical Discussion of the Debate on "Alternative Concepts for Organising Work" ', Labour Resource Centre, Melbourne, October 1978.

4   Australian Bureau of Statistics, *The Labour Force.*

5   Australian Bureau of Statistics, *Evening and Night Work*, November 1976.

6   'The Great Australian Weekend: Penalty rates Under Attack', Labour Resource Centre, Melbourne, 1979.

7   Judy Willis, 'Women and Part-time Work: the Waverley Survey', forthcoming.

8   Denise Cusack and John Dodd, *Outwork: an alternative mode of employment*, CURA, Melbourne, 1978.

9   Australian Bureau of Statistics, *The Labour Force*, May 1979.

10   Judy Willis, *Unemployed Women: a Research Report*, NSW Council of Social Service, Sydney, 1978; and Cox, Jobson and Martin, op. cit.

11   Throssell, op. cit.

12   Gallagher, op. cit.

13   Karen Throssell, 'Rip-off Ronald: how McDonald's exploits kids', Labour Resource Centre, Melbourne, 1980.

14   Women's Bureau, 'Part-time Employment', *Women at Work*, No. 13, Commonwealth Department of Labour, Canberra, january 1974.

15   'Alternative Working Hours', Working Women's Centre. Discussion Paper No. 8, Melbourne, June 1976.

16   Jozefa Sobski, 'Effects of permanent part-time work on women', unpublished paper, 1979.

17   Australian Post and telecommunications Union (Victorian Branch), correspondence.

18   ACTU Charter for Working Women.

19   ACTU, 'Draft Guidelines and Negotiating Exhibit on Part-time work', Melbourne, September 1979.

20   Penny Giles, 'Permanent part-time work: some objections answered', paper to Australian Teachers' Federation Seminar, October 1979.

21 Joan Ford, 'Permanent Part-time Work Study', Future Lobby and the NSW Association for Mental Health, 1977.

22 'Alternative Working Hours', Working Women's Centre, Discussion Paper No. 8, Melbourne, June 1976.

23 Jan Harper and Lyn Richards, *Mothers and Working Mothers*, Penguin, Melbourne, 1979.

24 Patrick Kinnersley, *The Hazards of Work: How to Fight Them*, Wild & Woolley, Sydney, 1978.

25 Rubinstein, op. cit.

26 J. Carpentier and P. Cazamians, *Night Work*, ILO, Geneva, 1977.

27 Australian Bureau of Statistics, *Evening and Night Work*, November 1976.

28 Women's Bureau, *Facts on Women at Work in Australia*, AGPS, Canberra, 1978.

29 Rubinstein, op. cit.

30 Cusack and Dodd, op. cit.

7 Health and Safety

1 Marion I. Ireland, M.B., B.S., *A Survey of Women in Industry, Victoria, 1928*, Division of Industrial Hygiene, Commonwealth Department of Health, 1928.

2 'Your job . . . his profits or your life?', Liverpool Women's Health Centre, 1977.

3 Dr H. Halse, *Fatigue in Working Women*, Commonwealth Department of Health, undated.

4 See, for example, Dr Margaret Raphael, "The Dual Role Dilemma of Women Today', Women's Health Conference, Brisbane, 1975.

5 'Tougher Safety Laws for Industry', the *Sun-Herald*, 1 August 1976.

6 'Migrants and Occupational Health' (Preliminary Report), Centre for Urban Research and Action, Melbourne, 1978, p. 7.

7   ibid.

8   *Encyclopedia of Occupational Health and Safety,* Vol. II L-Z, ILO Office, Geneva, 1972, pp. 1501-7.

9   Lyn McKenzie, 'Women's Work is a Health Hazard',

10   Dorothy Hewitt, *Bobbin Up,* Seven Seas Books, Berlin, 1961.

11   Gill Armstrong, *A Hundred a Day,* Sharmill Films, Melbourne, 1973.

12   Zelda D'Aprano, *Zelda: the becoming of a woman,* Widescope International, Melbourne, 1978.

13   'Family Planning Needs', Discussion Paper No. 14, Working Women's Centre, Melbourne, December 1976.

14   Working Women's Charter Campaign Conference, *Resolutions,* Sydney, August 1977.

15   'Warning: Work is a health hazard . . . especially for women', *Link,* undated.

16   ibid.

17   Raphael, op. cit.

18   See, for example, the film *Me and Daphne,* Sydney Film and television School, 1977.

19   'This Job Mutilates Women', *Women at Work,* No. 16, Working Women's Centre, Melbourne, April-May 1979.

20   'Your job . . . his profits or your life?', Liverpool Women's Health Centre, 1977.

21   Ian Davis, 'Survey of Control of Sound', *Australian Financial Review,* 21 March 1977.

22   'Chemical Health Hazards', Circular letter No. 27/76, ICF, Geneva, 1976.

23   'Human factors and the work environment in the process industry: the trade unions' viewpoint', address given by Brian O'Neill, Executive Officer, the AWU and NSW Secretary, SDA, to the Institute of Chemical Engineers, June 1976.

24 Anne George, 'Occupational Health Hazards of Women: a Synoptic View', Advisory Council on the Status of Women, Ottawa, 1976.

25 Jim Walker, 'Tenosynovitis, A Crippling New Epidemic in Industry', *New Doctor,* number 13, Doctors' Reform Society, Sydney, 1979.

26 Deborah Vallance, 'Repetition Complaints of the Upper Limb in Female Workers - A Case Study', thesis for M.B., B.S. Department of Social and Preventive Medicine, Monash University, Clayton, December 1979: see also, address given to Women and Labour Conference planning group, Melbourne, 1979.

27 'More Health Checks Needed', *Women at Work,* Working Women's Centre, Melbourne, August 1977.

28 'Meat Wrappers' Asthma', *Women at Work,* No. 12, Working Women's Centre, Melbourne, Oct.-Nov. 1978.

29 L. Jorgensen, *Health Problems of Women in the Workforce,* background paper, Health Services research and Planning Branch, No. 1, Canberra, April 1977.

30 Linda Rubinstein, 'Computer Jobs Make Telephonists Sick', *Women at Work,* No. 18, Melbourne, Oct.-Nov. 1979.

31 'In an Office', *Women at Work,* Working Women's Centre, Melbourne, undated.

32 See, for example, 'Psychotropic Drug Abuse', Working Women's Centre, Discussion paper No. 21, Melbourne, September 1977.

33 Mary Owen and Sylvie Shaw, *Working Women,* Sisters, Melbourne, 1979, p. 36.

34 ibid.

35 'Slow down the line', *Women at Work,* No. 15, Working Women's Centre, Melbourne, April 1979.

36 'In the Meatworks', *Women at Work,* No. 16, Working Women's Centre, Melbourne, June 1979.

37 'Your job . . . his profits or your health?' Liverpool Women's Health Centre, 1977.

38 Ben Bartlett and the Workers' Health Centre Collective, 'The Politics of Occupational Health', *New Doctor,* number 13, Doctors' Reform Society, Sydney, 1979.

8 Child Care

1 Winsome McCaughey, 'History and Development of the Child Care Movement', in *Child Care: an industrial issue,* ACSPA, Melbourne, 1979.

2 'Action for Adequate Child Care', leaflet, Amalgamated Engineering Union, Sydney, undated.

3 McCaughey, op. cit.

4 ibid.

6 Women's Bureau, 'Child Care Centres', *Women in the Workforce,* No. 7 Department of Labour and National Service, Melbourne, January 1970.

7 Australian Bureau of Statistics, *Child Care,* Canberra, May 1977.

8 *The Need for Children's Services in Victoria,* Community Child Care Information Paper, Melbourne, February 1979.

9 Ailsa, Burns, 'Needs of Children and Families', in *Child care: an industrial issue,* ACSPA, Melbourne, 1979.

10 Rosalind Dey, 'WTUC - Film on Child Care', Sydney, September 1977.

11 FILEF Women's Group, 'Child Care and the Working Mother', in *Women at Work,* No. 3, Working Women's Centre, Spet.-Oct. 1976.

12 Storer, *'But I Wouldn't Want My Wife to Work Here'.*

13 Ailsa Burns, Maureen Fegan, Ashley Sparkes and Pat Thomson, *Working Mothers and their Children: the Electrical Trades Union*

Study, School of Behavioural Sciences, Macquarie University, 19743

14 Barbara Gayler, 'The Multi-cultural society: what about child care?' in *Ekstasis,* No. 15, CURA, Melbourne, August 1976.

15 *The Need for Children's Services in Victoria,* Community Child Care Information Paper, February 1979.

16 Ruth Crow, the *Melbourne Times,* 23 March 1977.

17 Merle Brown, 'Child Care and Working Women', position paper, undated.

18 *Royal Commission into Human Relationships,* AGPS, Canberra, 1977.

19 Minutes of meeting held at the Victorian Council of Social Service, July 1979, between representatives of welfare, child care and union peak council

20 'Should Unions Be Concerned About Child Care?', Working Women's Centre, Discussion Paper No. 2, Melbourne, October 1975; and 'Child Care - an important industrial issue?', Working Women's Centre, Discussion Paper No. 19, Melbourne, July 1977.

21 ibid.

22 Linda Rubinstein, 'The Role of Unions in the Child Care Movement', in *Child Care - an industrial issue,* ACSPA, Melbourne, 1979.

23 Anna Stewart, 'Unions and Employers: Current Policies and Attitudes', in *Child Care - an industrial issue,* ACSPA, Melbourne, 1979.

24 ibid., p. 55.

25 Rubinstein, 'The Role of Unions in the Child Care Movement'.

9 Women and Unions

1 Australian Bureau of Statistics, *Trade Union Statistics,* December 1978.

2   Australian Bureau of Statistics, *Trade Union Members*, November 1976.

3   D. W. Rawson, *Unions and Unionists in Australia*, George Allen & Unwin, Sydney, 1978.

4   Ross Martin, *Trade Unions in Australia*, Penguin, Melbourne, 1975.

5   Storer, '*But I Wouldn't Want My Wife To Work Here*'.

6   Galbally, op. cit.

7   ibid.

8   Martin, op. cit.

9   Leslie Falkiner, 'Women Join Union Movement', the *Age*

10 Storer, '*But I Wouldn't Want My Wife to Work Here*'.

11 Sol Encel *et al.*, *Women and Society: an Australian study*, Cheshire, Melbourne, 1974.

12 Chris R. Phillips, 'The Disadvantaged Worker', in *The Worker in Australia*, by Allan Bordow (ed.), University of Queensland Press, St Lucia, 1977.

13 Hurwitz, op. cit.

14 Stella Nord, 'New COnditions, New Demands', in *Australian Left Review*, Oct.-Nov. 1969.

15 Christine Curry, 'Union Lobby or Job Action?' in *Scarlet Woman*, No. 5, Melbourne, March 1977.

16 *Women and Politics Conference*, AGPS, Canberra, 1976.

17 Helen Prendergast, 'Women and Unions', Women's Trade Union Commission, unpublished paper, 1975.

18 'Women March for Jobs . . . The "Conspiracy" Affair', in *Voice*, Sydney, March 1975.

10 Prospects for the 1980s

1   Prerost, op. cit.

2   Ann Forward, International Women's Day Seminar, Melbourne, 1980.

3   Prerost, op. cit.

4   Gail Shelston, 'Unemployment and Girl School Leavers', unpublished paper.

5   *Employment Prospects by Industry and Occupation,* Department of Employment and Industrial Relations, Canberra, 1979.

6   Peter Robson, 'The Impact of Technological Change on Employment in the 1980s', unpublished paper, Labour Resource Centre, Melbourne, May 1978, p. 16. 7 ibid., p. 7.

7   ibid., p. 7.

8   *Structural Change in Australia,* Industries Assistance Commission, AGPS, Canberra, 1977, p. 86.

9   New Fixed Capital Expenditure by Private Enterprises in Selected Industries, Australian Bureau of Statistics Cat. No. 5626.0.

10 *Australia Ripped Off,* AMWSU, Sydney, undated, p. 22.

11 Robson, op. cit.

12 Joe Lo Bianco and Anna Boland, *The Rag Trade in Brunswick: Its Problems and Potential,* CURA, Melbourne, November 1978.

14 Prerost, op. cit.

15 *Women at Work,* Working Women's Centre, Melbourne, August-September 1979, p.1.

16 Working Women's Centre, Submission to the Committee of Inquiry into Technological Change in AUstralia, Melbourne, November 1979.

17 Linda Rubinstein, 'Women, Work and Technological Change', in *Women, Class and History,* edited by Elizabeth Windschuttle, Fontana, Melbourne, 1980.

18 Women's Bureau, 'Preliminary Investigation into the Effects of Technological Change on Employment Opportunities for Women', AGPS, Canberra, December 1978, pp. 9-10.

19 ibid., pp. 7-8.

20 Game and Pringle, op. cit.

21 Ellen Goodman, 'Working their hearts out', the *Age*, 14 May 1980, p. 19

22 Trans National Brief: 1, Workers' Plans, Trans National Co-operative Ltd., Sydney, 1980.

23 Working Women's Centre, Submission to the Committee of Inquiry into Technological Change in Australia, Melbourne, November 1979.

24 ibid.

25 Robson, op. cit.

26 Red Fems, 'Some Thoughts on the Implications of Technological Change for Women and Part-time Work in the Public Sector', Second Women and Labour Conference Papers, Vol. 1, Sydney, May 1980.

27 Shelston, op. cit.

28 Forward, op. cit.

29 Shelston, op. cit.

30 Trans National Brief: 1, Workers' Plans, Trans national Co-operative Ltd., Sydney, 1980.

31 *Australia Ripped Off,* AMWSU, Sydney, undated.

32 Trans National Brief: 1, Workers' Plans, Trans national Co-operative Ltd., Sydney, 1980.

33 Bruce Macfarlane, 'Imperialism in the 1980s', in *Selected Papers from the Second Australian Political Economy Conference,* Australian Political Economy Movement, Melbourne, 1978.

34 E. L. Wheelright, 'S.E. Asia, Australia and the New International Division of Labour', paper delivered to Australia and South-East Asia: Directions for the 1980s Conference, Melbourne, May 1980.

Index

9 781958 381908